"A fascinating page-turner. . . . There's something undeniably gratifying about an elegantly crafted morality tale—and the business reporter Christopher Leonard has written a good one. . . . A fascinating and propulsive story about the Federal Reserve—yes, you read that right. Leonard, in the tradition of Michael Lewis, has taken an arcane subject, rife with the risk of incomprehensibility (or boredom), and built a riveting narrative in which the stakes couldn't be any clearer."

—*The New York Times*

"Skillfully tells the story of how, over several decades, a phalanx of economic sophisticates at the Fed have badly misunderstood the U.S. economy and often come up with policies that fail to produce the intended results."

—*The Wall Street Journal*

"A timely addition—appearing just as inflation is making headlines. . . . Leonard writes vividly about a technical subject. . . . By focusing on a regional banker, Leonard offers a refreshingly non-Washington view. . . . The author is surely correct that many Americans view the Fed as an unelected power aligned with elites, perhaps contributing to the disaffection that exploded on January 6, 2021."

—*The Washington Post*

"It's tough to turn the nuances of monetary policy into personality-driven narrative. But Christopher Leonard has succeeded in doing just that with *The Lords of Easy Money*. . . . He turns [an] unassuming economist into the protagonist of a compelling tale about how the Federal Reserve changed the entire nature of the American economy. . . . Weaving together narrative nonfiction with big ideas can be difficult. One of the best things about this book is that through Hoenig, Leonard, a business journalist, is able to tell the whole, complicated half-century story of how we got to where we are now in a way th̲a̲t̲ ̲i̲s̲ ̲r̲e̲a̲d̲a̲b̲l̲e̲.̲ ̲T̲h̲e̲r̲e̲ are real people here, making real decisions al̲

"[A] bracing and closely reported chronicle. . . . Leonard's book is an indispensable account in many respects—his coverage of the invisible bailout of the repo market alone stands as a bracing case study in how the false pieties of quantitative easing directly stoked ruinous asset bubbles. But Leonard is also that rarest of financial reporters who conscientiously tracks the real-life consequences of the Olympian deliberations undertaken by the paper economy's gatekeepers. . . . Richly reported, accessible, biting, and long overdue."

—*The New Republic*

"The book is a timely read to understand what could happen next through a thorough analysis of what this policy intervention looks like on the ground."

—*Enterprise*

"We get his point and it is a good one. This has been an era of loose money and the benefits have been very unevenly distributed. . . . The office politics of the Fed are well captured by Leonard, as is the intimidating physical setting."

—*The New York Times*

"Leonard is skilled at explaining complicated financial maneuvering in a way normal people can understand. . . . A good reminder of how uncertain a lot of monetary policy is."

—*The Washington Free Beacon*

"Leonard's wonderfully readable new book is about one of the most important, yet least covered and least understood, changes in American life. That's the effect of the dramatically increased role in financial markets played by the Federal Reserve. As Leonard convincingly argues, it might be nothing short of catastrophic."

—Bethany McLean, *New York Times* bestselling co-author of *The Smartest Guys in the Room*

THE
LORDS
OF EASY
MONEY

HOW THE FEDERAL RESERVE BROKE
THE AMERICAN ECONOMY

CHRISTOPHER LEONARD

SIMON & SCHUSTER PAPERBACKS

NEW YORK   LONDON   TORONTO   SYDNEY   NEW DELHI

This book is for Joan and John Miller.
Thank you so much for the support you have given,
and the example you have set.

Simon & Schuster Paperbacks
An Imprint of Simon & Schuster, Inc.
1230 Avenue of the Americas
New York, NY 10020

First Simon & Schuster trade paperback edition January 2023

SIMON & SCHUSTER PAPERBACKS and colophon are
registered trademarks of Simon & Schuster, Inc.

For information about special discounts for bulk purchases, please contact
Simon & Schuster Special Sales at 1-866-506-1949
or business@simonandschuster.com.

The Simon & Schuster Speakers Bureau can bring authors to your live event.
For more information or to book an event, contact the
Simon & Schuster Speakers Bureau at 1-866-248-3049 or
visit our website at www.simonspeakers.com.

Interior design by Ruth Lee-Mui

Manufactured in the United States of America

5   7   9   10   8   6   4

Library of Congress Cataloging-in-Publication Data has been applied for.

ISBN 978-1-9821-6663-2
ISBN 978-1-9821-6664-9 (pbk)
ISBN 978-1-9821-6668-7 (ebook)

CONTENTS

PART 1

"RESPECTFULLY, NO"

CHAPTER 1

GOING BELOW ZERO

(2010)

Thomas Hoenig woke up early on November 3, 2010, knowing what he had to do that day, and also knowing that he was almost certainly going to fail. He was going to cast a vote, and he was going to vote no. He was going to dissent, and he knew that this dissent would probably define his legacy. Hoenig was trying to stop something: A public policy that he believed could very well turn into a catastrophe. He believed it was his duty to do so. But the wheels were already turning to make this policy a reality, and the wheels were far more powerful than he was. The wheels were powered by the big banks on Wall Street, the stock market, and the leadership of America's Federal Reserve Bank. Everyone knew that Hoenig was going to lose that day, but he was going to vote no anyway.

Hoenig* was sixty-four years old, and he was the president of the Federal Reserve Bank of Kansas City, a position that gave him extraordinary power over America's economic affairs. He was in Washington that morning because he sat on the Federal Reserve's powerful policy-making

*Pronounced HAW-nig.

3

committee, which met every six weeks to effectively determine the value and quantity of American money. Most people in America don't think very much about money—meaning the actual currency, or that thing we call a dollar. The word *dollar* is, in fact, just a slang term for American currency, which is actually called a Federal Reserve note. People spend Federal Reserve notes every day (if they're lucky enough to have them), but they rarely think about the complex, largely invisible system that makes money appear out of thin air. This system is the U.S. Federal Reserve System. The Fed, America's central bank, is the only institution on Earth that can create U.S. dollars at will.

Because he was a senior official at the Federal Reserve, Thomas Hoenig had to think about money all the time. He thought about it in the same way that a very stressed-out building superintendent might think about plumbing and heating. Hoenig had to think about money as a system to be managed, and to be managed just right. When you ran the system that created money, you had to do your job carefully, with prudence and integrity, or else terrible things might happen. The building might flood or catch on fire.

This is why Hoenig felt so much pressure when he woke up that November morning in Washington, D.C. He was staying at a very nice hotel, called the Fairmont, where he always stayed when he traveled from his home in Kansas City to the nation's capital. Hoenig was in town for the regular meeting of the Federal Open Market Committee, or FOMC for short. When the committee met in Washington, its members voted and set the course of the Fed's actions. There were twelve members on the committee, which was run by the powerful chairman of the Federal Reserve.

For a year now, Hoenig had been voting no. If you tallied his votes during 2010, the tally would read: no, no, no, no, no, and no. His dissents had become expected, but they were also startling if you considered Tom Hoenig's character. He wasn't, by nature, anything close to a dissident. He was a rule-follower. He was born and raised in a small town, where he started working at the family plumbing shop before he was ten years old. He served as an artilleryman in Vietnam, and when he came home he didn't protest against the war. Instead, he studied economics and banking at Iowa State, earning a PhD. His first job out of school was as an economist with the Federal Reserve regional bank in Kansas City, in the supervision department. At the Fed, he went from being a rule-follower to being a rule-enforcer. Hoenig rose through the ranks to became president of the Kansas City Fed in 1991. This was the job he still held in 2010. His responsibilities as one of twelve regional Fed bank presidents illuminate the structure of America's money system. The Federal Reserve system is unlike any other in the world; it is a crazy genetic mashup of different animals, part private bank and part government agency. People talk about the Fed as if it were a bank, but it is really a network of regional banks, all controlled by a central office in Washington, D.C. Hoenig had all the fiery disposition that one might expect from a regional Fed president, which is to say none at all. He was soft-spoken, civil, wore cuff links and pin-striped suits, and spent his days talking about things like capital requirements and interest rates. Hoenig was an institutionalist, and a conservative in the little "c" sense of the word.

And yet here he was, in late 2010, a dissident.

After he woke up in his hotel room, Hoenig had some time alone before the big day started. He gathered his thoughts. He shaved, put on a suit, knotted his tie, and gathered his papers. If he had any doubts about what he was going to do that day, he didn't advertise them. He had spent months, years, even decades preparing for this action. His vote would reflect everything he'd learned during his career at the Fed. He was trying to apply what he knew to help the Federal Reserve navigate through extraordinary times.

The American financial system had broken in late 2008, after the investment bank Lehman Brothers collapsed. That moment marked a threshold for people like Tom Hoenig. Economists and central bankers

describe the ensuing panic as the Global Financial Crisis, eventually be-
stowing the moment with its own biblical label, the GFC. The world of
central banking was neatly divided into two eras. There was the world
pre-GFC and the world post-GFC. The GFC itself was apocalyptic.
The entire financial system experienced a total collapse that risked creating another Great Depression. This would mean years of record-high
unemployment, economic misery, political volatility, and the bankruptcy of countless companies. The crisis prompted the Federal Reserve
to do things it had never done before. The Fed's one superpower is its
ability to create new dollars and pump them into the banking system.
It used this power in unprecedented ways after Lehman's collapse. So
many of the financial charts that capture the Fed's actions during this
period look like the same chart—a flat line that bounces along in a
stable range for many years, which then spikes upward like a reverse
lightning bolt. The upward spikes capture the unprecedented amount
of money the Fed created to combat the crisis. Between 1913 and 2008,
the Fed gradually increased the money supply from about $5 billion to
$847 billion. This increase in the monetary base happened slowly, in a
gently uprising slope. Then, between late 2008 and early 2010, the Fed
printed $1.2 trillion. It printed a hundred years' worth of money, in
other words, in little over a year, more than doubling what economists
call the monetary base. There was one very important characteristic of
all this new money. The Fed can create currency in just one way: It
makes new dollars and deposits them in the vaults of big banks. Only
about twenty-four special banks and financial institutions have the privilege of getting these pristine dollars, making those banks the seedbed of
the money supply. The amount of excess money in the banking system
swelled from $2 billion in 2008 to $1.2 trillion in 2010, a level 800
times higher than before.

In doing all of this, the Fed had created a new foundation for the
American financial system, built on extraordinary amounts of new
money. Hoenig had a chance to watch firsthand as this system was

created because he sat on the very committee that created it, the FOMC. In the beginning, during the crisis years of 2008 and 2009, he had voted to go along with the extraordinary efforts.

The dispute that Hoenig was preparing for, on that morning of November 3, 2010, was about what the Fed would do now that the days of crisis were over. A difficult and slow recovery was just beginning, and it was one of the most important moments in American economic history. It was the moment when one phase of economic conditions was ending and giving way to the next. The Fed had to decide what the new world was going to look like, and Hoenig was increasingly distressed by the path the Fed was choosing.

It is commonly reported that the FOMC meets every six weeks to "set interest rates." What this means is that the Fed determines the price of very short-term loans, a number that eventually bleeds out into the entire economic system and has an effect on every company, worker, and household. The basic system works like this: When the Fed raises interest rates, it slows the economy. When the Fed lowers interest rates, it speeds up the economy. The FOMC, then, is like a group of engineers in the control room of a nuclear power plant. They heat up the reactor, by cutting rates, when more power is needed. And they cool down the reactor, by raising rates, when conditions are getting too hot.

One of the most important things the Fed did during the Global Financial Crisis was to slash the interest rate to zero, essentially for the first time in history (rates had briefly flirted with zero in the early 1960s). Economists called the 0 percent interest rate the "zero bound," and it was once seen as some kind of inviolable boundary. You couldn't go below zero, it was believed. The rate of interest is really just the price of money. When interest rates are high, money is expensive because you have to pay more to borrow it. When rates are low, money is cheap. When rates are zero, money is effectively free for the banks who can get it straight from the Fed. The cost of money can't get lower than zero, economists believed, so the zero bound reflected the limits of the Fed's power to control interest rates. The Fed hit the zero bound shortly after Lehman Brothers collapsed, but the more important thing is what happened next. After hitting zero, the Fed didn't try to lift rates again. The Fed even started telling everyone very clearly that it wasn't *going* to try to lift rates. This gave the banks confidence to keep lending in a free-money environment—the banks knew that life at the zero bound was going to last for a while.

But by 2010, the FOMC faced a terrible dilemma. Keeping interest rates pegged at zero didn't seem to be enough. The economy had revived but remained in terrible health. The unemployment rate was still 9.6 percent, close to the levels that characterize a deep recession. The people who ran the FOMC knew that the effects of high and sustained unemployment were horrific. When people are out of a job for a long time, they lose their skills and they lose hope. They get left behind, compounding the economic damage of having been laid off in the first place. Even the kids of people who lose their jobs suffered a long-term drop in their earning potential. There was an urgency, inside the Fed, to stop this process. There was also the risk that the economic rebound might stall altogether.

That is why the committee began considering ways to break past the zero bound in 2010. The Fed's leadership was going to vote in November on a radical experiment, one that would effectively take interest rates negative for the first time, pushing yet more money into the banking system and shifting the Fed to the very center of American efforts to boost economic growth. No one knew what the world might look like after that. The experimental program had, like all things at the modern Fed, a name that was intentionally opaque and therefore difficult for people to understand, let alone care about. The plan was called "quantitative easing." If the program was enacted, it would reshape the American financial system. It would redefine the Federal Reserve's role in economic affairs. And it would make all of the things that Hoenig had been voting against look quaint. He was planning to vote against quantitative easing, and his dissent was going to be a lonely one. There was a tense debate inside the FOMC about quantitative easing, but the public barely knew about it. Political fights over America's money supply had become increasingly insular, even hidden, as they were decided by the Fed's leaders.

The politics of money used to be a charged political issue. It was once debated with the heat and passion that defined fights over taxes or gun control in 2010. Back during the presidential election of 1896, the Democratic nominee, William Jennings Bryan, made monetary policy one of his primary issues. He was a populist, and he used the topic to rile up crowds. This led to the most potent and most famous political statement ever made about American money, when Bryan proclaimed during a campaign speech, "You shall not crucify mankind upon a cross of gold!" Bryan was specifically talking about the gold standard in that speech, but he was also talking about short-term interest rates and the monetary base—exactly the issues regularly debated, in secret, by the twelve members of the FOMC. There was a reason the politics of money was so heated back in Bryan's day: The Federal Reserve hadn't yet been created. Managing the money supply was still in the public realm of democratic action. All of that ended when the Fed was founded in 1913. Power to control the money supply then belonged exclusively to the Fed, which then consolidated the power under the FOMC, which then debated behind closed doors. A big wall went up around the decision-making on money.

The things that bothered Hoenig about quantitative easing were just as important to the American people as the things that bothered Williams Jennings Bryan. The FOMC debates were technical and complicated, but at their core they were about choosing winners and losers in the economic system. Hoenig was fighting against quantitative easing because he knew that it would create historically huge amounts of money, and this money would be delivered first to the big banks on Wall Street. He believed that this money would widen the gap between the very rich and everybody else. It would benefit a very small group of people who owned assets, and it would punish the very large group of people who lived on paychecks and tried to save money. Just as important, this tidal wave of money would encourage every entity on Wall Street to adopt riskier and riskier behavior in a world of cheap debt and heavy lending, potentially creating exactly the kind of ruinous financial bubble that had caused the Global Financial Crisis in the first place. This is what Hoenig had been arguing inside the secret FOMC meetings for months, his arguments growing sharper and more direct, punctuated by his dissenting votes.

As it turned out, Hoenig was almost entirely correct in his concerns and his predictions. Perhaps no single government policy did more to reshape American economic life than the policy the Fed began to execute on that November day, and no single policy did more to widen the divide between the rich and the poor. Understanding what the Fed did in November 2010 is the key to understanding the very strange economic decade that followed, when asset prices soared, the stock market boomed, and the American middle class fell further behind.

At first, when Hoenig started casting "no" votes, he was trying to convince his peers that they might take a different path. But this effort was undermined by the Fed's chairman, Ben Bernanke, who was quantitative easing's author. Bernanke was an academic who had joined the Fed in 2002 and became chairman in 2006. Bernanke led the response to the Global Financial Crisis, which made him famous. He was anointed *Time* magazine's Person of the Year in 2009 and appeared on *60 Minutes*. In bailing out the financial system, Bernanke made the bank more influential than it had ever been. In 2010, he was determined to push things further. Bernanke saw Hoenig's concerns as wrongheaded, and disarmed them masterfully by personally lobbying the other members of the FOMC.

It eventually became obvious that Hoenig's "no" votes were unlikely to sway any of his peers on the FOMC. His dissents now had a different effect. He was sending a message to the public. He wanted people to understand that the Fed was about to do something profound, and that someone had fought against it. He wanted to telegraph that the politics of money wasn't just a technical affair involving smart people who solved equations. It was a government action that imposed a public policy regime, affecting everyone.

After Hoenig was dressed and ready for the meeting, he made his way to the hotel lobby, where he would face his fellow FOMC members before they cast their votes.

When the Fed's regional bank presidents came to town in 2010, the bank put them up in the Hotel Fairmont and, in the mornings, they gathered in the lobby, where they waited to be picked up by one of the most powerful car pools in America. The Fed sent vehicles to ferry them as a group to its headquarters building, about fifteen minutes away in D.C.'s dense morning traffic. Sometimes the regional bank presidents rode together in a van, at other times they rode one or two to a town car.

There was a deep feeling of collegiality among the bank presidents, and Hoenig fit in with them. His appearance could be described as standard-issue banker. He had a square jaw, a dimpled chin, and blue eyes; he was good-looking in a conventional, almost generic way. He had the face of someone that you might expect to see across the desk from you, about to extend you a reasonable thirty-year home loan. He was tall, and dressed conservatively. The cadence of his speech and his vocabulary matched the subdued color and cut of his wardrobe. He unspooled sentences methodically, in a measured way, never letting his words race ahead of his intended message. When Hoenig got agitated, he repeated the phrase "lookit" a lot, but that was about as salty as it got.

For many years, Hoenig got along quite well with everyone on the FOMC. When he came down to the lobby, he could easily make small talk with the other regional bank presidents. They shared a bond that few outsiders could understand. They operated a large part of the

American economic machine, and they shouldered a heavy burden in doing so. They were also, to a person, pretty brilliant people. There was Janet Yellen, for example, president of the San Francisco Federal Reserve. She was arguably one of the most accomplished economists in the country, having served as a Fed economist in the late 1970s before teaching stints at Harvard, the London School of Economics, and U.C. Berkeley. She had been chairwoman of the White House Council of Economic Advisers in the late 1990s and was fluent in the complex language of macroeconomics. But she had never lost her Brooklyn accent. She could be blunt as well as charming when talking about what the Fed might do next.

Then there was Richard Fisher, the president of the Dallas Fed, who looked every part the investment banker that he'd once been. Fisher slicked back his white hair, wore sharp suits, and spoke in a baroque and grandiloquent way during FOMC meetings, mixing poetic metaphors and jokes throughout his long monologues. Just a couple of months prior, Fisher had opened his remarks by saying: "Mr. Chairman, I'll tell a story to frame my comments. Three Texas Aggies apply to be detectives . . ." This was a typical Fisherian opening. There was also Charles Plosser, president of the Philadelphia Fed, a reserved academic, and Charles Evans, the young president of the Chicago Fed and a self-described "inflation nutter."

These were Hoenig's people. They all spoke the same language. They shared the same burden. Hoenig had worked around people like this his entire career, since joining the Fed in 1973. But his position inside the FOMC had grown increasingly strained with each "no" vote that he cast. Hoenig was pushing himself further and further to the fringe of the Fed's power structure.

There were two reasons why Hoenig's dissents were causing so much tension. The first had to do with the way the Fed was run. Consensus, and unanimous votes, had become all-important inside the FOMC. The world needed to have faith that the Fed's leaders knew what they were doing, and that what they were doing was something much more like math than like politics. The mighty brains who ruled the FOMC were portrayed to the public as PhD-educated civil servants who were essentially solving complex equations rather than making policy choices. When an FOMC member dissented, it shattered this illusion. It pointed out that there might be competing points of view, even heated debate, about what path forward the Fed ought to take. Unanimous votes helped the FOMC keep its power by essentially denying that it had power—it was just a group of smart engineers operating the power plant according to the rule manual.

The second reason Hoenig's dissents caused so much tension was tightly linked to the first. Consensus was ever more important at the FOMC because the decisions it was making were more consequential. America's democratic institutions were increasingly paralyzed, which left more work to be done by its nondemocratic institutions, like the Supreme Court and the Federal Reserve. This reality was literally blaring from TV sets and splashed on the front pages on the morning that Hoenig went down to the lobby. The Hotel Fairmont offered guests free copies of *The New York Times*, and, on that morning of November 3, the *Times* carried one of those bold-type headlines across the top of the front page that telegraphs emergency. "G.O.P. TAKES HOUSE," the headline read. Below that, in smaller type, it proclaimed: "SETBACK FOR OBAMA AND DEMOCRAT AGENDA; CUOMO WINS; SHOW OF STRENGTH BY TEA PARTY."

The previous day had been Election Day across America, the first midterm election of Barack Obama's presidency, a crucial vote that would determine who controlled Congress. Just two years prior, voters had hit the "change" button and hit it hard, giving the Democratic Party control of the White House and both chambers of Congress. Now voters hit the change button again, taking away control of the House of Representatives and crippling the Democrats' control of the Senate by narrowing their majority. This was a rebuke to Obama's administration, but it was also just one in a long string of rebukes against the democratically elected government in Washington. Almost every election was a change election by 2010. Voters threw the bums out, then threw the new bums out. The American electorate seemed motivated primarily by anger and discontent, and this anger found a new form in the conservative Tea Party movement. If the Tea Party had a single animating principle, it was the principle of saying no. The Tea Partiers were dedicated to halting the work of government entirely. The *Times* quoted a Tea Party activist stating that her goal was to "hold the line at all hazards."

It was a shame that America's democratic institutions, like Congress, stopped working at the very moment they were needed most. The Global Financial Crisis of 2008 didn't come out of nowhere. The collapse came after many long years of decay inside an economic system that had stopped working for a majority of Americans. The problems were varied and complex, and they all helped create the conditions for crisis, with indebted workers, powerful banks extending risky loans, and wildly overvalued market prices. People were borrowing more money in part because the decline of labor unions had taken away the bargaining power of workers, depressing their wages and degrading their working conditions. Trade deals shifted jobs overseas as new technology meant that fewer workers were wanted. An aging population relied more and more heavily on underfunded government programs like Medicare, Medicaid, and Social Security, creating huge levels of government debt. The education system was falling behind that of peer nations. Years of deregulation meant that the banking system was dominated by a few titanic firms that specialized in making and selling opaque and risky debt instruments. These were huge challenges facing the nation, and the federal government had not substantially addressed any of them. There were conservative ways to deal with these problems, and there were liberal ways to deal with these problems. But, with the election of the Tea Party, Congress was not going to deal with the problems at all.

The federal legislative machine had been switched off, beginning an era of stasis and dysfunction.

This put a tremendous burden on each member of the FOMC. On November 3, the Federal Reserve became the central driver of American economic policy making. If American voters had just voted to halt government action, they did so at the very moment when the Fed was about to embark on a program of unprecedented activism. This is why the Fed was able to act so quickly. Back in 2008, the Fed had gotten about $1 trillion out the door before Congress was even able to tie its shoes and start debating stimulus bills and bank bailouts. The twelve FOMC members couldn't ignore that they were charting the course of American economic development.

And it was exactly at this historical moment that Thomas Hoenig decided to embark on his string of dissents, among the longest of any FOMC member in history. Hoenig dissented so frequently that it seemed like he enjoyed it. A columnist at *The Wall Street Journal* wrote a regular column called "The Lone Dissenter" in which he interviewed Hoenig after each "no" vote. Hoenig wasn't just undermining the image of a consensus-driven Fed, he was helping draw attention to the fact. This echoed loudly inside the cloistered world of the FOMC members, who spoke often and who traveled to the same conferences and award ceremonies. Hoenig had been well liked in that world, but now his peers talked to him with unease. They asked if he was *sure* he needed to do what he was doing. The relationship between Hoenig and Chairman Bernanke, though never close, was now adversarial. Years later, when Bernanke wrote his memoir, the book included relatively few mean-spirited comments, and many of them were reserved for Hoenig. Bernanke painted Hoenig as disloyal, obstinate, and maybe even a little unbalanced.

When the cars arrived, Hoenig and the other bank presidents walked outside through the glass doors of the hotel lobby, to the half-circle driveway sheltered beneath a broad portico where their ride awaited. Hoenig got in, and the vehicle nosed out of the driveway and into the busy morning traffic. The route from the hotel to Fed headquarters passed through the Foggy Bottom neighborhood of northwestern Washington, a quiet part of the city that feels far removed from the Capitol building and the busy streets surrounding the White House. One route to the headquarters passed through Washington Circle, a small park with a statue of America's first president in the middle, riding a horse, leaning back slightly with a sword in his hand as if preparing to enter the battlefield.

As the scenery passed by, Hoenig had a few final minutes to think, and to fortify himself for the day. Each member of the FOMC would present an argument during the daylong meeting, and Hoenig had been working hard on his statement. What was going to happen that day was basically a political debate, and Hoenig needed to carefully marshal his facts.

Even the basic politics of the Federal Reserve are confusing to outsiders. In the broader American world, the battle lines of political argument were relatively clear. You had your conservatives, who wanted to limit the government's reach, and you had your liberals, who wanted to expand the government's reach. The angry debates that played out on cable news each night tended to flow from these two broad theories of governance. But the politics of the Fed were scrambled, and didn't make a lot of sense within this broader framework. The basic tension within the Fed was described with language that had been borrowed from the world of foreign policy, using the terminology of "hawks" and "doves." In foreign policy, it was the hawks who advocated for aggressive military intervention and it was the doves who pushed against aggressive intervention by supporting diplomacy. Curiously, these terms were reversed when applied to the Fed. It was the doves inside the Fed who argued for more aggressive intervention and it was the hawks who tried to limit the Fed's reach.

The debate between hawks and doves at the Fed was usually talked about in terms of inflation, that dangerous state of affairs when prices rise quickly and the value of a currency falls. If the Fed is seen as a team of nuclear engineers who supervise economic growth, then inflation is seen as the meltdown to be avoided at all costs. The last time inflation hit America was in the 1970s, and it was remembered as a chaotic time when prices for everything from meat to gasoline to houses were rising uncontrollably. Central banks cause inflation when they keep interest rates too low for too long. Hawks hated inflation, and therefore wanted to keep interest rates higher and limit the Fed's reach. Doves were less afraid of inflation, and therefore more willing to print lots of money.

It is unclear exactly who started the hawk-and-dove motif inside the Fed, but it stuck. Janet Yellen, for example, was often described as dovish because she supported low interest rates and more intervention. Tom Hoenig and Richard Fisher, in contrast, were described as hawkish because they sought to raise interest rates and limit the Fed's reach into markets. Needless to say, among the public, the doves got better press. Who could take issue with a dove? The theory seemed to be that doves were compassionate and wanted to help the economy and working people, while hawks were harsh and severe and wanted to *stop* the Fed from helping people.

Hoenig's actions during 2010 had turned him into the FOMC's ultra-hawk. It even turned him into something worse. In economic terms, he was seen as a type of prehistoric brute, something economists called a "Mellonist," a term that refers to Andrew Mellon, who was secretary of the Treasury when the Depression began. There aren't many actual villains in the world of economics, but Mellon is one of them. Mellon is famous for one thing: being heartless and delusional. This reputation came from a single piece of advice that he gave President Herbert Hoover as the markets collapsed. Mellon told Hoover to let the fire burn, let the people go broke. He believed the crash was a type of moral cleansing that was necessary to clear the way for a better economy in the future. "Liquidate labor, liquidate stocks, liquidate the farmers, liquidate real estate," Mellon is reported to have told Hoover. The reason this advice was delusional, as well as heartless, was that Mellon's economic theory was mistaken. It wasn't cleansing to liquidate the farmers and the stocks. The liquidation created a downward cycle of unemployment, weak spending, and slow growth that only grew harder to reverse the longer it lasted. By urging Hoover to liquidate so much value, Mellon liquidated years of future economic growth.

It seemed inconceivable that someone could push Mellon's view in 2010. And it appeared that this was exactly what Hoenig was doing. The Fed was trying to help. It was trying to boost economic growth. The Fed was trying to be dovish. By voting against these plans, Hoenig was apparently trying to keep the Fed on the sidelines as people suffered under a 9.6 percent unemployment rate. Hoenig, the extreme hawk, the Mellonist, was out of step with the times. This was, in fact, the reputation that solidified around Thomas Hoenig over time. Years after his string of dissents, a liberal financial reporter in New York, when asked about Hoenig, immediately responded: "Yeah, he's a crank." Around the same time, at a cocktail party in Washington, D.C., an economist with the American Enterprise Institute, the conservative think tank, immediately said about Hoenig: "He was wrong." Hoenig's concerns were universally remembered as being concerns over inflation, concerns that proved to be unwarranted because inflation never arrived. Over the years, the story about Hoenig became that of a misplaced Old Testament figure who had somehow wandered onto the modern economic landscape, clinging to outdated scripture and frantically warning about inflation, more inflation, and even hyperinflation.

The historical record shows that this narrative is entirely wrong. Hoenig didn't dissent because he was worried about inflation. He was also no Mellonist. During the Global Financial Crisis, Hoenig voted repeatedly to take emergency actions that were both far reaching and unprecedented. He believed in the Fed's role as a crisis responder that could flood the banking sector with money in times of panic. He believed in robust money-printing policies when banks were in trouble.

Hoenig only began dissenting in 2010, when it appeared that the Federal Reserve was committed to keeping the American money supply at the zero bound. A review of Hoenig's comments during the 2010 FOMC meetings (the transcripts of which become public five years after the fact), along with his speeches and interviews at the time, show that he rarely mentioned inflation at all. Hoenig warned about quite different things, and his warnings turned out to be prescient. But his warnings were also very hard to understand for people who didn't closely follow the politics of money. Hoenig, for instance, liked to talk a lot about something called the "allocative effect" of keeping interest rates at the zero bound.

The allocative effect wasn't something that people debated at the barbershop. But it was something that affected everyone. Hoenig was talking about the allocation of money, and the ways in which the Fed shifted money from one part of the economy to another. He was pointing out that the Fed's policies did a lot more than just affect overall economic growth. The Fed's policies shifted money between the rich and the poor, and they encouraged or discouraged things like Wall Street speculation that could lead to ruinous financial crashes. This whole way of talking about the Fed undermined the very construct of hawks versus doves. He was pointing to the fact that the Fed could cause meltdowns that had nothing to do with price inflation.

Hoenig didn't just say these things behind the closed doors of FOMC meetings. In May 2010, he laid out his views, and explained his dissents, in an interview with *The Wall Street Journal*. "Monetary policy has to be about more than just targeting inflation. It is a more powerful tool than that. It is also an allocative policy, as we've learned," Hoenig said.

When Hoenig talked about allocative effects, he was describing how 0 percent interest rates created winners and losers. When interest rates hit zero, and money becomes cheap, it pushes banks to make riskier loans. That's because the banks can't earn a profit by saving money, as they might be able to do in a world where interest rates are higher, like at, say, 4 percent. In a 4 percent world, a bank can earn a decent return by stashing its money in ultrasafe investments like government Treasury bonds, which would pay the bank 4 percent for the loan. In a 0 percent world, things are different. A bank earns much closer to nothing for stashing its money in an ultrasafe bond. This pushes the bank to search for earnings out there in the risky wilderness. A riskier loan might pay a higher interest rate, or a higher "yield," as the bankers call it. When banks start hunting for yield, they are moving their cash further out on the yield curve, as they say, into the riskier investments.

Life at the zero bound pushes banks way down the yield curve. What does a bank have to lose? A risky bet beats nothing. And this isn't just a side effect of keeping rates at zero. "That's the whole point," Hoenig explained, many years later. "The point was to get people willing to take greater risk, to get the economy started again. But it also allocates resources. It allocates where that money goes."

Hoenig was worried about what would happen when the Fed pushed all that money from safe investments out into risky investments. When cash is pushed out onto the yield curve, it leads to the second big problem that Hoenig warned about in 2010: something called an asset bubble. The housing market that collapsed in 2008 was an asset bubble. The dot-com stock market crash of 2000 was the bursting of an asset bubble. When an asset bubble crashed, the general public tended to blame the people at the scene of the disaster, who were inevitably greedy Wall Street types. It was the shortsighted stockbrokers who bid up the stock market, or the dishonest mortgage lenders who fueled the housing boom. But Hoenig had sat on the FOMC during both of these asset bubbles, and the following crashes, and he'd seen firsthand the Fed's vital role in creating them. Hoenig was worried, in November 2010, that the Fed was repeating this mistake. Just a few months earlier, at the

August FOMC meeting, Hoenig's frustration seemed to boil over. He said something that most Fed officials never acknowledged, at least in public. The central bank hadn't just rescued the economy from the crash of 2008. The Fed bore a great deal of responsibility for it.

"The financial and economic shocks we've experienced did not just come out of nowhere," he said. "They followed years of low interest rates, high and increasing leverage, and overly lax financial supervision, as prescribed by both Democratic and Republican administrations." He was explaining his dissent at that meeting, and warning that the Fed might be making the same mistakes that led to 2008. "The continued use of zero-interest rate will only add the risk to the longer-run outlook," he said.

Hoenig lost that fight, and all the other fights of 2010. The Fed didn't just keep rates pegged at the zero bound, but was now voting on the plan to go below the zero bound, with quantitative easing. Hoenig had fought against quantitative easing for months, and today he would lose that fight as well.

Hoenig's ride continued south toward the Fed headquarters, which were located in the Marriner Eccles Building. The Eccles Building was down on the quiet side of the Mall, near the opposite end from the Capitol dome. The building was modest by the standards of Washington. It wasn't very imposing. It was barely notable, in fact, next to the museums and trade buildings that populated the mall. The Eccles Building had a bright white marble façade and rectangular columns, as pristine as an engraving on a dollar bill: neat lines, sharp angles, and quiet authority.

The cars carrying the regional bank presidents were guided to a side entrance of the building, where they drove into a private basement lot. The passengers got out and walked down a hallway into the building itself, taking an elevator up to the second floor, where Hoenig and the other bank presidents made their way to the boardroom.

The décor inside the Eccles is what you'd get if a big bank and a museum had a child. The hushed, carpeted hallways were lined with fine art. The offices alongside them were large and well appointed. The boardroom was the most famous feature of the Eccles Building, and the most famous feature of the boardroom was the enormous ovoid table at its center, a gleaming slat of polished wood that seemed to go on forever. The FOMC members gathered around this table when they debated. An ornate gilded chandelier hung directly above the table for lighting. There was a yawning fireplace, framed by a large mantelpiece, on one side of the room. On the opposite side were rows of chairs where staffers assembled and sat during the meeting, offering presentations when called upon.

Tom Hoenig took his seat as the FOMC members made small talk and found their places. Hoenig first joined this table, as a voting member of the FOMC, when the legendary Alan Greenspan presided as chairman of the Fed. But Hoenig's experience at the central bank went back even further than that. He had worked at the Fed under the leadership of five chairmen, starting with Arthur Burns back in the 1970s, and including the legendary tenure of Paul Volcker, who raised interest rates into the double digits in the early 1980s to beat inflation (causing a brutal recession in the bargain).

There had never been anything like a peaceful, stable period at the Fed. Things were always changing and one crisis always led to another. But there had also never been a period quite like the one under Greenspan's successor, Ben Bernanke, who changed everything.

When Ben Bernanke published a memoir in 2015, he entitled it *The Courage to Act*. This captured the theory of Bernankeism. It held that monetary intervention is necessary, courageous, even noble.

It was Bernanke, after 2008, who pushed the Federal Reserve to do things it had never done before, to grow the monetary base larger than what it had ever been, to push the interest rate down to zero, to offer a "forward guidance" that promised interest rates would stay at zero, inducing banks and investors to take more risk. These aggressive actions were at odds with Bernanke's demeanor. He was soft-spoken, friendly, and approachable. His closely trimmed, graying beard gave him an avuncular look. He seemed happy enough, at first, to be something like a caretaker chairman, after Greenspan's long tenure: a low-key manager who would quietly pull the levers of monetary policy in a cautious way. But the crash of 2008 turned Bernanke into a global celebrity, along with the secretary of the Treasury, Hank Paulson, and the New York Federal Reserve Bank president, Timothy Geithner. They were the trio at the center of things, bailing out the giant insurance conglomerate AIG, letting Lehman Brothers fail, pushing for a $700 billion bank bailout. Bernanke became the face of the American economic rescue effort.

If Bernanke was bold during the crisis, it was partly because the Fed had moved too slowly before the crash, when it let the housing bubble inflate, infect the financial system, and explode. In 2007, when mortgage borrowers started defaulting in large numbers, Bernanke said during an industry conference that the problems in subprime mortgages weren't that dangerous. "We believe the effect of the troubles in the subprime sector on the broader housing market will likely be limited," Bernanke said, "and we do not expect significant spillovers from the subprime market to the rest of the economy or to the financial system."

When the system did fall apart, Bernanke had a chance to define his legacy. He was, in many ways, perfectly suited for the job. As an academic, Bernanke had focused on the Great Depression and written extensively about ways in which a new depression might be averted. One of his central ideas was that the Fed hadn't acted boldly enough back in the 1930s. The central bank had actually worsened the Depression by tightening the money supply. The solution, Bernanke believed, was to be as aggressive as possible after a crash. He had spent many years thinking up new ways that the Fed could boost economic growth even after pushing interest rates to zero. He didn't see the zero bound as an inviolable limit, but just as another data point. Bernanke published papers on this concept as far back as the early 2000s, when 0 percent rates were still just a wild idea. Some of Bernanke's ideas were outlandish. He suggested that the Fed could set a limit on the long-term interest rates of Treasury bonds* by purchasing unlimited amounts of them, for example. He discussed something called a "helicopter drop" of money, in which the U.S. government would give people a huge tax cut by simply selling all of its debt to the Fed, which would print the money to buy it. Bernanke had suggested that the central bank of Japan could end that nation's slump by depreciating the value of its currency to stimulate exports, even though inflation would jump to a very high 3 or 4 percent. Bernanke had backed off most of this by the time he became Fed chairman, but he had never lost his interest in experiments.

The stagnant economy of 2010 encouraged such experiments. Economists knew that it would take years to recover from the banking crisis, but the reality of high unemployment so long after the crash was still shocking. The unemployment rate was still above 9 percent and economic growth remained weak. There was a crisis gathering strength in Europe thanks to deeply indebted nations like Greece and Spain. These problems, if left unaddressed, could create a cascading effect across the world. The American stock market started to sink again during the spring of 2010, with the Dow Jones Industrial Average falling about 1,000 points, or 9 percent, between May and June.

Members of the FOMC were worried about this, but they generally agreed that another recession was unlikely. Still, there was always a risk, and the Fed didn't want to be caught underestimating a problem. At first, Bernanke was only pushing to keep interest rates at zero. It seemed like the safe thing to do. But Hoenig started dissenting. He explained his heightened worries during the FOMC meeting in August. "I think of it more as planting the seeds of a briar patch that we will have to deal with not in a year from now, but three or four years from now, as we have in the

* Financial traders use specific terms to discuss U.S. Treasury debt. They call short-term U.S. Treasuries Treasury "bills," while longer-term Treasuries are called Treasury "notes" and very-long-term Treasuries are called Treasury "bonds." This book uses common vernacular terms "Treasury Bills" or "Treasury Bonds," while specifying the duration of Treasurys when relevant.

past. So I very much oppose this policy," he said. The dissents didn't mean that much to Bernanke because Hoenig remained a lone voice. There was a lot of debate inside the FOMC meetings, but the actual votes kept coming out in the lopsided tally of 11 to 1, with Hoenig being the one.

In August, Bernanke began a public campaign to initiate his greatest innovation, and one of the greatest experiments in the Fed's history. This was the program called quantitative easing. The program had been used on a large scale once before, during the financial crash. But it had never been used in the way that Bernanke believed it should be used in late 2010, as an economic stimulus plan to be employed outside a crisis. Bernanke built public support to use quantitative easing this way, strangely enough, at an event that Hoenig himself helped host. Every summer, the Kansas City Fed held a symposium in Jackson Hole, Wyoming, a gathering of global central bankers and economists that was the closest thing that monetary policy had to the Academy Awards. It was a place for red carpet strolls and moments captured by news photographers. The Fed chairman's speech was always a major event, and in 2010 Bernanke did not disappoint. He announced the program that would help the Fed push interest rates below zero and stimulate the economy when no one else was willing to do so. The mainstream press, which covered Bernanke's speech, didn't yet have the vocabulary to describe what the chairman was talking about. It was only months later that the term *quantitative easing* entered the broader lexicon (to the degree that it ever did). Even the best financial reporters filed muddled-sounding stories from Jackson Hole about a Fed plan to buy bonds, long-term debt, and Treasurys. It sounded dry, technical, and harmless.

But the members of the FOMC knew otherwise, because they knew how the plan would work and what it was intended to do. The Fed had done quantitative easing once before, during the heat of the 2008 financial crisis. It was an emergency effort, an extraordinary thing for an extraordinary moment: The Fed directly bought mortgage debt to stabilize the mortgage market. Now Bernanke was suggesting that the

Fed turn quantitative easing, for the first time, into a normal operating tool to manage the economy.

The basic mechanics and goals of quantitative easing are actually pretty simple. It was a plan to inject trillions of newly created dollars into the banking system, at a moment when the banks had almost no incentive to save the money. The Fed would do this by using one of the most powerful tools it already had at its disposal: a very large group of financial traders in New York who were already buying and selling assets from the select group of twenty-four financial firms that were known as "primary dealers." The primary dealers have special bank vaults at the Fed, called reserve accounts.* To execute quantitative easing, a trader at the New York Fed would call up one of the primary dealers, like JPMorgan Chase, and offer to buy $8 billion worth of Treasury bonds from the bank. JPMorgan would sell the Treasury bonds to the Fed trader. Then the Fed trader would hit a few keys and tell the Morgan banker to look inside their reserve account. Voila, the Fed had instantly created $8 billion out of thin air, in the reserve account, to complete the purchase. Morgan could, in turn, use this money to buy assets in the wider marketplace. This is how the Fed creates money—it buys things from the primary dealers, and it does so by simply creating money inside their reserve accounts.

Bernanke planned to do such transactions over and over again until the Fed had purchased $600 billion worth of assets. In other words, the Fed would buy things using money it created until it had filled the Wall Street reserve accounts with 600 billion new dollars. Bernanke wanted to do this over a period of months. Before the crisis, it would have taken about sixty years to add that many dollars to the monetary base.

There was one more thing about quantitative easing that made it so powerful. Bernanke was planning to buy long-term government debt, like 10-year Treasury bonds. This was a bigger deal than it sounds. The

---

*Of course, in modern times this reserve account wasn't a physical vault at all, but more like a digital account on an electronic ledger.

Fed had always bought short-term debt because its job was to control short-term interest rates. But the central bank was now targeting long-term debt for a strategic reason: Long-term debt was Wall Street's equivalent of a savings account. It was the safe place where investors tied up their money to earn a dependable return. With quantitative easing, the Fed would take that savings account away. It would reduce the supply of 10-year Treasury bonds that were available. All the money that the Fed was creating would now be under a great deal of pressure because it could no longer find a safe home in a 10-year Treasury. All the new cash would be pushed out on the yield curve, out there into the risky investments. The theory was that banks would now be forced to lend money, whether they wanted to or not. Quantitative easing would flood the system with money at the very same moment that it limited the refuge where that money might be safely stored. If economic growth was weak and fragile during 2010, then quantitative easing would shower the landscape with more money and cheaper loans and easy credit, enticing banks to fund new businesses that they might not have funded before.

Hoenig had spent a whole year complaining about the dangerous "allocative effects" of 0 percent interest rates. Now, at Jackson Hole, those complaints looked quaint. The allocative effect of quantitative easing would be like nothing ever seen in American finance.

Inside the FOMC meetings, quantitative easing was debated for being what it was—a large-scale experiment that carried unclear benefits and risks. There was more opposition to the plan than was publicly known at the time. Hoenig wasn't the only FOMC member with strong objections to the plan. The regional bank presidents Charles Plosser and Richard Fisher expressed concerns about it, as did the president of the Richmond Federal Reserve Bank, Jeffrey Lacker. But if quantitative easing was radical, Bernanke insisted that it was called for by extraordinary times.

During the FOMC meeting in September, Hoenig offered his most condensed, straightforward critique of what the Fed was doing. He pointed out that the deep malaise in American economic life wasn't caused by a lack of lending from banks. The banks already had plenty of money to lend. The real problem lay outside the banking system, in the real economy where the deep problems were festering, problems that the Fed had no power to fix. Keeping interest rates at zero, and then pumping $600 billion of new money into the banking system—money that had nowhere to go but out into risky loans or financial speculation—wasn't going to help solve the fundamental dysfunctions of the American economy.

"I am not arguing for high interest rates at all—I never have been. I am arguing for getting off of zero, getting away from thinking that if we only added another trillion dollars of high-powered money, everything would be okay. It won't," Hoenig said.

He warned that another round of quantitative easing would push the Fed into a "new regime" that wouldn't easily be ended. "At this point, the crisis should have taught us that we need to increase our emphasis on longer-run macroeconomic and financial stability and not just on inflation goals. We have allocative effects, and I think we should be very, very mindful of that."

At this moment, there did seem to be a chance that Hoenig might sway some of his colleagues. When Bernanke responded to Hoenig, later in the meeting, Bernanke argued for quantitative easing with a defense that would become his primary defense in the coming years, one he repeated many times. He pointed out that the Fed faced risks if it *didn't* intervene.

"This is very, very difficult," he said. "We don't have good options. It feels safer not to do anything, but then, on the other side, we have an economy which is underperforming very severely—we have very high unemployment. So there's no safe option. Whatever we do, we're going to have to make our best judgment and hope for the best."

While Bernanke debated inside the FOMC, he had very skillfully shaped the terms of the debate. By announcing quantitative easing in Jackson Hole, he had raised expectations that the plan would happen. This prompted speculators to start trading as if the program were a certain thing, driving up prices for some assets. Within a few months, the market might have fallen if the Fed didn't follow through.

It was during this period, in autumn, when the relationship between Bernanke and Hoenig became as outright hostile as it could be within the genteel world of monetary policy. Months earlier, in May, Hoenig had given the interview to *The Wall Street Journal* in which he directly criticized the 0 percent interest-rate policy, explicitly warning that it might stoke asset bubbles. Now, during a public speech, Hoenig said that quantitative easing was akin to making a "deal with the devil." This was not the polite language usually employed by FOMC members. This was a public condemnation.

These comments irritated Ben Bernanke, perhaps even more than Hoenig's dissenting votes had irritated him.

When the Fed gathered to vote on the quantitative easing plan in November, the two-day meeting began on an unpleasant note. Bernanke opened the meeting with something of a scolding for the gathered FOMC members. He said that there had been too many leaks of information about their meetings and, just as worrisome, some Fed officials seemed to feel increasingly free to express their opinions on important policy matters during their public speeches. It was hard not to see this complaint as directed squarely at Tom Hoenig. Bernanke said that airing such "very strong, very inflexible positions" undermined the FOMC's credibility.

Janet Yellen agreed. "I personally see them as damaging our credibility and our reputation at a time when the institution is under enormous scrutiny, and we can ill afford it," she said.

Consensus was important. Presenting a unified front to the outside world was important. Vocal dissent was disloyalty. That was the message on November 2, the first day of the meeting. Now, on November 3, Tom Hoenig and the other members took their seats around the giant table and prepared to hold their final debate on quantitative easing.

———

"Good morning, everybody," Bernanke said as he began the meeting. "We made an awful lot of progress yesterday. FOMC productivity is up," he joked, drawing laughter from the crowd. But there wasn't much need for small talk. Bernanke quickly handed over the stage to one of his deputies, Bill English, who gave a long presentation about how quantitative easing might work and what effect it might have.

The Fed's own research on quantitative easing was surprisingly discouraging. If the Fed pumped $600 billion into the banking system, it was expected to cut the unemployment rate by just .03 percent. While that wasn't much, it was something. The plan could create 750,000 new jobs by the end of 2012, a small change to the unemployment rate but a big deal to those 750,000 people.

After English was finished, the FOMC members asked him questions, mostly technical in nature. But it didn't take long for the criticism to begin.

Jeffrey Lacker, president of the Richmond Fed, said the justifications for quantitative easing were thin and the risks were large and uncertain. "Please count me in the nervous camp," Lacker said. He warned that enacting the plan now, when there was no economic crisis at hand, would commit the Fed to near-permanent intervention as long as the unemployment rate was elevated. "As a result, people are likely to expect increasing monetary stimulus as long as the level of the unemployment rate is disappointing, and that's likely to be true for a long, long time."

Charles Plosser, the Philadelphia Fed president, was more blunt. "I do not support another round of asset purchases at this time," he said. "The economy has been through a soft patch this summer but it appears to be emerging from it." Plosser suggested that the Fed might be misleading the public about its plans, presenting a false sense of certainty about its path forward and the risks associated with it. "I think it would be a mistake to convey to the public that we know how to fine-tune an asset-purchase program to achieve our objectives when, in fact, we don't," he said. "Again, given these very small anticipated benefits, we should be even more focused on the downside risks of this program."

Fisher, the Dallas Fed president, said he was "deeply concerned" about the plan. Of course, he didn't let pass the chance to use a nice metaphor: "Quantitative easing is like kudzu for market operators," he said. "It grows and grows and it may be impossible to trim off once it takes root." Fisher echoed Hoenig's warnings that the plan would primarily benefit big banks and financial speculators, while punishing people who saved their money for retirement. "I see considerable risk in conducting policy with the consequence of transferring income from the poor, those most dependent on fixed income, and the saver to the rich," he said.

It was widely believed that it would be disastrous if three or four members of the FOMC voted against any given plan. This level of dissent would telegraph to the world that the Fed was divided, even uncertain, and maybe liable to reverse course.

Bernanke, however, didn't face the risk of three dissents in November. The reasons for this had to do with the bizarre makeup of the FOMC. The committee had twelve seats, but a majority of those members were not regional bank presidents. Seven of the FOMC seats belonged to members of the Fed's board of governors, who oversaw the bank from their offices in the Eccles Building in Washington. The governors worked full-time there, in offices that were just down the hall from the boardroom. Because there were twelve regional bank presidents, but only five seats available to them on the FOMC, the bank presidents rotated as voting members. In 2010, Plosser, Lacker, and Fisher were not voting members of the FOMC. They could attend the meetings and speak their mind, but they could not affect the final vote tally.

One member of the board of governors, named Kevin Warsh, was seriously opposed to quantitative easing. Warsh had a vote, and he had criticized quantitative easing since the day it was introduced. He was a former investment banker, only forty years old, with thick dark hair and a boyish face. Because he had spent his life in the financial markets, rather than academia, Warsh seemed to appreciate just how distortive Bernanke's plan could be. During a conference call in October, Warsh had bluntly stated that he was against it. The experiment was just too risky. "My sense is that none of us really know the probabilities of the downside risks associated with a second round of quantitative easing, but I do think we have an idea of how bad the situation could get if those downside risks materialized," he said.

Bernanke personally lobbied Warsh to put aside his concerns and vote with the majority. Less than a month before the vote, on October 8, Bernanke promised Warsh that if he voted for quantitative easing, they could quickly end the program if it appeared to be a mistake. Warsh was still not convinced, but during a second meeting on October 26, Warsh agreed to side with Bernanke. As a compromise, Warsh would publish an op-ed that expressed his reservations about quantitative easing, but only after he voted for it.

This left Hoenig, alone as a voting member, to make the case against the policy. During that day's meeting, Bernanke called on each member to share their comments, going around the table. When it was finally Hoenig's turn to speak, he began by acknowledging that his opposition had become almost entirely symbolic. But he would oppose it nonetheless.

"I strongly disagree with the course being charted here today," Hoenig said. "We may see some short-run improvement, but not long run. There will be, I'm sure, in the end, a lot of givebacks. Experience tells us that. This course sows the seeds of instability, in my opinion."

Hoenig warned that the Fed might be laying the groundwork for another financial crisis, even if the timing and cause of that crisis could not be predicted. "In the most general terms, the purported benefits are small and the risks are large," he said.

In his final dissent, Hoenig narrowed his argument to three points. The first risk he pointed out was that the Fed would find it extremely difficult to end a quantitative easing program once it began. It would be the financial equivalent of a military quagmire. Once the money printing began, where would it stop? When unemployment had been pushed down to 9 percent, or 8 percent, or lower?

"We will chase an open-ended commitment, I think" he said. "The Federal Reserve doesn't have a good track record of withdrawing policy accommodation in a timely manner, no matter how much we say we will."

The second risk was that the Fed might compromise its independence because it would be purchasing so much government debt. The explicit goal was to lower long-term interest rates on that debt. This could put the Fed in a bind. If the Fed pulled back on quantitative easing, it might cause interest rates to rise. That, in turn, would put more pressure on the Fed to keep buying to keep the price of government borrowing artificially low.

Finally, Hoenig said the program could "unanchor" inflation expectations. This was different than saying it would cause inflation. He was warning that companies and financial speculators would start anticipating higher inflation in the future thanks to the inflow of new money, and they would start to invest accordingly. This is partly what he was talking about when he used the word *instability*. Risky loans would drive up asset prices to unsustainable levels, and when those prices crashed it would cause mass unemployment.

In short, once the Fed started this program, it would create so many distortions and side effects that it would almost certainly not be able to end the program without causing massive instability or even a crash. "If we ease further, or if we leave the accommodation there too long, we will overshoot, and that's not consistent with our long-run mandates," Hoenig concluded. "Thank you, Mr. Chairman."

It was Bernanke's turn to speak next.

"Thank you," the chairman said to Hoenig. "It's eleven o'clock. I understand that coffee is ready. Why don't we take twenty minutes for refreshments?"

Hoenig had a choice, during the coffee break. He had spoken his piece. Now he could follow a path like Warsh's, expressing his reservations but then voting with the committee to show solidarity. Or he could dissent. Hoenig had been an institutionalist his whole life. And this was his last year on the FOMC. He was set to retire in 2011, and a "yes" vote could ease his retirement. The outcome of the vote was all but preordained. Hoenig wouldn't change it by dissenting.

After the break, the attendees settled back into their seats. There was more debate and then, at the end of the long day, the vote began. Each voting member of the FOMC would speak their verdict on quantitative easing as they went around the table.

Bernanke opened the process.

"Yes," he said.

William Dudley, vice chairman of the Fed: "Yes." Jim Bullard, of the St. Louis regional bank: "Yes." Betsy Duke, a Fed governor: "Yes."

Then it came to Hoenig.

"Respectfully, no."

After Hoenig, the votes were predictable: Yes. Yes. Yes. Yes. Yes. Yes. The final tally was 11 to 1.

When Bernanke wrote his memoir, he engraved this moment in history. "Surprising no one, Hoenig dissented—and, to boot, gave an interview the day after the meeting to Sudeep Reddy of *The Wall Street Journal* in which he criticized the Committee's action," Bernanke wrote. "Hoenig's comments had irked me . . ."

Virtually all of the predictions Thomas Hoenig made about quantitative easing, and 0 percent interest rates, would come true over the next decade. Years later, he didn't say that he voted the way he voted because he was smart. He said he voted that way because of what he'd learned over more than thirty years working inside the Federal Reserve. Hoenig became a dissenter against the Fed because of what he learned inside that very institution. He had seen firsthand how much devastation the Fed could cause when it got things wrong.

CHAPTER 2

SERIOUS NUMBERS

(1946–1979)

When Thomas Hoenig was nine years old, he was given a clipboard and sent into the back room of his father's business. It was Christmas vacation. Hoenig spent his break helping his dad, Leo, who ran a small plumbing business in the family's hometown of Fort Madison, Iowa. Leo had been raised on a farm outside of town, so he only knew a certain kind of life. It was a life where the kids woke up before dawn and did chores when they weren't at school. "You just—you were part of that family, and this is what families did. That was your responsibility," recalled Tom Hoenig's older sister, Kathleen Kelley.

So, rather than go sledding or make a snowman or run around in the woods, Tom took the clipboard and went in the storeroom, as he was told. His job was to take inventory. This wasn't busywork. Hoenig tabulated the make and number of various parts that were piled on the shelves. If he was lazy or careless, his dad wouldn't know what parts were on hand for a job, and might show up empty handed. Tom Hoenig concentrated, trying to make sure he got the numbers right.

Fort Madison was a small town that hugged a bend in the Mississippi

River and was a transit point for barge traffic. There were a couple of big factories, one of which made ink pens. The downtown was thriving and populated by small businesses. Hoenig remembers going to the soda counter downtown, and playing basketball with friends. He was the second oldest in a household with seven children. The Hoenig plumbing business was an all-consuming affair for the family. Tom and his siblings worked there, as did their mother, Arlene. She was the most educated member of the family, having graduated from high school. Leo left the family farm when he was young and got shipped out to fight in World War II. When he came back, he decided he didn't want to have anything to do with farming anymore. He got work as a plumber, learned the trade, and eventually ran his own contracting firm.

Leo and Arlene wanted their children to have a better station in life. Arlene encouraged her children to study hard and attend college. If Arlene stoked the dream of going to college, then Leo showed his kids exactly what they could expect if they decided against it. Leo seemed determined to give Tom jobs that were increasingly unpleasant and miserable as he grew older. Tom dug ditches, cleaned out muddy ravines, and carried heavy parts of a disassembled boiler up from a basement, leaving him covered in filth. The message was clear: This was the life of a high school dropout.

Tom decided to go to college. He attended a Catholic college in the small farming town of Atchison, Kansas, run by the religion's Benedictine order. It was a liberal arts school, and Tom was exposed to a wide range of subjects, but he quickly realized that he was attracted to just one of them. It only took a single introductory class in economics to change his life.

Economics seemed like the hidden key to explaining everything. It was presented to Hoenig as the scientific study of choices that people made to get by in their daily lives. It wasn't just about math or money; it was about the way a society of millions of people managed to somehow organize itself and function without the all-powerful hand of a tyrant.

The chaotic swarm of independent-thinking people made all these choices about what to do with their limited time and money, and slowly all of those choices began to aggregate into big social forces. When people suddenly decided that they wanted to buy cars, for example, it made the price of cars go up, which then stimulated companies to make more cars, in turn stimulating engineers to design cheaper cars, which further stoked demand. But then, when there were too many cars and not enough people who wanted to buy them, the prices fell. These were the kinds of dynamics that fascinated Tom Hoenig.

Hoenig met with his college advisors, and they told him that if he wanted to be an economist, he needed to earn a PhD, which would require at least three years of graduate school. He was going to surpass his parents' education level by several degrees. He had it all mapped out. And then, shortly after he graduated from college, he got a draft notice. Hoenig had the luck of graduating in 1968, the year of the Tet Offensive in Vietnam. The war escalated and draft deferments were suspended for graduate students.

When he got his draft notice, Hoenig was placed in the middle of a terrible storm that was battering America's civic life. It wasn't entirely clear, in 1968, what might be the best course of action to take for a good citizen. On the one hand, Hoenig believed in America's institutions. He was patriotic and religious. He said the Pledge of Allegiance at school, just like everyone else. He attended Catholic church, Catholic schools, and a Catholic college. So when the government told him that he was legally obligated to go into the Army, he felt he should obey. On the other hand, Hoenig wasn't blind to what was happening in Vietnam. Even in rural Kansas, students were protesting the war. The atrocities of Vietnam were broadcast on the nightly news. Hoenig didn't want to go to a jungle to kill people or risk being blown apart by a land mine. But he decided that he wasn't ready to dodge the draft or move to Canada. He knew that his dad would be deeply ashamed of him if he did so. Faced with the inevitability that he'd be drafted, as the notice informed him, Hoenig decided to enlist instead. That way he could get his service over with sooner. He explained his decision to his older sister in terms that defined how he thought about such things. "I remember him saying: 'You know, I'm an American citizen and I hope to be able to enjoy all the benefits this country offers, so it's my responsibility,'" Kelley recalled.

Hoenig went to basic training, where he got yelled at by drill sergeants and taught how to fire a rifle. He was relieved to discover that he wouldn't be assigned to the infantry, but would become an artilleryman instead. Artillery units were located farther away from the front lines, where infantry soldiers fought the Viet Cong at close quarters. "I'm nothing like an infantryman. Nothing. That was hell on Earth," Hoenig later remembered.

Hoenig was deployed to the field in Vietnam for roughly seven months. His job title was "fire direction control specialist," meaning he was an expert in firing heavy artillery. At one point, he was sent to a base north of Saigon to help a New Hampshire National Guard unit. That's where he met Jon McKeon, who would become a lifelong friend. Both men were in their early twenties, and had been trained in the fine science of artillery fire. This was another phase in Hoenig's life when he was given the job of recording and computing serious numbers, with serious consequences at stake.

Hoenig and McKeon worked together in a small bunker, located in the center of an encampment called a firebase. The base was laid out in a big circle, surrounded by sandbags and concertina wire, guarded at night by infantry soldiers. Hoenig's bunker, in the center, was made from a large metal storage container stuffed with chairs, a desk, and a large metal computer. Photos from the era show cramped conditions in such a bunker, with loose wires hanging from the ceiling, makeshift lamps clipped overhead, and protractors and charts hanging from the walls. The soldiers went shirtless in the heat. They slept on cots at night and took turns burning the contents of 55-gallon barrels that they used as latrines. Between three and six howitzer cannons were located outside the circle. The howitzers fired heavy shells, as long as a person's forearm, that weighed about 100 pounds. The shells could hit targets more than a mile away and their destructive impact was immense. When infantry soldiers were in combat, they radioed the firebase for supporting fire. The howitzer shells had to be fired quickly and aimed with almost perfect precision. A missed shot could kill U.S. soldiers or decimate nearby villages where families might be hiding.

As fire-control specialists, Hoenig and McKeon sat on a committee of three soldiers who worked twelve-hour shifts, directing the fire of the artillery cannons. This committee did the math and decided how to fire each shell to protect troops they couldn't see. Each of the three committee members did a series of complex calculations for each artillery strike, as fast as they could. If they made a mistake, people died. They divvied up the work and rotated between jobs. One soldier plotted out the coordinates of battle on a map and stuck a pin in the exact location where the artillery shells needed to land. Then he collected weather data gathered each day by balloons, charting the wind speeds and humidity levels that would affect the shells' trajectory.

All of this data was handed over to the second soldier, who did the calculations to determine how the cannons should be aimed, then fired. This was a lot more complicated than it sounds because there were so many variables to consider. The soldier had to figure out how much powder should be loaded into the cannons, how steep the arc of the shell's trajectory should be, and where to set the cannon's side-to-side axis (called the azimuth). Then the soldier who did these calculations fed the data into a giant metal box with keypads on the front, called a FADAC computer. "We didn't have one hundred percent faith in the computer," McKeon recalled. They often redid the calculations by hand. Finally, the third soldier operated the radios, commanding the team outside that was working the cannons.

None of this was easy for Hoenig. All his life he'd been taught a Christian doctrine that emphasized nonviolence and loving one's neighbor. He had no illusions about what was going on. "You're trying to kill people. The whole purpose of the program here is to kill as many of 'em as you can," he said. He also knew that if his team made a mistake, the consequences could be catastrophic. Hoenig dealt with these thoughts by shutting them out. He and his team took in all the data that they could, did the math as quickly and efficiently as possible, checked their work, and gave the order to fire. "I just did the calculations, sent the signal, put it out of my mind."

As far as he knew, the team never made a mistake that killed U.S. soldiers or civilians.

After about seven months near the front lines, Hoenig was transferred to a larger camp, where he joined a team of specialists who analyzed artillery accidents. He studied how bad data, bad decisions, or miscommunications could lead to catastrophe. Mistakes could be made quickly, in ways that a committee of three soldiers didn't realize at the time. One wrong assumption, one bad piece of information about air pressure, or one misspoken command, could set off a chain reaction.

Hoenig was spared close-quarters combat, but he saw up close how chaotic and senseless war could be. A group of his friends from the artillery unit were shipping home when, on the way to an air base, their truck hit a land mine and everyone on board was killed. Hoenig had known all of them well, and it seemed cruel that they should die with just two days left on their tour. He, on the other hand, made it home safe.

When he got back home to Fort Madison in 1970, Hoenig faced the same challenge as other soldiers who had served in Vietnam. They had to make sense out of the terrible things they had seen and done overseas. And they had to do it at the very moment when Americans were losing faith in their government. A lot of soldiers were protesting, and Hoenig understood why. The war blew a permanent hole in the foundation of trust that Americans had in the democratic institutions that governed them. In 1971, *The New York Times*, *The Washington Post*, and a series of regional newspapers published a secret government report, known as the Pentagon Papers, which showed that America's leaders had lied to the public for years about the war in Vietnam. Just two years later, President Nixon was caught up in a criminal conspiracy to bug his opponent's campaign headquarters at the Watergate Hotel. This was a time when any young person might lose faith in American institutions, and many of them did.

Hoenig turned to his father for advice. Leo Hoenig had fought his own war in the 1940s and managed to make a good life afterward. His advice to his son was clear and simple: "Move forward."

It helped that Hoenig had a new life to move toward. When Hoenig and McKeon had talked during the quiet moments in Vietnam, Hoenig had talked a lot about the fiancée who was waiting for him at home. Her name was Cynthia Stegeman, a Kansas City girl whom Hoenig started dating while he was going to college in Kansas. They'd met on a blind date. It didn't start out great. Cynthia considered herself a creative type, who loved art. When she asked Tom what he was into, he said his passion was mathematics and economics. They went to see *The Godfather* and then got a drink at a lounge in downtown Kansas City. The lounge was dim, and while trying to take Cynthia to the dance floor Hoenig walked straight into a wall. "He bounced back from that, and actually just laughed about it to himself. Didn't try to recover with a lot of bravado, or try to impress me that he knew it was there or anything," Cynthia said. "And I thought: 'This guy is terrific because he can laugh at himself.'"

Tom and Cynthia got married after he returned from combat. Tom had returned in March, and by June, he had enrolled at Iowa State University, where he planned to earn a PhD in economics. He would move forward.

———————

When Tom Hoenig studied economics at Iowa State, he studied it in a way that seemed quite strange in later years. By the 1990s, the field of economics would transform into something that seemed like the science of how to get rich quick. Modern economists developed theories that justified the actions of large corporations and banks, paving the way for international trade deals, new financial trading in exotic derivatives, and a relentless push toward maximizing profit for people who owned stock. But, in the early 1970s, Hoenig applied himself to a different kind of economics. This economics studied how America's democratic government could coexist with free markets. Hoenig studied the ways that capitalism, democracy, and regulation might be mutually supportive.

His master's thesis, for example, was an in-depth study of the income tax in the state of Iowa. He began his paper by pointing out that the obligations of state governments had expanded dramatically since World War II. States had once been confined to passing and enforcing laws, but now they were committed to a growing range of public services, like operating highways and providing welfare benefits. This expansion of the regulatory state was already stoking anger in American politics. But Hoenig bypassed that controversy in his thesis. He didn't criticize the regulatory state, but tried to figure out how economists might help it function. The size of the regulatory state was the result of accumulated choices made by American citizens. If that was the case, then it ought to at least work well. He examined the tricky issue of how the state could meet its budget while collecting taxes that rose and fell every year. Hoenig was more agitated by the idea that a state might miss its budget targets because it failed to analyze the right numbers. His thesis employed exclamation points on this matter: "A 5 percent decline in personal income would imply a fall in revenue of perhaps 2 or 3 percent, just at a time when larger [state] expenditures had already been authorized!"

Hoenig argued that the state should hire serious number crunchers and economists to help project, as accurately as possible, what future sales and income taxes might be. After 155 pages of charts, tables, and citations, his ultimate conclusion was unsatisfying in its humility. Setting budgets would always be maddeningly unpredictable and uncertain. "The best that can be done is to look at the available data and make the best judgement possible," he wrote.

For his PhD dissertation, Hoenig turned his attention to the banking system. By the late 1960s, banks were merging with one another at a fast pace. If this continued, Hoenig worried, it might create a banking system that was dominated by very large institutions. "I could almost see the beginning of the end of the community bank," he later recalled. Hoenig studied this issue in a narrow way, similar to how he studied state tax issues. He wrote a deeply technical report that aimed to help federal regulators decide if they should approve or reject a given bank merger. He did this by examining the market for consumer loans—the type of loan people used to buy cars or send their kids to school. Hoenig noted that when there wasn't a lot of competition between banks, they tended to charge people more money to borrow (by charging higher interest rates) and pay them less money to save (by offering lower interest rates). Hoenig compiled loan data from all fifty states and parsed it. He found evidence that the market for consumer loans was "segmented," meaning that banks didn't have to compete directly with other institutions like credit unions for loan business. This meant that regulators should only consider the impact that a bank merger had on the concentration of ownership among banks, rather than considering what impact it might have on the concentration of all lending in a given area. This wasn't the kind of finding that generated big headlines, but it could help a lot of people and keep banking competitive.

Decades later, these papers would illuminate how Hoenig thought about banking and finance. He didn't study how to boost profit margins or make a market more efficient. Instead, he studied the structure of banking institutions and thought about how it impacted society. This reflected a viewpoint that was widespread in the era when Hoenig grew up. It held that bankers were motivated to make money, but that it was up to the government to make sure that the banks served a broader purpose, feeding economic growth and providing a healthy circulatory system for money. The structure of banks mattered a lot, in this view.

It might not have been surprising, considering his studies, that when Hoenig graduated with a PhD, he pursued a job not in banking but in banking policy. Hoenig heard that the Kansas City Federal Reserve was looking for a research economist in the department of bank supervision. Hoenig wrote a letter to the Fed, laying out his qualifications for the job. In 1973, he was hired. Tom and Cynthia moved to Kansas City. For Cynthia, it was coming back home. For Tom, it was a move to the big city. Each morning, he went downtown to the Federal Reserve building and joined a team of economists analyzing the conduct and operations of banks throughout the Kansas City Fed's district, which included Colorado, Kansas, Nebraska, Oklahoma, Wyoming, and portions of Missouri and New Mexico. This is where Hoenig began his long education in the inner workings of the institution that would define his entire career in public life. This is where he started to see how powerful the Federal Reserve really was, and how it actually worked.

There is nothing in the U.S. Constitution that demands, or even specifically authorizes, the creation of a central bank. But it turned out to be impossible for a modern nation to survive without a central bank, and the United States proved it. America tried to get by, for about a century, without a establishing a government-run bank that controlled the currency. Between 1776 and 1912, the United States twice created and then destroyed a central bank. The country resisted having a central bank because it concentrates so much power into so few hands. This concentrated power would undermine the entire American project, which was, ideally, to put control of the government into the hands of average citizens. When Andrew Jackson revoked the charter of the second U.S. national bank in 1836, he called it "dangerous to the liberties of the people." It's not hard to understand why. Imagine if one bank had dominion over the entire financial system, and the leaders of that bank could decide who got loans and who didn't. Those bank leaders would be the most powerful people in the country. Such a scenario is, by any measure, anti-American.

The early American banking system was decentralized, and it was a disaster. The reason things can't work without a central bank is that every modern nation needs a reliable form of currency. Currency is the medium of exchange that holds value and transfers value from one person to another. Without currency, people would still be trading corn for tobacco and trying to figure out the exchange rate.

Without a central bank to issue a national currency, creating money becomes a cottage industry. In the mid-1800s the United States had thousands of different currencies floating around (one count put it at 8,370 currencies). This was called the "free banking" era, and it was lunacy. Any bank could issue money, and the currency was backed by the bank itself. So, if the bank went bust, the money went bust with it. Every person had to make a judgment about the health of a given bank to figure out if they wanted to use its currency. A person could get money from a bank in Illinois, and then travel to Oregon only to argue with a clerk at a hotel whether the Illinois currency was any good.

Congress passed a law after the Civil War that chartered a series of national banks around the country, which issued a more uniform currency. But even if the currency problem got ironed out, there was a second reason that a central bank was necessary. The American banking system was still hyperfragile and subject to regular panics and failures. Major bank panics broke out, one after the next, in 1893, 1895, and 1907. Bank runs were inevitable in panics because there wasn't an all-powerful central bank that could print money and act as a "lender of last resort," providing loans when every bank needed money at the same time. Without a lender of last resort, the banks were left to bail out one another, using whatever reserves they happened to have on hand, or to fail. The Fed was given power to print money and loan it out freely to otherwise sound banks during a panic, which had the effect of stopping panics in the first place because borrowers knew the Fed was there. The Fed disbursed its emergency loans through a program called the "discount window."

Finally, on top of the bank panics, there was a third problem. There was no central bank to manage the overall supply of money itself. Demand for currency went up and down in unpredictable ways but the money supply couldn't change along with it.

Every autumn, for example, farmers withdrew from their local banks to hire workers to harvest their fields. This drew down the limited cash reserves at banks in the Midwest, which made them scared that they might not have enough cash on hand to meet their obligations. So, when those rural banks ran low on cash, they turned to the bigger regional banks in cities like Chicago to get cash. Those regional banks then turned to the New York banks, and the New York banks turned to the big banks in Europe. This could turn into a panic and be truly ruinous for everyone. The bank panic of 1873 led to a depression that lasted about six years.

This helps explain why the major push to form a central bank didn't come from bankers. It came from the hell-raising Populist and Free Silver movements, formed by angry farmers in the middle of the country who needed loans to survive. The politics of money was suddenly a riotous public issue. William Jennings Bryan was playing to the crowd when he did his "cross of gold" routine. People were already angry about monetary policy.

The popular effort to form a central bank gathered strength during the early 1900s. But the movement didn't become a realistic political possibility until the Wall Street bankers decided to get behind it. To the everlasting joy of every conspiracy theorist in America, a group of ultrapowerful bankers got together and held a secret meeting in 1910 in which they created the blueprint for an American central bank. The bankers met at a luxury resort called Jekyll Island, making it easy for future filmmakers and authors to talk about the Fed as the "Creature from Jekyll Island," as if it were a secret plot that the bankers foisted on America. But this isn't the case, as William Greider made clear in his seminal history of the Fed, *Secrets of the Temple*. The bankers did push their plan in the U.S. Senate, but they were riding a wave of public sentiment that had been building for decades. A central bank was inevitable by that point in the United States.

But the bankers at Jekyll Island did secure an important victory at their secret meeting. They made sure that the U.S. central bank would not usurp the power of the private banking system on Wall Street. This was very important. The populists had proposed all kinds of plans that would have democratized the process of controlling American money, even bypassing the big banks. One plan, put forward in 1889, called for the U.S. Treasury to establish a network of grain elevators and warehouses around the nation that would be decentralized "sub-treasuries," where farmers could deposit crops as collateral for loans. The bankers at Jekyll Island exterminated such wild notions. They put Wall Street at the center of the proposed Federal Reserve system. When the Fed increased or decreased the money supply, it would do so through the commercial banking system, letting the banks decide how the money would be distributed into the economy.

The Jekyll Island plan was debated and modified in Congress and passed in 1913, creating the first enduring central bank in U.S. history. But the deeper, very American tension over having a central bank never went away. America needed a central bank, but it didn't want one that was too powerful. This tension was encoded into the Federal Reserve's DNA. The Federal Reserve was both a government agency and a private bank. It was controlled in Washington, D.C., but also decentralized. It was given total control over the money supply, but didn't replace the private banking system. It was insulated from voters, but broadly accountable to politicians.

The tension was also encoded into the Fed's structure. It's why the Fed is a network of regional banks, governed from an office in Washington, D.C. The twelve regional banks might be one of Congress's strangest creations, mixing public government with private enterprise. Each regional bank is owned by a group of private banks in the district (the private banks own stock in the regional Fed, though they can't sell it). The private banks in each region are given seats on the regional Fed's board of directors, and the board selects the bank's president. This was designed to create a decentralized system, with powerful regional banks that are accountable to both the community banks in their region and to the Fed's governing board in Washington.

While the Fed was supposed to look like America—a federated nation of twelve regional banks—its governance became more centralized in Washington each time the Fed's charter was updated by Congress. The power at the Fed now rests largely with the bank's board of governors, of whom there are seven, nominated by the president and approved by Congress. The tension between the governors and the regional bank presidents is seen most acutely inside the Federal Open Market Committee. Because the governors have a majority of seats on the FOMC, they set the agenda, and the board's power only increases in times of emergency. When the Fed becomes the lender of last resort, the governors can take action without the approval of the full FOMC.

This was the institution that hired Tom Hoenig in 1973. It is not surprising that life inside the central bank appealed to him. The Fed embodied his worldview. It was the result of a series of unhappy compromises, and it seemed like the best system America could create to tackle difficult problems. One of the Fed's important roles is to regulate the banking industry, to help ensure that bank panics and bank failures don't destabilize the wider economy. Hoenig would spend nearly two decades in the supervisory department, meaning he was a bank regulator.

He was well suited to this work. As a kid, he'd helped his dad tally the family store's inventory. As a soldier, he'd helped calculate the trajectory of artillery shells. At the Fed, Hoenig helped analyze the constant inflow of data about banks inside the Kansas City Fed's large district.

This is how Hoenig got a front-row seat to observe the biggest banking crisis since the Great Depression.

Hoenig's job involved a lot of arguments with local bankers. The substance of the disputes usually centered on a topic of paramount importance: the value of assets. The bankers often thought that their assets were worth more than the bank examiners thought they were worth. The consequences of such disagreements were enormous. Hoenig and his team were trying to make sure that the banks weren't making dangerous loans or getting so overextended that they might fail. The assets in question were held as collateral at the banks. If a bank had more collateral, it could make more loans. But if the Fed ruled that its collateral was worth less than the bank said, then the bank needed to raise money to cover the value of its loans. In dire cases, the bank could be taken into receivership and essentially dissolved. If the arguments were heated, there was no doubt who held the power in the relationship. Fed examiners had access to the banks' records and employees. They could see what they were lending and to whom.

Hoenig was fascinated by this work, and he knew it was essential to keeping the financial system stable. The job was also a challenge; it was surprisingly complicated to determine the health of a bank. That's why the arguments over asset values were so important. If a bank in Oklahoma loaned $1 million to an oil-drilling company, the riskiness of that loan depended on the value of the assets the bank received as collateral. One common form of collateral was future revenue expected from oil wells. But that raised a lot of variables. If oil was going to be worth $20 a barrel, on average, over the term of the loan, then the collateral might be worth $1.5 million. In that case, the loan was super safe. But if oil prices fell to $10 a barrel, the collateral would only be worth $750,000. Now the loan was looking riskier. This is why bank examiners were entangled in arguments. The value of an asset is always open to debate.

As the 1970s progressed, such arguments became more heated, and eventually turned desperate. The reasons for this can be traced back to the Federal Reserve Bank itself. While Hoenig's team of examiners were trying to keep the banking system safe, they were being undermined by a different, far more powerful arm of the Fed: the FOMC. The policy board in Washington was doing things that fundamentally changed the behavior of the very banks that the Fed was supposed to be keeping healthy.

During the 1970s, the Federal Reserve encouraged the banks to extend riskier and riskier loans. The FOMC was keeping interest rates extraordinarily low, in part because there had been two recessions between 1970 and 1975. The Fed wanted to create jobs, encourage investment, and boost overall economic growth. So it kept rates low even as the ill effects of creating so much money became more apparent each year. The most obvious effects of this policy showed up in rising prices for consumer goods like food, fuel, and electronics. In 1973, the rate of consumer price inflation was 3.6 percent, meaning that the cost of goods most people bought rose 3.6 percent from one year to the next. By 1979, inflation had surged to 10.7 percent per year. The change was obvious to everyone; it showed up in prices at the grocery store and the gas station. It showed up in the payroll department of companies that needed to give big pay raises every year if employees were to keep up with the cost of living.

But the Fed wasn't just inflating consumer prices. It was inflating asset prices as well. This was the form of inflation that was alarming to bank examiners like Hoenig. The value of farmland, a key asset for banks within the Kansas City Fed district, was rising steeply. So was the value of commercial real estate, and the value of oil wells and drilling rigs. These assets were the collateral on banks' balance sheets, and their rising value encouraged more aggressive lending. Banks throughout the Midwest extended big loans to farmers, based on the theory that the value of farmland would keep rising and support the value of the loan. The same thing happened in the oil business, and real estate. Hoenig heard about short-term construction loans that were extended based on the theory that property values would rise so quickly that the loan could be refinanced as soon as the building was finished.

This was pushing the banks to make riskier loans. High inflation and relatively low rates discouraged banks and investors from saving money, because savings earned only small interest payments compared to the value it lost from inflation. The banks had to find something to do with their money that earned a good return. They were pushed out further on the yield curve. Hoenig and his team watched this happen, but there was very little that they could do about it. As asset prices rose, the banks could credibly argue that the loans were safe and the banks were stable. The examiners at the Fed could argue otherwise, but the bankers had the numbers on their side.

In 1981, Hoenig was promoted to vice president of the Kansas City Fed's supervision department, overseeing a team of about fifty bank examiners. He got the job just in time to learn his most important lesson about the role of the Fed in American economics. He got to see what happens when a long period of inflation comes to a sudden, unexpected stop.

"You have this enormous collapse," Hoenig said. "Failure upon failure, loss upon loss, crisis upon crisis."

CHAPTER 3

THE GREAT INFLATION(S)

(1980–1991)

Hoenig was thirty-three years old when the banking crisis started. But the forces that combusted in 1980 had been building for many years. Hoenig's team of examiners in Kansas City could see for themselves that banks had been making riskier and riskier loans for years. But the bankers could always justify what they were doing. They were using a certain logic that was made possible only by the wild distortions of the Great Inflation of the 1970s. Consumer prices were rising sharply every year, and asset prices were rising in sync with them. "Bankers are making these loans in an environment where asset values are strong and rising," Hoenig explained. This put the Fed examiners in a bind. They believed that bank loans were risky, because the asset prices underpinning those loans were probably overvalued. But the bankers argued back, pointing out that the asset prices were marked according to fair market value. The value of assets isn't a fixed or even a knowable thing. It's a matter of judgment. "Examiners are no more able to predict the future than the bankers are," Hoenig said.

This whole experience, and the massive financial ruin that followed in its wake, provided Tom Hoenig with the most important education of his career. It taught him, in very fine detail, about the powerful and unruly thing that economists call an asset bubble. Decades later, the Great Inflation was not usually described in terms of asset bubbles. When people look back on the 1970s, they tend to talk about only one half of the disaster: the shocking inflation of consumer prices, for things like meat and gasoline. But the Great Inflation was so destructive because it was actually two kinds of inflation that were intertwined, and which fed off each other. The other one was the inflation of asset prices, a phenomenon that later became the most important feature of American economic life. Asset inflation was the force behind the dot-com crash of 2000, the housing market crash of 2008, and the unprecedented market crash of 2020, which was precipitated by the coronavirus outbreak.

An asset is anything a person can buy that stores value. A ham sandwich is not an asset because it loses value with time, making it a consumer good. A bar of gold, on the other hand, is an asset. A share of stock is an asset. A painting is an asset. An apartment building is an asset. The Federal Reserve can stoke asset inflation when it keeps money too cheap for too long, pushing asset prices so high that they are no longer supported by the actual value of the asset. This is when asset prices become a bubble. One of the best examples of an asset bubble was described in 1955 by the economic historian John Kenneth Galbraith. In the department of some things never changing, Galbraith described an asset bubble in Florida real estate in the early 1900s. Developers were expecting a lot of people to move to the state, so they bought big tracts of land and subdivided it into neighborhood plots. Then they sold deeds of ownership for the plots. In this case, the actual land in Florida was an asset and the deeds to the land were an asset, because the paper deeds could be bought and sold. Speculation in Florida real estate took off. The price of land, and the price of deeds for the land, spiraled upward. The asset inflation was stoked by the very fact that asset prices were rising in the first place. One person bought a deed and sold it for more money, and this enticed yet a third person to buy the deed because its price was going up. If this cycle could go on forever, the world would be a much happier place. But, inevitably, the price of an asset converges with the actual value of the asset. In Florida, this convergence happened when it became clear that the expected hordes of people were not moving there. Hurricanes kept hitting the state, dissuading new homeowners. And a lot of the overhyped subdivisions were located on hot, humid stretches of swamp, without a beach in sight. People started selling, then everyone started selling. The bubble burst, and the asset price collapsed.

Tom Hoenig watched, in the 1970s, as asset bubbles inflated across the Kansas City Fed's district, which included both heavy farming states, like Kansas and Nebraska, and the energy-producing state of Oklahoma. The self-reinforcing logic of asset bubbles was painfully evident in farming. When the FOMC kept interest rates low, it encouraged farmers to take on more cheap debt and buy more land. This, in turn, stoked demand for farmland, which pushed up land prices. The higher land prices encouraged more people to borrow and buy yet more land. The bankers' logic followed a similar path. The bankers saw farmland as collateral on the loans, and they believed the collateral would only rise in value. More lending led to more buying, which led to higher prices, which led to more lending.

The same thing was happening in the oil and natural gas business. Rising oil prices and cheap debt encouraged oil companies to borrow money and drill more wells. The banks built a whole side business dedicated to risky energy loans. In commercial real estate, it was the same thing. This is how asset bubbles escalate in a loop that intensifies with each rotation, with the reality of today's higher asset prices driving the value of tomorrow's asset prices ever higher, increasing the momentum even further.

While Hoenig and his team were arguing with the bankers, the FOMC was stoking the Great Inflation even more by keeping interest rates low. But this stopped in 1979, and it stopped with a severity that has never been repeated. It was stopped because of one person, Paul Volcker, who became chairman of the Federal Reserve. Volcker was serious about beating inflation. He was willing to push the unemployment rate to 10 percent to do so, to force homeowners to take out mortgages that carried 17 percent interest rates or higher, and to make consumer loans so expensive that many Americans couldn't afford to buy cars.

Volcker recognized that when he was fighting inflation, he was actually fighting two kinds: asset inflation and price inflation. He called them "cousins," and acknowledged that they had been created by the Fed. "The real danger comes from [the Fed] encouraging or inadvertently tolerating rising inflation and its close cousin of extreme speculation and risk taking, in effect standing by while bubbles and excesses threaten financial markets," Volcker wrote in his memoir.

Volcker's predecessors had encouraged these risks, but Volcker would not. Under his leadership, the Fed raised short-term interest rates from 10 percent in 1979 to 20 percent in 1981, the highest they have ever been. When the history of interest rates is plotted on a graph, this period of super-high rates looks like a mountain peak. This is why Volcker's tenure as Fed chairman is such an important period in the history of U.S. monetary policy. He is remembered as one of the few people willing to initiate the brutal shock therapy necessary to correct years of mistakes. Volcker's rate hikes devastated the economy, put millions of people out of work, and ended the Great Inflation.

At first, people didn't think Volcker was serious about raising rates. Then they didn't think he'd actually be able to do it. Right after he started doing so, in October 1979, there were rumors that he had resigned under pressure. It seemed inconceivable that the Federal Reserve would go through with a plan that would push the economy into recession. Volcker held an emergency press conference in the Eccles Building on a Saturday evening to announce that he wasn't leaving, and that the Fed was serious about raising interest rates. "I'm still alive—contrary to the latest rumor," Volcker told reporters. That weekend, short-term rates were 11.6 percent. By the end of the month, they would be 16 percent. In less than a year, they reached the high of 20 percent.

The reporters pressed Volcker that Saturday night, asking if the rate hikes would damage the economy. He was largely dismissive of the question. "I would be optimistic in the results of these actions," he said. "I think the best indications that I have now in an uncertain world is that it can be accomplished reasonably smoothly."

Volcker was wrong on this point. Nothing went reasonably smoothly. The American economic ecosystem had settled itself around the North Star of low interest rates. Volcker moved the polestar overnight, and everything reoriented. A decade's worth of resource allocation would change and everything would shift back in from the edge of the yield curve, away from risk.

The change was wrenching. It played out very quickly in the Kansas City Federal Reserve's district. The bankers were caught totally off guard. "You could see that no one anticipated that adjustment, even after Volcker began to address inflation. They didn't think it would happen to them," Hoenig said.

When Paul Volcker and the Fed doubled the cost of borrowing, the demand for loans slowed down, which in turn depressed the demand for assets like farmland and oil wells. The price of assets began to converge with the underlying value of the assets. The price of farmland fell by 27 percent in the early 1980s; of oil, from more than $120 to $25 by 1986. The collapse of asset prices created a cascading effect within the banking system. Assets like farmland and oil reserves had been used to underpin the value of bank loans, and those loans were themselves considered "assets" on the banks' balance sheets. When land and oil prices fell, the entire system fell apart. Banks wrote down the value of their collateral and the reserves they were holding against default. At the very same moment, the farmers and oil drillers started having a hard time meeting their monthly payments. The value of crops and oil were falling, so they earned less money each month. The banks' balance sheets, which once looked stable, began to corrode and falter.

Hoenig's examiners had the unpleasant job of pointing out the obvious: The financial health of the banks was collapsing along with asset prices. Predictably, the banks fought back. The bankers almost always asked for more time. They promised that if they were given a chance, a few more months or a few more quarters, they could turn things around. Asset prices would rise. The balance sheet would improve.

Hoenig's team spent most of the early 1980s doing one thing: deciding which banks could actually survive if given more time, and which banks were doomed. John Yorke was a Fed lawyer who worked closely with Hoenig during this period, and he said that the debates with the banks had a desperate edge. There was a clock ticking behind the arguments that decided which banks were solvent, because banks were asking the Fed for emergency loans. The Fed was the lender of last resort, and its power in this role was almost limitless. It could print money, so it could lend as much money as it chose to. But Congress had imposed one limit on this power: The Fed wasn't supposed to lend to banks that were going to fail. The emergency loans were doled out through the Fed's so-called discount window. Tom Hoenig oversaw the Kansas City Fed's discount window in the 1980s. When his team decided who could borrow from the discount window, they were rendering life-or-death judgment on banks.

A true bank panic broke out in 1982, the worst since the Great Depression. More than a hundred banks failed that year, far more than in any single year since the 1930s. In 1986, the rate was higher, with more than two hundred banks failing. Overall, more than sixteen hundred banks failed between 1980 and 1994.

The bankers came to the Kansas City Fed, in a parade, pleading their cases. All of them pitched plans under which they would stay solvent, and Hoenig developed a broad rule of thumb to evaluate them. He noticed that the best plans had a lot of detail. The worst plans were vague, and peppered heavily with platitudes. Bankers, Hoenig came to believe, were like anyone else. Some of them were honest and hard-working. A small minority were hucksters. But it wasn't just the hucksters who were failing. Many of the failed banks had been in business for generations. They were the financial pillars of small communities throughout the region.

John Yorke was dispatched to the small town of Sedan, Kansas, where he had grown up and worked at a community bank as a teenager. Everyone at the bank still knew him as "Johnny," his childhood nickname. "I was the officer that went in and told the board that, you know . . . you're going to fail. It was terrible," Yorke said. "Particularly when they're calling you 'Johnny,' which only my mother called me." Hoenig had to deliver many such verdicts personally. He didn't seem to flinch from the responsibility. "Tom's German," Yorke said, referring to the ethnic origin of Hoenig's name. "He's strict. There's rules."

Hoenig was cursed at, shouted at, and informed in the clearest way possible that his decisions had ruinous consequences. "They could become quite stressed and quite vocal in their objections," Hoenig said of the bankers. "You could empathize with them enormously. You could understand the anguish. Lives were destroyed in this environment, people lost everything in this environment. I didn't blame them for yelling or being distraught."

It would have been easy enough for Hoenig to blame the bankers when the bubble burst. Examples of banking grotesquery were abundant. This is what happens in a speculative bubble. Stupidity and risk-taking thrive during the upswing, then cause misery on the downswing. But Hoenig didn't think the stupidity in lending was entirely the bankers' fault. They were, after all, responding to macroeconomic conditions like rising inflation, relatively low interest rates when compared to inflation, and rising asset prices.

It wasn't the bankers who created these conditions. It was Hoenig's own institution, the Federal Reserve. "The fact is, [bankers] made the loans," Hoenig said. "They made them in an environment of incredible optimism in terms of asset values. And that, really, was in part the fault of a decade of too-accommodative monetary policy."

This was the dynamic that so often gets lost in the discussion about the inflation of the 1970s and the collapse and recession of the 1980s. The Fed got credit for ending inflation, and for bailing out the solvent banks that survived it. But new research published many decades later showed that the Fed was also responsible for the whole disaster.

Perhaps the most detailed account of how the Federal Reserve handled the Great Inflation is related in *The History of the Federal Reserve*, a remarkable 2,100-page book, split into three volumes, that is dense to the point of being nearly unreadable. The author, the economist Allan Meltzer, reconstructed the Fed's decision making during the 1970s using transcripts of FOMC meetings, combined with other public documents and detailed economic studies and data. His verdict on the inflation of the 1970s was stark: It was monetary policy, set by the Fed, that primarily created the problem. "The Great Inflation resulted from policy choices that placed much more weight on maintaining high or full employment than on preventing or reducing inflation," he wrote. "For much of the period, this choice reflected both political pressures and popular opinion as expressed in polls."

This statement was combative and inflammatory, as far as Fed economic histories go. What Meltzer was saying was that the Fed basically didn't know what it was doing during the 1970s. Maybe even more damning, he was arguing that the Fed was not the independent agency it claimed to be. The members of the FOMC were not wise technocrats, making decisions about the money supply, guided by nothing more than high-minded economic theory. They were humans, driven at least in part by political pressures. Meltzer said the Fed kept struggling to boost job creation by printing more money, not because the economic equations dictated it, but because that's what the public and the politicians wanted the Fed to do. The FOMC believed the unemployment rate should have been close to 4 percent, but it never fell below 6 percent between 1975 and 1977 and was still near 6 percent in 1978. So the Fed kept printing money, and in doing so it stoked the asset and inflation bubbles that created ruinously high unemployment rates above 10 percent in the early 1980s.

Part of this was due to honest mistakes. The Fed was making decisions based on data that was eventually proven to be wrong. This was only uncovered years later, after the data was revised. One key piece of mistaken data was consistently low estimations of price inflation. This was the equivalent of artillery specialists firing off the howitzers while using data from faulty weather balloons—the outside conditions were different than the team inside the bunker believed them to be.

But the problem was more fundamental than mistaken data. There is strong evidence that the Fed, during the 1970s, didn't even truly understand how monetary policy was affecting the economy and stoking inflation. In a 2004 report, the Fed economist Edward Nelson wrote that the most likely cause of inflation during the '70s was something he called "monetary policy neglect." Basically, the Fed kept its foot on the money pedal through most of the decade because it didn't understand that more money was creating more inflation. This wasn't done out of malice but out of misunderstanding. The Fed, along with many prominent economists of the era, believed that the country was experiencing something called "cost push" inflation. This theory holds that a bunch of external forces that had nothing to do with the Fed were pushing up costs. Big labor unions, for example, were pushing up the cost of labor. And Middle Eastern cartels were driving up the cost of oil. It was these costs that pushed inflation higher and higher, not the Fed. Decades later, a very different understanding of inflation took hold at the Fed. This was the "demand pull" theory, which located the blame for inflation squarely inside the Fed's boardroom. By increasing the money supply, the Fed stoked demand for debt and loans, which "pulled" inflation higher. Cheaper money meant more loans, more borrowing, and more demand for everything, which further pulled up prices. This idea is commonly described as the phenomenon of "too many dollars chasing too few goods," meaning that when you print more money, people use that money to buy things and it drives up prices. The same force drives up consumer prices and asset prices alike.

In the 1970s, the Fed left the job of fighting inflation to others. The White House imposed price and wage controls, trying to keep costs lower. This gave the Fed freedom to keep interest rates low and increase the money supply. Every time unemployment rose, or economic growth slowed down, the Fed cut rates and printed more money. And this pointed to the deepest problem of all, at least in Meltzer's account of the fiasco. The Fed was reacting to short-term pressures, and in doing so it was pumping out new money that created long-term risks. The members of the FOMC were reading the news like everyone else, and they didn't want to be accused of making things worse during a decade of race riots, recessions, and protests. Whenever the FOMC tried to raise interest rates, which would have cooled inflation, the committee quickly retreated because unemployment rose or growth weakened. "Although many [FOMC] members understood that reducing inflation required consistent long-term action, there is scant evidence of longer-term planning," Meltzer wrote.

This lesson of the banking crisis stuck with Tom Hoenig. It would make him stubbornly passionate, decades later, when he debated quantitative easing. Hoenig had seen firsthand how an FOMC decision made in a day, in a single vote, took months or even years to express itself fully in the world as the effects filtered out through the banking system and economy. "Monetary policy operates with what they refer to as 'long and variable lags,'" Hoenig said later. He said this repeatedly, sometimes in a way that looked like he wanted to pound the table to get his point across. His frustration stemmed from the fact that this piece of hard-earned knowledge seemed to be ignored at every turn. When there was short-term trouble, like a drop in the market or a jump in unemployment, the Fed intervened. It printed more money and cut interest rates. It addressed short-term problems and left the long-term problems to grow.

During the 1980s, Hoenig and his colleagues in Kansas City were left to sort out the long-term problems the Fed's short-term thinking created during the 1970s. The biggest mess they cleaned up was the failure of Penn Square, a bank in Oklahoma that had extended a chain of risky energy loans during the 1970s. When Penn Square failed, it almost took down the entire U.S. banking system with it. It also illuminated a second important pattern that would harden in the coming years. The Fed didn't just stoke asset bubbles. It found itself on the hook to bail out the very lenders who profited most off a bubble as it rose. Some banks, the Fed was about to discover, had grown too large and too interconnected to fail.

Penn Square was run by a guy named Bill "Beep" Jennings. He was the sort of person who drank beer out of a cowboy boot to impress clients, so it wasn't surprising that he'd figure out creative ways to extend countless loans in an oil boom. Penn Square was an early pioneer of what's called securitization, whereby the bankers create risky debt and then sell it to someone else. Penn Square's version of securitization was the sale of a "participating loan." Jennings would loan money to an oil company, then sell most of the loan to another bank while keeping a small share of the debt on its own books. The idea was simple—extend as many loans as possible, collecting fees with each deal, and move the actual risk of a loan default onto someone else's balance sheet. This helped Penn Square avoid rules requiring it to keep a certain amount of cash reserves on hand.

Penn Square also gamed rules that limited how much money it could loan to any one person by using complex webs of interlocking shell companies and partnerships. There was a loan limit of $35 million per person, for example, but Penn Square still managed to loan $115 million to an oil executive named Robert A. Hefner. Going through all the schemes would fill a book (and in 1985 it did, with Phillip L. Zweig's *Belly Up: The Collapse of the Penn Square Bank*). But the result was simple: Between 1974 and 1981, Penn Square's assets jumped from $35 million to $525 million. Many of these new assets were energy loans written on the optimistic premise that oil prices would only keep rising. On the way up, Beep Jennings was hailed as a financial innovator and a charmingly brash risk taker.

When Paul Volcker and the Fed raised the cost of borrowing, it killed demand for the loans Penn Square was selling and turned Beep Jennings into a literal beggar. Jennings and his team desperately petitioned the Kansas City Fed for discount-window loans that would keep the bank afloat. Like so many others, they said they just needed more time. This effort grew more frantic in the summer of 1982. Penn Square was petitioning the Kansas City Fed along with the Federal Deposit Insurance Corporation, or FDIC, an agency created right after the Great Depression. The FDIC was the grim executioner that arrived when the Fed's discount window was no longer an option. The agency liquidated insolvent banks, using taxpayer money to repay retail customers who had accounts at the bank with $100,000 or less in deposits.* The FDIC and the KC Fed went back and forth about Penn Square. The Fed provided millions of dollars in emergency loans, but Hoenig and the Fed lawyer John Yorke were growing skeptical that the bank could survive. Letting Penn Square fail would wipe out millions of dollars in equity. But letting the bank stay alive, and continuing to borrow from the Fed and others, could make things worse. "That can be a real mistake, because that can lead to larger losses," Yorke said.

---

*The FDIC paid for these deposit losses by drawing on a fund that it collected in fees from banks. When that fund doesn't have enough money to cover losses, then taxpayers can be on the hook to cover losses.

Time ran out over the Fourth of July weekend in 1982. Hoenig worked on the holiday, poring over numbers to help determine if it was too risky to make another loan to Penn Square. The Fed's board of governors was also involved. At an emergency meeting in Washington that Sunday, Paul Volcker cast his own vote on the matter: Penn Square should be allowed to fail. On Monday, the verdict was rendered final through a series of letters between the FDIC, the Fed, and the Treasury Department's Office of the Comptroller of the Currency. The FDIC pronounced Penn Square insolvent. The Kansas City Fed declared Penn Square was ineligible for more emergency loans.

Tom Hoenig had the duty of breaking the news to Penn Square. The bankers' response fit the pattern that Hoenig had grown accustomed to. "They would say: 'It's *your* fault that we're failing. If you gave us more time we could work out of this,'" he recalled.

But the really important thing about the failure of Penn Square is that the damage was not contained. The failure was just the first shock in a large cascade of shocks. There were still all those "participating loans" to contend with. It was only when the loans started failing that it became clear just how broadly they had infected the banking system. The loan failures revealed that a very large bank in Chicago, called Continental Illinois National Bank and Trust Co., was one of the biggest customers for Penn Square's assembly line of risky debt. Continental Illinois had purchased $1 billion worth of these loans in just a few short years toward the end of the 1970s. This caught everyone by surprise. Continental was seen as a conservative, even boring bank. It lent money to auto companies and steel makers in the Midwest. But the forces unleashed during the Great Inflation were too much for it. Continental Illinois pushed out along the yield curve, straight to Oklahoma.

Continental had become the biggest commercial and industrial lender in the country. In 1984, it had $40 billion in assets. Things fell apart quickly when the oil loans went bad. Continental was the problem of the Chicago Federal Reserve, which extended a $3.6 billion emergency loan to the bank. Even this wasn't enough. New York's J. P. Morgan pulled together a group of lenders to assemble a $4.5 billion line of credit for Continental, but that also wasn't enough. Continental's customers lost faith in the bank and started a bank run, withdrawing about $10.8 billion in a year. Continental was going to fail.

Even Paul Volcker became nervous when he was faced with the failure of Continental Illinois. He communicated constantly with the FDIC as the bank teetered. He was warned that Continental's collapse could not be contained. The bank was simply too large, and too deeply connected with too many other banks. The FDIC estimated that 2,300 banks had money invested in Continental. About 179 banks had so much money in Continental that it amounted to more than half of their equity. Its failure might drag them down with it. Even more worrisome, about half of those banks were insured by the FDIC in case of failure. This would put unprecedented strain on the FDIC, which was already handling about eighty bank failures.

The FDIC and the Fed came up with an alternative. The FDIC provided an extraordinary rescue package, injecting $1.5 billion into Continental. But, most important, the FDIC promised to cover bank losses above a previously set threshold of $100,000, protecting all bondholders and depositors. This was a huge increase in the safety net for banks that invested money in Continental while knowing that the FDIC would only insure part of it. Now all of it was insured by taxpayers. Simultaneously, the Fed promised that it would give Continental emergency loans until the crisis passed.

The Continental bailout was one of the most important legacies of the Great Inflation. If a bank got big enough, and spread enough risk to other banks, then that bank would be rescued in a crisis. The previously existing rules would be bent or rewritten to save the bank. This precedent brought a new term into the vocabulary of American banking. During a congressional hearing about the Continental bailout, a Republican congressman from Connecticut named Stewart McKinney described the situation in a pithy statement: "Mr. Chairman, let us not bandy words. We have a new kind of bank. It is called too big to fail."

Paul Volcker's career as chairman did not end pleasantly. He had whipped inflation, and was then driven back to the wilderness. FOMC members cast dissenting votes against Volcker more often than at almost any chairman in modern Fed history. He asked not to be reappointed after his term ended in 1987. Volcker's halo would only be bestowed in later years, when economic historians decided that his efforts against inflation had been independent-minded and uniquely effective. But he was never again at the center of American power.

Things worked out better for Thomas Hoenig.

The wave of bank closures eventually receded in the Kansas City Fed's district. The Penn Square failure was the worst of it. Hoenig's performance during the crisis was noted by the people around him, like Yorke, who believed Hoenig had handled himself during a brutal period with integrity and competence. This reputation proved important when the Kansas City Fed president Roger Guffey announced he was retiring in 1991.

The Kansas City Fed had never hired a president from its own ranks. But Hoenig put his name forward anyway. There were about 150 applicants for the job. Guffey would choose his replacement with the help of the Kansas City Fed's board of directors. The Fed's chairman and board of governors in Washington would also need to approve the hire.

Guffey had seen up close how Hoenig handled the Penn Square crisis, and thought he was right for the job. Hoenig won approval from the Kansas City Fed's board and then he flew to Washington to sit for interviews with each Fed governor. Finally, Hoenig was ushered into the office of the new Fed chairman, Alan Greenspan. A soft-spoken economist with many decades of political experience in Washington, Greenspan had worked on Wall Street and in the White House under Presidents Nixon and Ford. Greenspan became chairman shortly before the stock market crash of 1987, and he won nearly universal praise for his deft handling of the crisis. He developed a reputation for maneuvering the Fed's levers of power gracefully, like a surgeon. Greenspan was inscrutable behind his large, owlish eyeglasses. During the job interview with Tom Hoenig, Greenspan listened more than he talked.

Greenspan asked Hoenig about his theories on monetary policy. Hoenig said that the crisis of the 1980s had allowed him to see the powerful consequences of the FOMC's decisions. Hoenig had overseen the banks when prices and asset values were climbing, and he had seen the long and variable lags that occurred when the FOMC kept money too cheap for too long. It had fallen to him to dispatch the failed banks after Volcker brought inflation to a violent end. "I was someone who was aware of the effects of easy policy for too long," Hoenig recalled. "I thought policy should be done very carefully, with an eye toward inflation."

More than that, Hoenig believed that monetary policy needed to be made with restraint, and a long-term view. "Every action you take has long-run consequences," he said. Greenspan was silent on this matter, as Hoenig remembered it. But the chairman apparently approved. Hoenig got the job.

After news got out that Hoenig was president, one of his elderly neighbors approached him with a gift. It was a framed copy of a piece of German currency, a single bill with a face value of 500,000 marks. Below the bill was a simple inscription that read: "In 1921 this note would buy a large home. In 1923 this note would buy a loaf of bread." It was a living memento of Germany's era of hyperinflation.

Hoenig hung it in his office downtown. It was a good reminder of the destructive power of inflation. Or at least the first kind of inflation, meaning price inflation, which can make a currency almost worthless. But Hoenig was worried about the other kind of inflation that he'd seen, in asset prices. He could have just as easily hung mementos on the wall, such as the bank charters for Penn Square and Continental Illinois, to remind him what happens when rising asset prices exert their own logic on borrowers and lenders, and what happens when fragile bubbles bring the entire financial system to a halt.

Within a year, Hoenig was sitting at the giant wood table in the Eccles boardroom, at the same table as Alan Greenspan, as a member of the FOMC. He never forgot what his neighbor told him when he imparted the gift. "I want you to have it, to remind you what can happen if you do your job poorly."

CHAPTER 4

FEDSPEAK

(1991–2001)

On October 1, 1991, Tom Hoenig walked into the Federal Reserve boardroom for the first time as a sitting member of the FOMC. He had spent his career observing the ground-level effects of Federal Reserve policy. Now he would help direct the Fed's policy, and carry responsibility for it. This was the first time that Hoenig was chauffeured to the building as a regional bank president, and led in through the side entrance to the private elevator. The gravity of that day was driven home by the majesty of his new surroundings. The lobby of the Marriner Eccles Building is a cavernous chamber, rising two stories up to a vaulted ceiling. The wide hallway is inlaid with an immaculate checkerboard pattern of black and white marble, with twin stairways leading to the mezzanine level, bordered with white columns extending to the ceiling. Down the hallway was the boardroom, where the FOMC members took their seats around the big table. Alan Greenspan sat at the center.

"Good morning, everyone," Greenspan said. "We have Tom Hoenig with us—officially this time. And I gather, Tom, that this is your first day as president."

"As a matter of fact it is," Hoenig replied. "And that's a warning to all of you."

In the spirit of ribbing the rookie, Edward Boehne, the president of the Philadelphia Fed, called out: "It's all uphill from now on!"

Greenspan immediately terminated the small talk.

"Would somebody like to move the minutes of the August twentieth meeting?" he asked. And so began the hours-long deliberations that characterized a typical FOMC meeting. The deliberations, at the end of 1991, were more urgent than most people knew.

Hoenig joined the FOMC at a very strange inflection point in America's economic history. The decade of the 1990s is remembered as a boom time: the decade when the Internet exploded, the stock market skyrocketed, when unemployment almost disappeared. But on the committee, members worried constantly over the economic machinery that underpinned America's power. There was a corrosive layer of weakness beneath the surface. In some ways, the economic weakness was hidden. The economy was growing, and the dark days of Volcker's interest-rate hikes and high unemployment were long forgotten. The mid-to-late 1980s had been a gold rush on Wall Street characterized by massive borrowing and gluttonous spending. This was the era of the junk-bond kings, who used cheap debt to buy companies and then merge them with other companies for a profit, or break them up for a quick sale. But there was an underlying weakness beneath the churning markets that was visible to millions of working Americans. Gas prices were high, layoffs were common, and business investment was slow. The economy slipped into a recession in August 1990 that lasted eight months, ending just a few months before Hoenig joined the FOMC. The recession itself wasn't that worrisome. It's what happened next that disturbed the Fed. The economy started growing again, but the jobs didn't come back. This broke the basic pattern of economic cycles going back to World War II. Jobs were supposed to disappear during a downturn, but then come back when growth resumed. This time, the unemployment rate kept rising even as the economy grew.

This was the puzzle faced by Greenspan during the October meeting. What was the Fed supposed to do in a recovery when unemployment rose? And why was it happening?

"We have a very unusual set of problems," Greenspan said. The sluggish recovery, the slow investment, and the lack of hiring wasn't easily explained. "It's very much as though an economy which is picking up steam is running against a fifty-mile-an-hour headwind," he said.

A key problem, Greenspan explained, seemed to be the debt-fueled growth of the 1980s, and the bank failures that followed. These remarks were prescient. Greenspan was describing a problem that would repeat itself, intensify, and become a defining feature of American economic life in the twenty-first century. Cheap debt produced fast growth for a while, but it was followed by an extended crash and a period of weak growth. Economists would deepen their understanding of this new pattern during the 1990s, and they determined that the recession of 1990 really was different, as Greenspan suspected. Businesses and households weren't spending money because they were still paying off their debts from the 1980s. It was the recessionary equivalent of a bad hangover. The damage was unusually widespread and affected white-collar workers, who were once more insulated from layoffs during a downturn.

In 1993, a young Princeton economist wrote a paper that outlined the risks posed by this heavy burden of cheap debt. His name was Ben Bernanke. When explaining the 1990 recession, he called the debt problem "the overhang." He pointed out that corporate debt had ballooned in the 1980s and left the economic system fragile in 1990, when the economy was shocked by rising gasoline prices during the Gulf War. In essence, even a small shock was enough to push heavily indebted companies to quickly fire workers and abandon expansion plans. "When a recession causes a general decline in sales and profits, firms with already high levels of debt and interest burden face a tighter cash flow squeeze," Bernanke wrote.

In October 1991, the Fed was still trying to make sense of all this.

Greenspan concluded Hoenig's first FOMC meeting by urging caution. Things would eventually get better. He just didn't know how long it would take. It ended up taking a long time.

When Hoenig became a voting member of the FOMC in January 1992, the economy was still stagnant. This was the beginning of a period that would coin a new phrase, the "jobless recovery." Hoenig could see it playing out in his own district. There were signs of strength, with high grain prices and plenty of new home construction. But a continued slump in manufacturing employment was wiping out many of the higher-paying jobs in the Midwest. About one thousand auto workers in Hoenig's district had recently been laid off. During his first meeting as a voting member, Greenspan asked Hoenig for an update on the midwestern economy. "We think our district is growing somewhat more slowly; it might be described as flat at best," Hoenig said. He would say basically the same thing during almost every meeting in 1992 using words like *mixed* and *sluggish*.

Even Greenspan was perplexed. Toward the end of 1992, during a news conference, he sounded exasperated. He said the Fed was doing its part to boost hiring, but the economy wasn't responding. "No models can explain the types of patterns we are having," Greenspan said. "This is really a quite extraordinarily difficult type of environment."

If the economy had broken with past patterns, then Greenspan was willing for the Fed to do the same thing. He guided the central bank to cut interest rates in the early 1990s, even though the economy was growing, which was the opposite of what the Fed should be doing according to the traditional models. In 1991, the Fed cut the short-term interest rate from a little more than 5 percent to just under 4 percent by early 1992, hoping to give the economy some sweet, palliative medicine that might counteract the debt overhang. But it quickly became clear that a lot more medicine was going to be necessary. Throughout 1992, the Fed cut rates steadily, meeting after meeting, bringing them all the way down to 2.9 percent at the end of the year. This emergency measure turned into something like the status quo. The Fed would keep rates around 3 percent until early 1994.

Hoenig voted yes, in line with Greenspan, at every single meeting during his first year as a voting member. If Hoenig was a born dissenter, he was hiding it well. He did express concern, at some meetings, about inflation. He said he was reluctant, at times, to keep making money cheaper. The lessons of the 1970s were still very much on his mind. But the weakness of 1992 convinced him the Fed's intervention was warranted, whether the recession was over or not.

Greenspan's actions were not a short-term emergency response. They marked the beginning of a new era of easy money. The easing that Greenspan oversaw in 1992 was mild compared to what was to come. And the overhang of bad debt in 1991, which the Fed had helped create, was modest compared to the overhangs it would help create later. Greenspan became a major public figure in these years, maybe the most famous chairman in the history of the Federal Reserve. But even as more people learned who Greenspan was, they seemed to learn less about what he was doing. The 1990s was the decade when the Fed truly moved into the center of economic policy making. But Greenspan worked very hard to make sure that this truth was obscured.

The Fed was created in such a way that its actions would be shielded from the accountability of voters. But there was still a general sense that the central bank should at least make regular reports to politicians in Congress to explain what it was doing and why. This idea led to a strange ritual during the Greenspan era. The wise chairman, with his dour demeanor and his big-framed glasses, would travel from the dignified confines of his office at the Eccles Building down the National Mall to the offices of Congress. There, he would sit before the lawmakers and explain the Fed's actions. The hearings were odd because it wasn't at all clear that Congress had any authority over Greenspan. Congress couldn't cut funding to the Fed. It couldn't fire or demote Greenspan.

Yet Greenspan permitted himself to sit for the hearings, which were televised on C-SPAN. He tolerated the questions and the long-winded soliloquies of elected lawmakers and then gave his own prepared statement. In these meetings Greenspan had the air of foreign royalty. He listened politely. He answered questions. And then he left.

A typical hearing occurred on June 10, 1998, when Greenspan testified before Congress's Joint Economic Committee. The hearing was billed as an "update on economic conditions in the United States." Of all the people in America, Alan Greenspan was believed to be the one who could best determine and describe the state of the American economy. He was described as an oracle, the maestro who dwelled at the zenith of the economy and had insight into every corner of it. He played this part well. Greenspan wore a dark pin-striped suit, a white shirt, and a maroon tie. He sat alone at a table with a white tablecloth and a microphone.

That day in June, the Republican committee chair, Rep. Jim Saxton of New Jersey, opened the hearing with a long statement praising Greenspan's leadership of the Fed. There was good reason for the praise. The period of weak growth and rising unemployment in the early 1990s was long gone. The economy grew steadily between 1993 and 1998, with unemployment falling to 4.4 percent and wages rising steadily. Saxton showed good political instincts when he started talking; he gave most of the credit for the boom to workers and entrepreneurs. But he said that if any governing entity had a hand in feeding the economic growth, it was the Fed. "To the extent policy factors are relevant, monetary policy has been the main factor in sustaining economic expansion," he said. "It appears to me that the Federal Reserve has been on the right course, and I commend its leadership."

As Saxton expressed his admiration of the Fed chairman, Greenspan looked down at the table and put his hand on his chin, like someone trying to stay awake during a movie. He tended to nod vaguely when elected officials finished their comments and to mumble his gratitude.

When the lawmakers were done speaking, the financial press would sit up, alert. It was the oracle's turn to talk. His words could move markets if he betrayed the slightest hint as to what the Fed might do in the future. With a few words about Treasury yields, or a stray comment about commodity price inflation, Greenspan might signal if the Fed was about to tighten or loosen the money supply. At least, this was what the financial press had decided to believe. They scrutinized his every word, searching for patterns that might make headlines and that a bond trader might find useful.

People who didn't trade bonds for a living still had good reason to be interested in what the Fed was doing. The Fed's actions affected every aspect of economic life—albeit with long, variable lags—and its policies could spell the difference between prosperity and calamity. But if any citizen was eager to find meaning in Alan Greenspan's statements, he made a fine art of frustrating their efforts. He intentionally spoke in a way that was not just inscrutable, but incomprehensible. This type of speech earned a nickname on Capitol Hill: "Fedspeak." It was a language so studded with jargon and with so many concepts nested within one another that a person needed an economics PhD (or many years' worth of experience trading on Wall Street) to make sense of it. When Alan Greenspan started to talk, everybody's brains immediately downshifted into a low gear to do heavy uphill climbing as they struggled to figure out exactly what he was saying.

Greenspan's testimony that day, for example, included this statement:

The fact that economic performance strengthened as inflation subsided should not have been surprising, given that risk premiums and economic disincentives to invest in productive capital diminish as product prices become more stable. But the extent to which strong growth and high resource utilization have been joined with low inflation over an extended period is nevertheless extraordinary. Indeed, the broadest measures of price change indicate that the inflation rate moved down further in the first quarter of this year, even as the economy strengthened.

This was typical. The curious thing about these statements is that they seemed more opaque and difficult to understand than the things that Greenspan said during FOMC meetings, when he was surrounded by PhD economists. Back in 1991, for example, when Greenspan addressed the committee members at the end of Hoenig's first meeting, the chairman was direct and concise in talking about debt problems in the financial system. To be sure, he talked about complex financial systems, but even a layman reading his comments later could understand them. This all changed when Greenspan opened his mouth in public. A cloudy veil drew down over his words.

Greenspan's use of Fedspeak had a lasting and important impact. It accelerated the long process that removed the politics of money from the center of American public life, just as those politics were becoming more important to the nation's economy. Any average citizens who heard snippets of Greenspan's comments couldn't be blamed if they came to believe that whatever the Fed was doing, it must be so complex that no normal human could dare to talk about it, let alone criticize it. Greenspan's speeches entrenched the image of the Fed as a group of genius-level decision makers, operating on an Olympian plane as they grappled selflessly with hypercomplex matters.

There was a tension to this arrangement that bubbled around the edges of the public discourse, even during public congressional hearings. While Jim Saxton claimed that the Federal Reserve was the main driver of economic growth of the 1990s, his Democratic counterpart Maurice Hinchey of New York politely rebutted the idea.

"I believe that monetary policy follows fiscal policy," Hinchey said during his remarks.

This comment highlighted an important divide that would soon widen beyond the point of repair. On one side of the divide there is monetary policy, controlled by the Federal Reserve. On the other side, there is fiscal policy, which belongs to the democratically controlled institutions like Congress, the White House, and state governments. Fiscal policy involves the collection of taxes, the spending of public money, and regulation.

America's ability to conduct fiscal policy deteriorated slowly over the years as the Fed's ability to conduct monetary policy strengthened. There were many reasons for this fiscal decay: money in politics, the rise of corporate lobbying, the birth of television cable news, and growing income inequality all played a role. But the one important fact about the deterioration of executive and legislative power is that it was not inevitable. For at least a century or so, fiscal policy led the way in America, and the Fed, with its money-printing power, followed.

The largest burst of fiscal action in U.S. history happened after the Great Depression and the election of Franklin Delano Roosevelt in 1932. Over the following decade, Roosevelt and a Congress with huge Democratic majorities passed a set of sweeping and interlocking laws that came to be known collectively as the New Deal. This is important to consider because of the effect it had on the economy and its arrangement of winners and losers. The New Deal laws empowered labor unions, broke up or regulated big monopolies, created the first transparency laws for Wall Street, and put the banking system on a tight leash. The New Deal was confrontational. It antagonized powerful interests, and it took away their power. Literally the first day after his inauguration, FDR shut down the banks because the banking system had triggered the Great Depression after years of reckless speculation. FDR called this temporary shutdown a bank "holiday," and he used the time to send in examiners and determine which banks were solvent and which were not. After that, the government restructured and reregulated the banks in a way it never did again.

The New Deal banking laws were like commandments from the

Old Testament—they were short, simple, and sweeping in their reach. The most famous of these laws was called the Glass-Steagall Act, which neatly divided the entire banking industry into two spheres—commercial banking, where customers put deposits into banks, and investment banking, where the banks speculated in the markets. This kept people's bank deposits safe. The safety was further enforced by the creation of the FDIC, which created a government-backed insurance program to protect consumer deposits.

This gave birth to the world Tom Hoenig inhabited, when bank regulators had strong oversight over lending. FDR famously embraced the conflict during a 1936 campaign speech. "We had to struggle with the old enemies of peace—business and financial monopoly, speculation, reckless banking, class antagonism, sectionalism, war profiteering," Roosevelt said. "Never before in all our history have these forces been so united against one candidate as they stand today. They are unanimous in their hate for me—and I welcome their hatred."

FDR got his wish. These forces really did hate him, and their hatred endured. The hatred even intensified, during the 1960s, when Lyndon Johnson was president. Johnson was a New Deal acolyte, and he expanded the reach of government even further when he passed the Great Society programs like Medicare and Medicaid. Backlash against these programs and the New Deal animated the conservative movement that would gain power with the two-term presidency of Ronald Reagan. In the mid-1990s it fueled the rise of a more radical Republican-controlled Congress under Speaker of the House Newt Gingrich. He personified the antigovernment spirit of the New Deal critics, which portrayed their grievance as a defense of the little guy. This birthed a new era of politics as warfare and made-for-TV conflict, characterized by the government shutdowns in 1995.

The Federal Reserve presented elected politicians with a convenient escape hatch. It could print money when recessions began, and tighten the money supply if inflation became too intense. This method didn't cause nearly as many fights as imposing financial legislation. It seemed like no one had to pay a price for letting the Fed gain more authority and more responsibility. The journalist and economic historian Nicholas Lemann has pointed out that the Fed-centric model follows the theories of John Maynard Keynes, the eminent economist who argued that government should spend money in times of recession to boost growth. "Keynesian economic management had no immediate natural enemies," Lemann wrote. Economic management became the art of filling a bathtub with money, increasing the money level when times were tough and reducing it when inflation looked like a danger. The Fed's primary power was to make money cheaper and more plentiful, and Greenspan used this power generously. In 1989, interest rates had been close to 10 percent. During the 1990s, they fell to as low as 3 percent before rising again. Between 1995 and 1998, rates were held at about 5 percent.

Hoenig sat on the FOMC during this entire period, serving as a voting member every third year. In 1998, he was a voting member again. This timing happened to coincide with one of Alan Greenspan's more aggressive actions, a series of rate cuts in the late 1990s that fueled a stock market bubble. The rate cuts illustrated that while using the Fed's power might not generate any natural enemies, it did come with very high costs for the American people.

Behind the cloud of Fedspeak, there were, in fact, serious political disputes unfolding inside the FOMC during the 1990s. One of the most important policy decisions, in retrospect, had to do with inflation. In Paul Volcker's formulation of two inflation "cousins," one for consumer prices and the other for asset prices, the Greenspan Fed made the consequential decision over time to focus on only one of them: consumer price inflation. The Fed could keep cutting rates and keep increasing the money supply, just as long as the price of consumer goods didn't rise too quickly. The price of assets was left to behave according to its own unruly nature.

There doesn't appear to be any single meeting where this policy was officially adopted. It happened over time, and as it solidified it became an increasingly uneasy fit for Tom Hoenig. He'd built his monetary philosophy on the hard ground of his experience in the 1970s, when asset inflation and asset bubbles had been so destructive. He was wary of letting asset prices run away uncontrolled. But Hoenig also held genuine respect and admiration for Alan Greenspan. He had cast only one dissenting vote on the FOMC before 1998. It happened in the summer of 1995, when Greenspan was pushing to cut interest rates at a time when Hoenig believed rates were already low enough. Hoenig was haunted by the rule of long and variable lags, and the experience of watching the FOMC create the Great Inflation without even realizing it. Rate cuts were often presented as a form of "insurance" against a future downturn, and that's how the cut of 1995 was being presented.

"I am concerned that that insurance comes with its own price," Hoenig said before casting his "no" vote. He was the only member to vote against the cut, and over the next year or two it appeared that his analysis had been wrong. The rate cut helped boost growth, and the much-dreaded signs of inflation never arrived. This economic data compounded the sting that Hoenig felt from voting no.

One of the more delicate lessons that Hoenig learned during his time on the FOMC was the unwritten lesson about dissent. There was a reason that FOMC votes were wildly lopsided, and it had nothing to do with the Fed's bylaws. On paper, at least, the FOMC was supposed to be a voting body, not unlike the Supreme Court. This might make it seem like there would be close votes on the FOMC as there were on the high court, where decisions were sometimes split almost evenly. Just like the Supreme Court, the FOMC was voting on complicated issues with unclear outcomes. But close votes were unheard of. The reason for this was the FOMC's culture, and the tradition of deference to the Fed chairman.

"I will tell you, there are instances where people kind of are surprised that you might vote against the chairman," Hoenig said. "I don't know how to describe it. There is kind of a message that it's, you know, it's very unusual to vote against the chairman. You have to do it with great care . . . There's not a manual that says you don't vote against the chairman. But there is kind of an uneasiness you see in the room if you're voting against the chairman."

It was easy, during most of the 1990s, for Hoenig to vote with the committee because he agreed with Greenspan. But the decision to essentially ignore asset bubbles made it harder for Hoenig to cooperate.

Greenspan had a solid rationale for focusing only on consumer price inflation. For one thing, it was easier to track: The price of gasoline, bread, and television sets is easy to collect. It was also more politically popular to fight price inflation than asset inflation. Very few people complained if the Fed took action to bring down the price of consumer goods. But bursting an asset bubble caused immediate pain, and it caused pain especially in the households of the very rich. "To raise interest rates in the face of a bubble is always to pay a certain price to head off an uncertain threat—and to incur the wrath of politicians and the public, who love nothing better than a soaring market," wrote the financial journalist Sebastian Mallaby. His biography of Greenspan, *The Man Who Knew*, captured the policy history of Greenspan's Fed in minute detail. It showed that the decision to fight price inflation rather than asset inflation happened gradually, but was unmistakable by the 1990s. This wasn't just a quirk of the Greenspan era. It set a permanent pattern.

Greenspan was rewarded for the decision. It helped explain why lawmakers in both parties praised him at the public hearings. Greenspan appeared to be the most talented financial engineer of his generation, and the key to this success, along with the mystery of it, was that he managed to stimulate the economy without stoking price inflation.

Asset inflation, however, was out of control by 1998. But this didn't raise much public concern. When asset inflation gets out of hand, people don't call it inflation. They call it a boom. Much of the asset inflation of the late 1990s was showing up in the stock market, where share prices were rising at a level that would have been horrifying if it was expressed in the price of butter or gasoline. The entire Standard & Poor's stock index rose by 19.5 percent in 1999. The Nasdaq index, which measured technology stocks, jumped more than 80 percent. The financial press covered the activity in these markets in the way ESPN covered sports, with a short-term, hour-by-hour storytelling that focused on which player was up and which was down. The big star of this performance, the Michael Jordan, was the crop of newly born technology stocks, like the Web-browsing firm Yahoo! and newly minted Internet retailers like Amazon, eToys, and Value America.

What was less prominently discussed was the relationship between these stock prices and the increasing supply of money that the Federal Reserve was pumping into the banking system. By 1998, it was undeniable that the stock market boom was closely tied to the Fed's policies. In July, Greenspan warned that stock prices might be unsustainably high, which made traders panic at the thought that the Fed would raise rates and tighten the money supply. Between July and August, stock market prices fell by about 18 percent. In response, the Fed cut rates again from 5.5 percent to about 4.8 percent in just a couple of months. The stock market bounced back.

This is why Hoenig was worried when he arrived in Washington for the FOMC meeting in mid-November. It was a pivotal moment for the Fed: By cutting rates, it had made money cheaper and encouraged more lending and stock purchases. The Fed could now wait and see how the stimulus worked its way through the system, or it could accelerate the money flow even further, potentially inflating the stock market bubble. Hoenig had to decide if he would cast his second dissenting vote if Greenspan pushed for another rate cut.

Fed chairmen usually downplay the impact of low interest rates on the stock market, but Greenspan was blunt about the connection during the November meeting. He acknowledged that the stock market might be a bubble, which made him hesitate about cutting rates even more. "The one area where things have eased regrettably more than I would have liked is the stock market," Greenspan said. "In a certain sense that has created a major question in my judgment as to whether we should move [rates]. . . . If the Dow Jones industrial average were two hundred to three hundred points lower, I think the case for moving [rates] one additional time and then putting policy on indefinite hold would be fairly strong. . . . I do think the concerns about an asset bubble are not without validity, and that is where I have my greatest concerns about easing."

But even in the face of this asset bubble, Greenspan pushed for another rate cut. Price inflation wasn't rising, he said. Labor costs were barely rising. And there were reasons to cut rates in November. The biggest worry at the time was the worsening debt crisis in Russia, where the government was unable to pay back its loans, and the IMF appeared unwilling to bail it out. This might destabilize foreign markets, and the chaos could reach U.S. shores. Cutting rates might help inoculate the financial system against these stresses, he argued. "The cost of the insurance is very small, and I suspect it is probably not a bad thing at this stage to take out the insurance but then to stop at that point, stay on hold, and watch events as they materialize over the weeks and possibly even months ahead," Greenspan said.

William Poole, the president of the St. Louis Federal Reserve Bank, said he would go along with a rate cut, but only reluctantly. Pushing more money into the banking system could be risky. "I am concerned that we are pouring gasoline rather than water onto this economy," Poole said.

When it was Hoenig's turn to speak, he echoed these worries. "I think President Poole said it best, that we could be pouring gasoline on this economy. I have concerns that a bubble economy syndrome may be building," he said. But Hoenig also said there were three good reasons to cut rates. First, he appreciated the danger posed by the foreign debt crises. Second, he didn't see signs of an immediate inflation threat. And finally, he believed that the Fed could raise interest rates again if the cuts proved unnecessary.

Poole and Hoenig voted with Greenspan to cut rates.

In 1999, shares of stock in a wireless telecommunications company called Qualcomm rose by 2,600 percent. This was the year that the S&P index jumped by 19.5 percent, and the Nasdaq nearly doubled. In an interview with *The New York Times*, Greg Maffei, the CEO of a fiber optics company called 360networks, explained the era succinctly. "We had an enormous amount of relatively low-cost capital," Maffei said. "When people throw a lot of money at things quickly sometimes, it's not all rational."

Signs of price inflation were starting to emerge in 1999. In early 2000, Greenspan warned, during a public hearing in Congress, that the small rate hikes taken in the previous year would not be enough to slow economic growth that had grown overheated. Price inflation was gathering strength and would only rise more if the Fed didn't do something.

The FOMC increased rates sharply after that, from 5.7 percent to 6.5 percent. This was the equivalent of hitting the emergency brakes on a subway train. The traders made a rapid transition in their thinking as they adjusted to a world where costs would be higher for money and for debt. They imposed a new framework on the value of the assets they were buying and selling. One such asset was shares of stock in a San Francisco–based company called Pets.com, which went public in February 2000. These shares were like those Florida land deeds Galbraith had written about. Quite suddenly, the traders started to reexamine the value of the real-world asset that underpinned the paper asset. They saw that Pets.com had failed to think about the high cost of shipping dog food. The company's stock had debuted at $11 a share, but began to fall steadily. This was the signal that the self-reinforcing logic of ever-rising asset values was over, and it was over because the Fed was raising rates. Pets.com declared bankruptcy in November.

The stock market crash of 2000 wiped out $1.76 trillion of value in 280 Internet stocks between March and November. The Federal Reserve had played a decisive role in creating, and then destroying, the multitrillion-dollar stock market bubble. But when the market crashed, bankers, traders, and politicians turned to the Fed for help. The disaster only seemed to enhance Greenspan's reputation as a financial rescue artist. Only the Fed was believed to hold the power to recalibrate markets and avert a larger disaster. This fact revealed a third pillar of Greenspan's policy framework as Fed chairman. He chose to control price inflation, ignore asset inflation, and then step in and bail out the system when asset prices collapsed. This might seem like an odd strategy for a libertarian-leaning thinker who was vocal in his distaste for government intervention. But over the years, Greenspan learned that bailouts were unavoidable. Letting big banks and debt-laden governments fail was simply too painful to consider. This was another policy that developed slowly, with the accumulation of many independent decisions. As Sebastian Mallaby wrote in his biography of Greenspan: "The Fed had bet its reputation on the proposition that it could clean up after the bubble; if it succeeded in that task, perhaps the downturn would be mild enough for the earlier boom to have been worth it."

The cleanup job in 2000 and 2001 was enormous. But the Fed began quickly and forcefully cutting interest rates to 3.5 percent by August 2001. Hoenig was once again a voting member of the FOMC, and he largely supported this action. The Fed was built to offer cheap money during a crisis, and nobody could deny the market crash was a crisis. But the question was how far the Fed should go. This was where Hoenig started to part ways with Greenspan.

In May, Greenspan wanted to cut the interest rate by a full half percent, an enormous change. Hoenig wasn't against easing, but he felt the Fed should move more slowly, giving time for its previous rate cuts to take hold. Hoenig's position was hardly radical—rather than making a half-point cut, he argued to make a quarter-point cut. "Mr. Chairman, I think we should pull back on the throttle today," Hoenig said. "We've added significant liquidity to the market. Now we should let it work through and we should be far more cautious about further moves." Hoenig lost this argument. His dissent that month was only the second in his career, and he was the only member who voted no.

On September 11, 2001, terrorists attacked the United States using hijacked airplanes, killing nearly three thousand people and throwing the economy into chaos. This was an emergency on top of the ongoing economic emergency. The Fed responded with more interest-rate cuts to cushion the blow, and nobody complained.

But in December, Hoenig would cast his second dissenting vote of the year. When it was Hoenig's turn to talk at the FOMC meeting that month, he once again counseled caution and restraint, worrying about long and variable lags. He pointed out that interest rates had already been cut to 2 percent from more than 6 percent just one year earlier. "Mr. Chairman, I really think we ought to stay where we are. A two percent Fed funds rate is stimulative," Hoenig said. "We are seeing some signs of improvement, and not all of the stimulus has come into play yet. While I recognize that inflation is not an immediate issue, and I appreciate that, I still think we need to take a little longer-run view at this time."

Hoenig lost the argument—again the lone dissenter—and the Fed cut rates. A month later, Hoenig rotated off his seat as a voting member of the FOMC.

Over the next two years, the Federal Reserve's state of emergency became almost permanent. The rate cuts of 2001 remained in place, with the cost of short-term loans staying below 2 percent until the middle of 2004. This era became comparable to the era of the 1960s, when monetary policy paved the way to an economic collapse. But this time would be different. Greenspan's policy of controlling price inflation and ignoring asset bubbles would take an extreme form during the 2000s. The Fed would play a pivotally important role in stoking the largest asset bubble, leading to the worst crash since the Great Depression. Once again, Tom Hoenig was there every step of the way. But this time he played an active role in the process. He rarely expressed regret about his votes on the FOMC. But the era of the housing bubble was an exception. Hoenig helped invite a bubble.

CHAPTER 5

THE OVERMIGHTY CITIZEN

(2002–2010)

It started in 2001, after the terrorist attacks and the stock market crash. The Fed was keeping rates low, and Hoenig was worried that the FOMC might once again be stoking asset bubbles in the Midwest. In March 2001, he cited a specific example: the housing industry. Hoenig was worried that low rates might push money out on the yield curve and into riskier loans in construction.

"Banks in our region are beginning to lend more aggressively on real estate," Hoenig said during that month's FOMC meeting. If rates stayed low, "we could see a fairly dramatic shift of funds into that sector as people look to deploy their assets, which might cause some—for lack of a better word—overbuilding in the real estate area."

During the meeting, Hoenig got into a back-and-forth with a Fed economist named David Stockton, who was presenting a national overview to the committee. Hoenig asked what effect low rates might have on the housing market, and Stockton said the low rates might indeed cause some investment "errors." "It's very difficult for me to forecast the errors that banks might make, but they certainly have traditionally made those kinds of errors in previous long periods of economic strength," Stockton replied. The dangers of a housing bubble were not some wild theory or unexpected consequence of low rates. They were a predictable danger of cheap debt, but it was a danger that Greenspan and others on the FOMC felt was acceptable.

Over the next few years, the Federal Reserve stimulated the economy by substituting one asset bubble for another, replacing the stock market bubble with the housing bubble. The theory was that a hot housing market would have spillover effects, creating jobs and encouraging spending and borrowing, and this theory proved to be true. During 2003 and 2004, the real estate business gained steam and the price of housing rose sharply across the county. Just as cheap debt increased farmland prices during the 1970s, low mortgage rates made it easier for people to borrow money and buy a house, increasing competition and pushing prices higher by the year. This dynamic was usually talked about in the same way that inflation in the stock market had been talked about during the late 1990s. It was described as a "boom." Houses, like stocks, were described as a key source of middle-class wealth and a vital retirement investment, so the inflation of their value was welcomed as an unalloyed good. And, just as in the 1990s, it was only the rising specter of price inflation that forced the Fed to consider raising rates.

By 2004, Alan Greenspan was worried that rates had been too low for too long. In May, the fingerprints of price inflation were unmistakable in the data that Greenspan reviewed. He pushed for the FOMC to tighten the money supply.

For the first six months of 2004, interest rates were essentially flat, at 1 percent. Starting in June, the FOMC began to raise them slowly but steadily, ending the year at a little more than 2 percent. Hoenig voted in line with the FOMC at every meeting that year. The committee was moving in the direction that he believed was prudent. It was only later, looking back, that Hoenig realized that the damage was done. The Fed had kept rates at 1 percent for too long, and when it started raising rates it raised them so slowly that they were still "accommodative," still incentivizing speculation and easy lending. "That left an impression on me," Hoenig recalled. "When you keep rates very low—even if you're raising them but you keep them very low—you are inviting bubbles."

Between 2003 and 2007, the average home price in the United States rose by 38 percent, to the highest level ever.

In 2006, Alan Greenspan retired as chairman of the Federal Reserve. He left with a virtually unblemished reputation. He was seen as the engineer of fifteen years of nearly unbroken American prosperity. This was the shadow that loomed over his successor, Ben Bernanke. Americans didn't have a strong impression of Bernanke when he took the job. He was soft-spoken, even shy, and didn't generate strong reactions. This was true even among his fellow members on the FOMC, where Bernanke had served since he became a Fed governor in 2002 (his tenure at the Fed was interrupted by a brief intermission, starting in 2005, when Bernanke was president of the White House's Council of Economic Advisers under George W. Bush). Hoenig, for one, didn't have much of a sense as to how Bernanke might lead the institution. He didn't know much about the former professor except that Bernanke was an "inflation targeter," meaning that he, like Greenspan, would most likely focus on price inflation rather than asset bubbles.

It was, in fact, the fear of price inflation that compelled Bernanke and the FOMC to raise interest rates sharply in the spring of 2006, pushing the short-term rate to roughly 5 percent, the highest it had been in years. Hoenig wasn't a voting member of the committee that year, but he supported what Bernanke was doing. In June, Bernanke proposed pushing rates even higher, raising them above 5 percent. This marks the first time that Hoenig expressed a serious disagreement with what Bernanke was doing, and the disagreement didn't make much sense to people who thought that Hoenig was a hard-money inflation hawk. Hoenig believed that the Fed should stop raising rates. During

the June meeting, he felt the need to voice his concerns, even if he wasn't
a voting member. At the meeting, Bernanke went around the big table
to hear from every regional bank president and gave the floor to Hoenig.

"Thank you, Mr. Chairman. I'm glad that everyone agrees that the
strength of a good committee is for someone to disagree, because my
preference, based on the assessment of the outlook, is to maintain the
funds rate at five percent, and I would vote accordingly if I were a voting member," Hoenig said. He pointed out that the Fed might be over-
shooting its target, raising rates so high that they might have more of a
disruptive effect on the economy than the Fed intended. "So I would
hold off, I would be patient, and I would be firm in keeping the rate at
five percent," Hoenig said.

"President Hoenig," Bernanke replied. "I think everyone around the
table admires you for your consistent position."

The comment evoked laughter in the room.

It wasn't entirely what Bernanke meant by "consistent," but Hoenig
took it as a reference to his reputation as a Fed "hawk." Hoenig replied:
"That's a generous word, but thank you."

Bernanke was correct that there was a certain consistency expressed
in Hoenig's concerns at that meeting. By 2006, Hoenig had a coherent view of how the Fed should conduct monetary policy, which he
had developed over thirty years at the central bank. It would be too
simplistic to say that Hoenig was an inflation hawk. But he also certainly wasn't a dove. If there was a single phrase that might capture his
philosophy, it was a "rules-based" approach. This was one that emphasized restraint, incrementalism, and limits on how far the Fed should
push its powers.

The first pillar of the approach was the law of long and variable
lags. If there was one thing Hoenig had learned, it was that the Fed's
leaders, who were only human, tended to focus on short-term events
and the headlines that surrounded them. But the Fed's actions were

expressed in the real world over the long term, after they had time to work their way through the financial system. When there was turmoil in the markets, the Fed leaders wanted to take immediate action, to do *something*. But their actions always played out over months or years and tended to affect the economy in unexpected ways.

The second pillar of Hoenig's view was that the Fed should focus on *both* of the inflation cousins, asset inflation and price inflation. It was true that detecting out-of-control asset inflation was more difficult than detecting price inflation. And asset inflation was harder to stop without disrupting markets and making prices fall. But the results of asset inflation were devastating. When asset prices eventually corrected, and they always did, it caused massive financial instability. If the Fed achieved 5 percent unemployment by encouraging asset inflation, it would have to contend with the 10 percent unemployment on the other side of the correction. This required the Fed to make ever-larger interventions to repair the damage from asset bubbles.

The third and final pillar of Hoenig's view was that the Fed should show restraint, and follow rules that it imposed on itself. It should not push interest rates too low, too fast, nor hold them there too long. And the Fed should show restraint on the other side of the equation as well: It should not raise interest rates too high, too fast, if it was worried about inflation, because it might cause a precipitous collapse. The need for restraint was made more important by the law of long and variable lags. Because it took so long for the Fed's actions to have an effect, Hoenig believed the FOMC needed to patiently monitor conditions in the real world to measure the effects of what they had already done before doing something more. Keeping their actions within a narrow band helped ensure they didn't overdo it on the upside or the downside of an economic cycle before they even knew how economic actors would react. This kind of restraint had once been imposed on the Fed by the gold standard, but the gold standard was arbitrary and unworkable in its own way.* If the gold standard worked, people would still be using it. But without the gold standard, central bank leaders had to figure out how to impose discipline on the money supply. There was really only one solution. They had to replace the tyrannical restraint of the gold supply with the restraining power of their own wisdom and discretion.

This view, Hoenig's view, was the opposite of heroic. It was a mode of leadership built on unhappy compromise, focused on results that wouldn't be evident for months or even years. Its unpopularity seemed guaranteed. No one wanted to celebrate a Fed official who sought to make the central bank more boring, more limited, or less central to American economic affairs.

When the laughter subsided after Bernanke's comment, Hoenig's consistency was disregarded. The short-term interest rate was hiked another quarter of a percent, to 5.25 percent, where it would remain through the year. At this time, some parts of the housing market were beginning to display signs of weakness, particularly in the category of riskier, "subprime," home loans.

In late October, Hoenig was invited to give a speech to a group of bank directors at their annual symposium in Tucson, Arizona. This was a regular part of his job. Hoenig had been interacting with bankers throughout the Midwest since the Fed first hired him in 1973. But the banks he interacted with in 2006 were very different from the banks he dealt with earlier. They were larger, more far-reaching, and more deeply intertwined with one another than ever before. After the banking crisis of the 1980s, Congress relaxed the laws that prohibited banks from doing

---

*The gold supply was influenced by geological factors that had nothing to do with monetary policy, for instance. The discovery of a big new gold mine in Alaska could randomly increase the money supply. This helps explain why the gold-standard era was characterized by bank panics, long bouts of deflation, and periodic depressions. Also, for the gold standard to work, nations need to accept punishing bouts of deflation at times, which very few are willing to do.

business in multiple states, hoping to make it easier for the survivors to stay in business. Loosening the interstate banking laws allowed stronger banks to buy up weaker competitors, paving the way for a new breed of giants. Continental Illinois had been deemed too big to fail in the 1980s, but it was a small bank compared to some of those the Federal Reserve was now charged with regulating. What worried Hoenig, as he traveled to Arizona, wasn't just the size and the scale of the new banking corporations. It was what they were doing. These bigger banks were making the same kinds of loans that marked the boom years of the late 1970s. Back then, Penn Square made risky oil loans and sold them off as "participations." In the mid-2000s, mortgage lenders extended risky home loans and sold them off as mortgage-backed securities.

The atmosphere at banking conventions tends to be chummy, and exclusive. The symposium in October was held at the JW Marriott Starr Pass resort on the edge of Tucson, and the resort felt like an island. It contained a golf course and a pool near an outdoor dining area with couches and small adobe firepits. The rooms had balconies from which guests could overlook the rolling mountain ranges to the west. This was the kind of place that bankers congregate to talk shop and make connections. Hoenig moved easily through such places and was treated like visiting royalty. His presence at such an event brought prestige and made attendees feel like they had inside access to power.

The symposium agenda said that Hoenig would deliver a speech entitled "This Time It's Different." This was catnip for a banker. It fed the general sense, in 2006, that banking and finance were driven by new and sophisticated insights. This was the age of the "quants"—meaning analysts who bought and sold stock using software algorithms—and the private equity kings who earned billions through buyouts and corporate turnarounds.

When the time for Hoenig's speech approached, the bankers filed into a conference room and took their seats, ready to hear how this time was different. Hoenig walked to the podium, looked out over the crowd, and began to speak. What followed was the equivalent of a close relative showing up at Thanksgiving dinner, standing up to offer a toast, and then proceeding to give a lengthy speech about Grandma's debilitating alcoholism and the emotional damage that it had inflicted on everyone at the table. The speech was not designed to comfort.

"Asset values are appreciating, farmland values are strong, and we are all well aware of what has occurred this year with the energy markets. In short, for many in this area of the country, times are good," he began. But then he pointed out that times had also been good back in the early 1980s, when asset prices were also rising. But the collapse wiped out 309 banks in the Kansas City Fed district alone.

"Let me share with you some statements that we actually heard from bankers and bank directors during the '80s," Hoenig said. He recalled bankers telling him, "If you understood this better, you wouldn't have a problem with it" and "Yes, we loaned a hundred percent on this project, but everyone knows that the collateral value can only go up during construction" and "Although this is unconventional, our accountant says it is perfectly legal" and "The corporate plane will save money for the bank in the long run."

In case the audience missed his point, Hoenig made it explicit: "Age-old behaviors, such as greed, shortsightedness, and arrogance, are at the center of these problems, and, I would caution, they are with us today just as they were in the 1980s."

Banks might be larger, and the financial instruments at their disposal more complex, but at root things were not in fact different in 2006 than they had been before. When asset prices were rising and debt was cheap, it induced reckless behavior. Hoenig told the story of Penn Square and Continental Illinois, and how the reckless behavior of one bank fed into the others. "The simple fact is there are times when it is wise not to jump on the bandwagon. In some instances, it is better to let the parade pass you by," Hoenig said. "As directors, you should be extremely cautious if your management can't fully and clearly explain the business lines they are about to enter or if there is too much of a rush to jump in."

Hoenig ended his speech by saying that if things were to end up differently in 2006, it would only be because bank directors, the very people in the audience that night, chose to be more skeptical, more restrained, and more focused on oversight.

"When I finished," Hoenig recalled, "I got stone silence."

A few months later, in March 2007, Ben Bernanke was invited to testify before the Congressional Joint Economic Committee. Bernanke did not have Greenspan's celebrity status, but he was still a trusted voice on Capitol Hill. He seemed to speak in actual English, even when delivering bad news, and the news wasn't good in 2007. "Economic growth in the United States has slowed in recent quarters," he said. "The principal source of the slowdown in economic growth that began last spring has been the substantial correction in the housing market."

Still, Bernanke assured lawmakers that they didn't need to be overly worried. The slowdown just meant that the economy was transitioning to a more "sustainable pace" of growth. The Fed wanted to slow the economy and was doing its job well, he suggested. Bernanke acknowledged that higher interest rates would probably cut demand for houses. Home foreclosures would probably increase, and there would be some damage. "At this juncture, however, the impact on the broader economy and financial markets of the problems in the subprime market seems likely to be contained," he said.

The problems were not contained. For roughly six years, the American financial system had arranged itself around the central, nourishing flow of cheap money. When the Fed raised interest rates throughout 2006 and 2007, the effects rippled outward through the economic system and shook it apart. The big tremors began in August 2007, when BNP Paribas, a French banking giant, said it couldn't accurately price some securities based on home loans. This meant that the bank couldn't figure out what the loans were really worth, raising questions about the value of underlying assets that banks depended on for their solvency. Things unraveled relatively quickly after that. The average housing price fell by 10 percent in a year, a wrenching downward correction for middle-class wealth. By the start of 2009, housing prices had fallen by 20 percent overall. In two short years, Americans lost about $10 trillion in wealth. The losses were felt at big banks and investment funds, which had been counting mortgage loans as valuable assets on their books. Many faced imminent collapse, just like Continental Illinois when the value of risky energy loans corrected. The stock market crashed in late 2008 when the banking wreckage became obvious, wiping out about $8 trillion in wealth over two years. It was the worst economic downtown since the Great Depression.

The crash of 2008 illuminated the deep disparity that had developed between the power of the Federal Reserve and the power of fiscal authorities like Congress and the White House. The fiscal authorities were exposed as slow and ineffective, while the monetary authority of the Federal Reserve emerged as robust, keenly maintained, and fast-moving.

The Obama administration first sought to ensure that the big banks were recapitalized. The secretary of the Treasury, Timothy Geithner, had previously been president of the New York Federal Reserve. Geithner's approach to the crisis embodied the modern Democratic Party's theory of bank regulation. The top priority was to protect the financial stability of banks rather than to close them down or restructure them as FDR had done during the Great Depression. Geithner famously described this strategy as putting "foam on the runway." He intended to help the banks make a smooth crash landing and to recover as quickly as possible. The foaming had begun before Obama took office, when Congress passed a $700 billion relief package for the banks. To repair the broader damage to the economy, the new administration followed the Keynesian path: spending government money at a moment when the private sector was pulling back. The goal was to stimulate demand and to cushion the downturn, but the effort was hobbled by strong Republican opposition to government spending. Obama began from a position of compromise, presenting a plan that his administration believed might appeal to Republicans. A large portion of the resulting stimulus package came in the form of tax cuts. The total package amounted to roughly $787 billion (although later estimates said the true amount added up to $862 billion). This was still not nearly large enough to replace the demand that had been lost.

These fiscal programs were dwarfed by the Federal Reserve's actions, the scope and speed of which weren't truly revealed for many years. The Fed had printed and disbursed more than $1 trillion while Congress was still arguing over the language of the stimulus bill. As Bloomberg News and the economic historian Adam Tooze later revealed, a lot of this money from the Fed went directly to foreign banks that were in danger of collapse. The Fed opened "swap lines" with foreign central banks, primarily in Europe, and traded newly created dollars for those banks' foreign currency, at a discounted rate. The Fed was also active on behalf of banks at home. In late 2008, the Fed engaged for the first time in quantitative easing. It bought about $600 billion in bonds from banks, placing all the new money it created for the purchase directly in their reserve accounts.

The Fed's actions seemed like they were very complicated and sophisticated, an impression that was reinforced when the emergency lending programs were labeled with a wild menagerie of incomprehensible acronyms like TAF (term auction facility), TSLF (term securities lending facility), and PDCF (primary dealer credit facility). But this was Fedspeak. The Fed's actions amounted to one basic thing: It created new dollars on Wall Street through the accounts of a small club of primary dealers. And it did so at a scale that was unprecedented.

It is easiest to grasp the scale of the Fed's actions by comparing them with what the central bank had done over the previous century. Between

1913 and 2008, the Federal Reserve printed more dollars every year at a steady gradual pace, increasing the supply of new money, called the "monetary base." Between 1960 and 2007, the Fed increased the monetary base by $788 billion.

During the bailouts of 2008, the Fed printed nearly $875 billion. It more than doubled the monetary base in a matter of months. Another way to measure the size of the Fed's interventions is to look at its balance sheet. When the Fed buys something, it takes it onto its balance sheet, which reflects how many dollars the Fed has injected into the banking system. In just a few months after the stock market crash of September, the Fed's balance sheet grew by $1.35 trillion, more than doubling the assets it already had on its books.

All of this was done with the understanding that these were emergency actions, an extraordinary attempt to confront an extraordinary danger. The financial panic of 2008 threatened to plunge the global economy into a deep depression. The financial system had seized up, and banks had ceased doing business with one another because nobody knew who was broke and who wasn't. The Fed stepped in, as it had been designed to do, and short-circuited the panic.

Tom Hoenig voted to support each and every one of these actions when they were presented to the FOMC in a series of emergency meetings. He believed that this was the Fed's job. But the question, for him, was what would happen afterward, when the emergency passed. This was where the hard decisions would have to be made.

When the crash of 2008 ended, it was immediately obvious that the damage would be long-lasting. Ben Bernanke himself had written the paper explaining how the downturn of 1991 led to a jobless recovery in part because of an overhang of bad debt. The overhang in 2009 was almost unimaginably larger. This wasn't just a matter of paying off old credit card bills or car loans. Millions of families were evicted, a wrenching process that played out over a decade, with 8 million mortgage foreclosures between 2007 and 2016. The long-term damage was foreseen at the time. Economists at the University of California, Los Angeles, estimated in early 2009 that the unemployment rate would still be above 9 percent by the end of 2011, when the country would still have about 4 million fewer jobs than in 2007. This was echoed by others, like the economist Mark Zandi, who estimated that the unemployment rate wouldn't fall back to 4 percent until 2014 unless Congress passed a major stimulus bill. Barack Obama did sign the stimulus bill a month later, but it was the last major fiscal action in response to the crash. Congress turned its energies after that to the passage of the Affordable Care Act and a financial reform bill called the Dodd-Frank Act. The conservative Tea Party movement gathered strength as these measures were debated and helped Republicans take control of the House during the midterm elections of 2010.

All of this put even more pressure on central banks to act. Paul Tucker, a senior official at the Bank of England, experienced the pressure firsthand. After Tucker left the central bank in 2013, he wrote the Fedspeak equivalent of a whistleblower's inside account of modern central banking. His book was called *Unelected Power* and discussed the ways in which democratic institutions were increasingly shifting power to nondemocratic institutions, like the military, the courts, and central banks. The banks were among the last institutions that could act quickly and decisively. This was by design. But the banks were also designed to operate with a narrow focus. "The most important constraint is that elected politicians should not be able, in effect, to delegate fiscal policy to the central bank simply because they cannot agree or act themselves," Tucker wrote. He pointed out that doing so creates a self-fulfilling prophecy: "The more central banks can do, the less the elected fiscal authority will be incentivized to do, creating a tension with our deepest political values."

When this happens, central banks became "overmighty citizens," Tucker wrote, capable of imposing sweeping changes on national life without the democratic accountability of democratic institutions. In 2010, as Congress effectively ceased to operate, the Federal Reserve took upon itself the job of stoking economic growth, a task that had once been the responsibility of fiscal authorities. If the Fed was an overmighty citizen, then its committee of twelve people on the FOMC faced more pressure with each vote that they cast.

In nearly twenty years as an FOMC member, Hoenig had cast forty-eight votes. He dissented four times in that period, or about 8 percent of the time. That might sound like a lot of dissent, by the standards of a consensus-driven committee, but it meant he still voted with the majority more than 90 percent of the time.

In 2010, it was Hoenig's turn to rotate back in as a voting member.

Hoenig could sense the uneasiness in the room when he voted against Chairman Bernanke. In 2010, when he voted against the chairman at every single meeting, the uneasiness spilled into almost every corner of his professional life. Each of his "no" votes telegraphed to the outside world that there was at least some level of dissension within the Fed, perhaps undermining faith in its actions. It also telegraphed that the Fed was making policy decisions, subject to debate. At professional conferences and meetings, Hoenig's peers expressed their uneasiness in the form of questions they asked him. Are you sure you're doing the right thing? Do you really think you should do this?

"It's not that you're being lobbied during the [FOMC] meeting at all. It's just that, as you vote no consistently, people kind of look at you as, 'This is very unusual,' as even the media is saying it's very unusual. So it's not hard to pick up the tone . . . It's a very serious matter," Hoenig recalled. "You really are affecting the economy and therefore the lives of many people, and to be an outlier is not the safest place to be."

Hoenig was pained at the memory of keeping interest rates too low during 2004, feeding the housing bubble. In 2010, the Fed kept rates at zero and gave "forward guidance" that assured bankers the rates would

stay at zero for a long time, giving them more certainty to make speculative bets. The zero rate incentivized bankers to reach for yield and make
risky loans. Once again, the Fed would try to stoke economic growth
by stoking asset bubbles, and betting that it could clean up the mess if
those bubbles collapsed.

In August, Ben Bernanke announced the plan to push the Fed's
efforts further, by pumping $600 billion into the banking system
through quantitative easing, even though the economy was starting
to grow again. It was true that unemployment was still high, but
the economists knew that it would remain high by the end of 2010.
The Fed's leadership felt the need to do something about it, to ease
conditions as the economy recovered in the hopes that it might speed
up the process. It was presented as an insurance policy that could be
reversed if needed.

On November 3, this proposition was put before the FOMC.
Bernanke called the roll, and it was Tom Hoenig's time to vote.

CHAPTER 6

THE MONEY BOMB

(2010–2012)

"Respectfully, no."

After he had cast his vote, Tom Hoenig sat through the formalities while the FOMC meeting wrapped up. When the proceedings were finished, the committee members and staffers gathered their things and chatted politely as they filed out into the hallway and toward the elevators. Hoenig's car was waiting for him downstairs, and he caught a flight to Kansas City. Back in Missouri, it took about forty-five minutes to drive from the airport to Hoenig's house, a stately red-brick Tudor that sat on a tree-lined avenue in the historic Brookside neighborhood. Cynthia could tell when her husband was under extreme stress, because he got really quiet. Hoenig was really quiet when he got home from the FOMC meetings in 2010. He retreated to his study, a converted bedroom upstairs, and closed the door. Hoenig couldn't talk about what had happened in Washington, because the FOMC proceedings were confidential. But Cynthia would read about the "no" vote in the media because the final vote tally was made public.

"I could see that it kind of physically wore him, to have to do that.

Because who wants to be not in the general consensus on things?" Cynthia said. Much later, Cynthia and Tom were at a social event, and she overheard him describe to a colleague how it felt to be the lone dissenter. "He said it was the most daunting thing you'll ever experience. To sit in a room, and your vote comes around, and you say 'No.' He said you never take that lightly."

Hoenig knew that his vote wasn't going to actually change anything. The FOMC had all but decided to undertake quantitative easing before the meeting even started. He voted no because he felt it was his duty. But there was another reason that he did it. He was sending a message to the American public. His vote was a signal that there was, in fact, dissent over what the Fed was about to do. There had been an argument about it, and at least one person had believed that the risks of quantitative easing were too high to justify.

Unfortunately, Hoenig's message could only reach the public in one way. The signal had to travel through the American media ecosystem of cable news shows, newspaper articles, financial wire services, and increasingly popular partisan websites. This media system was fractured and degraded in 2010 in ways that both mirrored and accelerated the decay of America's democratic institutions. This was a primary reason why quantitative easing and 0 percent interest rates were the most important economic policy of the decade, while also being one of the least discussed.

The Fed's policies were an obsession for only a small fragment of the conservative movement, but almost totally ignored by everyone else. Years later, an economist named Carola Binder analyzed media coverage of the Fed and quantitative easing between 2007 and 2011, using a database of more than 300,000 news stories. The results showed that the Fed's policies barely made the news. President Barack Obama, for example, was the lead newsmaker of about 8 percent of all stories. Ben Bernanke was the lead newsmaker in 0.13 percent of stories. When the Fed was written about, it was only written about when there was some kind of ready-made press conference, like Bernanke's testimony before Congress. FOMC meetings were virtually never covered. The only outlets that did regularly cover the Fed were specialized financial news services, like Bloomberg News, which sent reporters to cover even minor Fed events like speeches by regional bank presidents. But their coverage tended to focus on one thing: what the Fed was about to do and how it would affect markets. It was coverage written for Wall Street traders and barely written in English. It didn't penetrate the broader discussion. "I would say that most people wouldn't have any idea what quantitative easing even was," Binder said.

On the night that Hoenig cast his dissent, Fox News aired a segment about quantitative easing that lasted for more than fourteen minutes, an eternity by the standards of television news. The impact of this segment would be disproportionately large because roughly 47 percent of American conservatives relied on Fox for a majority of their news. There was no equivalent network for American liberals, who divided their attention among outlets that included National Public Radio, CNN, *The New York Times*, and MSNBC. Fox's prime-time segment on quantitative easing reached several million viewers. It was presented by one of the network's most popular personalities, the former radio show host Glenn Beck. His understanding of the Federal Reserve was like that of a very high drug user who had sat in a motel room, trying to eavesdrop through the wall as people in the next room talked about central banking. He sometimes said things that resembled the truth, but he ultimately left his viewers far less informed about the Fed than when he began talking.

Beck's preferred costume for television was a rumpled suit and tennis shoes. His thick-rimmed glasses and crew cut evoked a high school social studies teacher in the early 1960s. His viewers trusted him, almost to a religious degree; Beck was a driving voice of the Tea Party movement, and his primary expertise was describing wide-ranging and malevolent conspiracies. On the evening of November 3, Beck scrawled a long numeral on a chalkboard: 600,000,000,000. This represented the value of bonds the Fed just announced it would buy. "This is what they call quantitative easing," Beck said. Then he walked to a new chalkboard with a confusing flowchart written across it that included a series of large, cartoonish arrows that seemed to signify the flow of money, or influence, or something like that, behind the Fed's new program. Confusingly, the whole thing began with organized labor, depicted by a union boss wearing a bowler's cap and with a cigar dangling from his mouth. It got weirder and increasingly inaccurate from there. The final cartoon on the flowchart showed a group of top-hat-wearing bankers, at which point Beck delivered his final, climactic revelation.

"I thought we hated bankers, right? No, no, no. This is actually the *Fed*," he said, getting excited now, barking out his words. "What is the Fed? Don't worry—just a collection of big bankers. You know, the Goldman Sachs. We don't really know for sure because we're not allowed to look. Oh, that sounds honest! So you go to the bankers, and the bankers say: 'Don't worry! We're going to go to the Treasury and print more money. We'll just print more money. And then we'll take this money off the printing press and buy your bonds . . .'" he said. He concluded: "You know where that leaves us? Extra broke!" Most of this was wrong. The Fed isn't made up of a collection of big bankers; it doesn't rely on the Treasury to print money; and quantitative easing wasn't going to leave America broke but would leave it the opposite of broke, with trillions of new dollars injected into the financial system. The only important thing Beck got right was pointing out that quantitative easing would hurt people who saved money. But his speech overall was a significant tragedy. His broadcast helped set the agenda that conservatives cared about in 2010.

Conservatives cared about the Federal Reserve far more than liberals seemed to. On November 3, quantitative easing was the top story on the conservative Drudge Report website, which featured a headline written in big red letters that said: "BIG NEW PUMP." The liberal Huffington

Post, by contrast, appears not to have run any stories about quantitative easing on its home page in the days after it was announced. But the conservative media covered quantitative easing in a specific way—with a deep concern about price inflation. The coverage focused on the fact that the plan would likely devalue the dollar, which sounded vaguely unpatriotic, as if it weakened the nation. Glenn Beck repeatedly mentioned the threat of hyperinflation during his long segment. "It will be the Weimar Republic moment," Beck said, referring to the hyperinflation that plagued Germany before the rise of the Nazi Party.

The Fed was, in fact, trying to devalue the dollar. The Dallas Fed president, Richard Fisher, pointed this out during the internal FOMC debates. "Another desired benefit, as you outlined it yesterday, Mr. Chairman, is to devalue the dollar to stimulate demand for our exports—and I don't think we should ever say that publicly," Fisher said. Devaluing the dollar wasn't seen as all bad inside the FOMC. It made American products cheaper overseas, which could stimulate exports and create jobs. But conservative critics of the Fed saw devaluation as near treasonous. The conservative author James Rickards published a book in 2011 called *Currency Wars: The Making of the Next Global Crisis*. Rickards was a former lawyer for the hedge fund Long-Term Capital Management, which had nearly destroyed the financial system when it collapsed in the late 1990s. His book took fears of devaluation to their most extreme possible conclusion, warning that it would lead to coordinated efforts between Russia and China to dump American debt, devalue their own currency, and destabilize the American economy. The success of *Currency Wars* led to a series of books by Rickards, with thematically identical covers and titles like *The Road to Ruin*, *Aftermath*, and *The Death of Money*.

These books, and other conservative coverage, helped to dampen criticism of the Fed and quantitative easing because the program's critics looked like right-wing cranks. People like Rickards predicted the most catastrophic possible outcomes, like hyperinflation, but those outcomes never happened over the following ten years. The Fed's actions did pressure other central banks to follow its lead, and to print more money through their own quantitative easing programs, but it was hardly a currency war. And, as had been the case over the previous decade, price inflation never rose to a serious level, let alone hyperinflation. The extremity of conservative arguments made them easy to dismiss. These arguments swept up Tom Hoenig's dissent in their undertow. This is how the image hardened over the ensuing years that Hoenig had been opposed to quantitative easing because it would lead to price inflation or hyperinflation. The focus on price inflation allowed supporters of quantitative easing to declare victory each year that prices didn't rise sharply.

Ben Bernanke helped entrench this narrative.

Shortly after the vote on November 3, Bernanke appeared on *60 Minutes*. It was Bernanke's second appearance on the show. The year before, he'd given a long interview that featured a segment filmed in Bernanke's small hometown of Dillon, South Carolina. He and the *60 Minutes* host Scott Pelley sat on a bench on Main Street, outside the humble building where Bernanke's grandfather once ran a drugstore. "I come from Main Street. This is my background," Bernanke said.

In 2010, Bernanke defended the unprecedented experiment that the Fed was undertaking. Pelley gave an accurate overview of how quantitative easing would work. But when he asked Bernanke about the possible downsides of the program, Pelley only focused on one thing: price inflation. "Critics of Bernanke's Federal Reserve . . . say that the six hundred billion dollars, and holding down interest rates, could overheat the recovering economy, causing prices to rise out of control," Pelley said. This defined the line of questioning that was fired at Bernanke, and it dramatically narrowed the nature of the true criticism raised inside FOMC meetings by Hoenig, Richard Fisher, Charles Plosser, and Kevin Warsh. Bernanke did not correct the misperception.

"Well, this fear of inflation, I think is way overstated. We've looked at it very, very carefully. We've analyzed it every which way," Bernanke said. Then Bernanke said something that tainted the understanding of quantitative easing for years. "One myth that's out there is that what we're doing is printing money. We're not printing money," he said. "The amount of currency in circulation is not changing. The money supply is not changing in any significant way."

This statement was fundamentally untrue. The money supply was already changing in significant ways and would never return to the already elevated level where it had been on November 3. The people who understood this fact best were the people, like Hoenig and Bernanke, who understood how the mechanics of the Fed's power actually worked and who understood what it was actually beginning to do after the FOMC cast its vote.

Beginning on November 4, 2010, the American financial system began to orient itself around a central hub, located at 33 Liberty Street, in lower Manhattan. This was the address of the Federal Reserve Bank of New York, where the new era of quantitative easing would begin.

The New York Federal Reserve employs a team of financial traders who usually arrive for work early, sometimes before sunrise, so they can be ready for a regular morning meeting at 9:05. The trading floors are hushed and serene, with murmured conversations and the clacking of keyboards. The long rows of cubicles are filled with analysts who tend to skew young; jeans are not uncommon. The cubicles are decorated in the way of cubicle farms everywhere, with small personal effects that struggle to overcome the joyless conformity. A bright red Rutgers pennant was tacked to one wall at one point, family photos to another. Anemic-looking plants on windowsills struggle to survive in the weak light. In many ways, it resembles any other trading floor in lower Manhattan. But the Fed traders have special powers. Their first power is access to information that would make a big bank envious. Because every bank keeps a reserve account inside the Fed, the Fed's traders can see just how much money each bank holds in its reserve vaults. The Fed can also monitor the overnight loans exchanged between banks, because those loans are made through the Fed's own transaction system. This private information is then coupled with over-the-counter data services like Bloomberg terminals to give the Fed traders an unparalleled view into America's banking system. This knowledge is combined with the second, far-reaching power enjoyed by Fed traders. They are the only traders in the world who can buy things by creating new dollars. This is the basis of the Fed's ability to influence the economy and the banking system.

It is often said that the FOMC "sets" short-term interest rates, which is true, to a degree. The FOMC sets a target for the short-term rates. It is the traders at the New York Fed who make that target a reality. For many decades, they did it by buying and selling securities at exactly the right amount to make the cost of money exactly what the FOMC wanted it to be. If the FOMC wanted interest rates to go down, then the New York traders would go out and buy Treasury bills, using newly created dollars. This had the effect of sucking Treasury bills into the Fed and pushing out new dollars in return. This meant that there were more dollars to go around, which lowered the cost of borrowing money, which is just another way of saying it lowered the short-term interest rate on money. When the FOMC wanted interest rates to rise, the traders did the opposite, selling Treasury bills and sucking in cash in the process, making money more scarce and therefore more expensive to borrow, as expressed in higher interest rates. The New York Fed trading team did this with the skill and expertise of a piano tuner, managing to keep the money supply at exactly the right level of tension to produce the interest rate the FOMC asked for. Unlike so much of America's infrastructure, the Fed's system for influencing financial markets was pristine and assiduously maintained. Its power and reach were breathtaking.

The Fed would put this machinery to a new use on November 4 when it launched the second round of quantitative easing. Now the Fed wasn't just trying to control short-term interest rates. It was trying to stimulate the entire U.S. economy. The program was operated out of a surprisingly small room located at one corner of the trading floor, where the Fed traders bought and sold things in order to control the money supply. At an appointed time, sometimes twice a week, a Fed trader went into the room and closed the door behind them. They sat at a terminal accessing the Fed's proprietary trading system, called FedTrade. The Fed had used this system for decades, almost daily, to buy and sell short-term securities from the most exclusive group of financial institutions in the world. These were the roughly two dozen "primary dealers" that had the special privilege of doing business directly with the Fed. The primary dealers included big banks and investment houses like Goldman Sachs, J. P. Morgan, Citigroup, and Credit Suisse, and smaller players like Nomura Securities International and Cantor Fitzgerald.

From the terminal, the Fed trader put out a bid on a specific asset—like long-term Treasury bonds or mortgage-backed securities—then waited to see which primary dealer was willing to sell, at the best price. The Fed always drew bids for its auction for a simple reason: It was the most powerful buyer in the world. It could simply create however much money it needed to close a deal. When the Fed and J. P. Morgan agreed on a price, say $10 billion for a bunch of Treasury bonds, for example, then the trader at J. P. Morgan would send its Treasury bonds to the Fed. This was the moment when the Fed trader entered a few keystrokes at the computer terminal and created the money for the transaction. When the J. P. Morgan trader checked the balance of the bank's reserve account at the Fed, 10 billion new dollars had appeared to fund the transaction. This is how the Fed created money on Wall Street. It took in an asset, and paid for it by making new dollars inside the reserve accounts of primary dealers.

Starting in November, the Fed traders did this transaction over and over again until they had created several hundred billion dollars inside the Wall Street reserve accounts. There is one more important part of this process to understand. The primary dealers were not just selling the Treasury bills and mortgage bonds that they happened to have on hand. If that had been the case, it would have limited how much money the Fed could have pushed into the banking system (even the primary dealers only had a finite amount of such assets on hand). Instead, the Fed set up a conveyor belt of sorts, which used the primary dealers as middlemen. The conveyor belt began outside the Fed, with hedge funds that were not primary dealers. These hedge funds could borrow money from a big bank, buy a Treasury bill, and then have a primary dealer sell that Treasury bill to the Fed for new cash. In this way, the hedge funds could borrow and buy billions of dollars in bonds, and sell them to the Fed for a profit. Once the conveyor belt was up and running, it began magically transforming bonds into cash. The cash didn't stay safe and sound inside the reserve accounts of primary dealers. It started flowing out into the banking system, looking for a place to live.

The money changed the world, primarily by changing the behavior of people and institutions that already had a lot of money. Each dollar created by quantitative easing put pressure on the dollars that already existed, like water pushing into an overflowing pool. This pressure was intensified by the fact that the Fed was already holding short-term interest rates at zero. The Fed was essentially coercing hedge funds, banks, and private equity firms to create debt and do it in riskier ways. The strategy was like a military pincer movement that closes in on the opponent from two sides—from one direction there was all this new cash, and from the other direction there were the low rates that punished anyone for saving that cash. The Wall Street types developed a name for the strategy. They called it ZIRP, which was short for zero-interest-rate policy. Economists talked about ZIRP in terms of interest rates, but on Wall Street there was a deeper appreciation for the combined power of new money and low rates. The hedge funds and investors could see how ZIRP was reshaping the world, because they were the people who were doing it on ZIRP's behalf.

To understand the effects of ZIRP, it's useful to think about the whole thing from the perspective of a greedy hedge-fund manager who had to make a living in the world that ZIRP created. This hedge-fund manager might have participated in the debt-to-cash conveyor belt and sold Treasury bonds to the Fed for a profit of $1 million (a $1 million profit is unrealistically small for a hedge-fund owner, but the round number helps for the sake of this scenario). The first thing this hedge-fund manager is going to think about, when that $1 million lands in their account, is the prevailing interest rate. The interest rate imposes a lens through which they will view everything else, because the interest rate is what the $1 million can pay them for doing nothing. If the interest rate on a long-term Treasury bond is 4 percent, the hedge-fund owner can stash their money in Treasurys and earn $40,000 a year, essentially risk-free.

Lots of people are going to visit this hedge-fund manager to convince them *not* to stash their money in Treasurys but, rather, to invest their money in whatever scheme that particular visitor happens to be promoting. There are many kinds of people who visit hedge funds asking for money. There are pathologically optimistic oil executives from Texas, raising money to drill fracking wells. There are commercial real estate developers from Miami, with plans to build new luxury condominiums. There are stock portfolio managers who use the word *diversify* so much that it sounds like a holy incantation. These people parade through conference rooms and display their PowerPoint presentations, and they always have a sword hanging over their head. The sword is the 4 percent interest rate. They all need to make a very convincing case that their project, whatever it is, will produce a profit higher than 4 percent, which is the riskless return on a 10-year Treasury bond. This is how things worked for decades, but they no longer worked that way after 2010.

Short-term interest rates were held at zero for many years, which meant other interest rates were also historically low. Quantitative easing intensified this effect in an intentional and strategic way. The program's primary goal of quantitative easing was to make sure that the long-term benefit of saving money was lower with each passing month. The New York Fed traders achieved this effect by purchasing certain Treasury bonds, namely the longer-term bonds, such as the 10-year Treasurys. This was new. In earlier years, the Fed controlled the money supply by purchasing only short-term Treasury bills. The Fed was buying the long-term bonds because doing so was like closing the one safe deposit box where Wall Street investors could stash money. Before the financial collapse that started in 2007, the reward for saving money in a 10-year Treasury was 5 percent. By the autumn of 2011, the Fed helped push it down to about 2 percent.*

The overall effect of ZIRP was to create a tidal wave of cash and a frantic search for any new place to invest it. The economists called this dynamic the "search for yield" or a "reach for yield," a once-obscure term that became central to describing the American economy. The people who had real money, meaning billions of dollars, were set on the search for investments that yielded anything more than zero.

Now when a pathologically optimistic fracking wildcatter visited the hedge fund, they got a far more sympathetic hearing. Their Power-Points included figures on the productivity of oil wells that might seem riskily inflated. But the hedge-fund manager was more likely to think: Why not? It beats zero. The Miami condo developer talked up sketchy forecasts about the demand for new units, but taking a chance on the project still beat zero. And the well-dressed portfolio manager who was pushing shares of stock—shares that seemed wildly expensive when compared to actual profits of the company underpinning them— that investment also beat zero. The search for yield didn't just pressure

---

*There are many factors that affect the yield of 10-year Treasury bonds, and those factors worked in concert with the Fed's actions to drive down the rates over time. Bernanke estimated that the first rounds of quantitative easing alone probably drove down the 10-year yields by between 1.1 percent and 0.4 percent while the second round cut about 0.15 to 0.45 percent off the yield.

risk-hungry hedge-fund managers. It also pressured the most conservative and wealthy institutions, like big pension funds and insurance companies. These institutions had enormous sums of cash, and they depended on interest payments to remain solvent. When interest rates are 4 percent, a pension fund might be able to meet all of its payment obligations with just $10 million saved in Treasury bills, because the $10 million will kick off regular interest payments. When rates are pushed close to zero, the pension fund is suddenly insolvent and must start a search for yield. Now even the pension fund will be taking a hard look at fracking wells and luxury condo developments.

This is why ZIRP caused asset prices to rise. When people search for yield, they buy assets. This increased demand drove up the price for corporate bonds, stocks, real estate, and even fine art. The asset price inflation was not an unintended consequence of quantitative easing. It was the goal. The hope was that higher asset prices would create a "wealth effect" that bled out into the broader economy and created new jobs. It was entirely clear to senior leaders at the Fed that to achieve the wealth effect, ZIRP must first and foremost benefit the very richest people in the country. That's because assets are not broadly owned in America, according to the Fed's own analysis. In early 2012, the richest 1 percent of Americans owned about 25 percent of all assets. The bottom half of all Americans owned only 6.5 percent of all assets. When the Fed stoked asset prices, it was helping a vanishingly small group of people at the top.

The people who benefited most from this arrangement tended to talk about it the least. Very few hedge-fund operators seemed eager to complain about the way that ZIRP widened income inequality and fueled speculative debt bubbles. One of the unspoken rules of Wall Street, in fact, is that those who know, don't show. If a trade is turning a profit, then people who know about it don't talk about it because doing so might draw a crowd and risk the trade itself. So the public rhetoric around quantitative easing remained dominated by inflation doomsayers who focused only on price inflation, which never materialized. The arguments made by people like Tom Hoenig were mostly ignored. And, after 2010, he would no longer be making them inside the FOMC.

In early 2011, Hoenig retired from the Kansas City Fed at the age of sixty-five. When NPR did a story about it, they referred to him as "Fed Dissenter Thomas Hoenig." His reputation had been set. In January, Hoenig gave a speech in Kansas City to a local business group. It was basically his goodbye speech as a Fed president. He didn't use the occasion to press his arguments against quantitative easing, or 0 percent interest rates. He gave a short speech, instead, about the value of dissent inside the Fed. He pointed out that the FOMC had been constructed to include members from around the country, not just Fed governors who were appointed in Washington, D.C. "In this structure, it is a key point to remember that each [FOMC] member was given a vote, not an advisory role," Hoenig said. "A deliberative body does not gain credibility by concealing dissent when decision making is most difficult."

Hoenig had dissented, and he had lost. The monetary experiment was now under way.

"As for me, I recognize that the committee's majority might be correct. In fact, I hope that it is. However, I have come to my policy position based on my experience, current data, and economic history," he said. "If I had failed to express my views with my vote, I would have failed in my duty to you and to the committee."

Between November 2010 and June 2011, quantitative easing pushed 600 billion new dollars into the financial system. The monetary base of the United States—meaning the core pool of new money that only the Fed can create—rose by a total of $720 billion between November 2010 and June 2011. In about seven months, the Fed injected more money into the banking system than it had in the thirty years prior to 2008.

The banks were overflowing with more cash reserves than they had ever seen in history. By the summer of 2011, the value of excess cash reserves in the banking system reached $1.6 trillion, a level 800 times larger than precrisis levels.

At first, there were encouraging signs that ZIRP might be helping the broader economy. The unemployment rate began to fall, slowly but steadily, in the months after quantitative easing ended. But as time passed, the broader benefits that Bernanke and others had hoped for proved elusive. When quantitative easing was launched in November, the unemployment rate was 9.8 percent. When the program finished in the summer of 2011, the unemployment rate was still 9 percent. Economic growth was, by the Fed's own measures, still anemic and uncertain. To achieve these small gains, the Fed had distorted the financial system in ways that would not be easy to undo.

Ben Bernanke became single-minded in his drive to do more. If the new round of quantitative easing worked only marginally well, then maybe another, even larger round might work better. If the banks weren't lending as much money as the Fed desired under the pressures of ZIRP, then ZIRP could be intensified. This is what Bernanke proposed doing in the summer of 2012. But this time, Bernanke would face more opposition than he had faced in 2010. During an FOMC meeting in the summer of 2012, six out of the twelve FOMC members expressed skepticism about launching a new round of quantitative easing. If even three of these members voted against Bernanke's plan, it would show the world that the Fed was uncertain about its experiments. Bernanke worked hard to make sure this didn't happen. He began politicking within the FOMC, building support for his plan to escalate the Fed's intervention.

Bernanke's strongest opposition came from a group of three Fed governors who began to work together to slow or hinder his plan. One of these governors proved to be a formidable critic of ZIRP, at least within the closed sessions of the FOMC meeting. His name was Jerome H.

Powell, and he was a relatively new addition to the Fed board, having been appointed by Barack Obama in 2012.

Powell raised many of the same concerns that Hoenig had raised. But Powell came to those concerns from a different path. He had spent his career in the world of private equity dealmaking. He had grown wealthy helping create and sell risky debt. When he joined the Fed, he began to point out just how risky that debt could become to the broader economy.

Unlike Thomas Hoenig, Jerome Powell would actually be listened to. He would, in fact, rise to the highest levels of power inside the Fed. And during the years that he ascended to the role of Fed chairman, he provided some of the clearest warnings of just how dangerous quantitative easing might become.

PART 2

THE AGE OF ZIRP

CHAPTER 7

QUANTITATIVE QUAGMIRE

(2012–2014)

When Jerome Powell joined the Fed board of governors, he joined one of the strangest, most isolated workplaces on Earth. The Fed governors work out of well-appointed offices that line a long hallway in the Eccles Building, near the cavernous, ornate boardroom. Though they work on the same floor of the same building, the governors didn't simply pop into one another's offices to ask for advice or share a thought. Discussions were set up by appointment, through the governors' assistants. One of Powell's neighbors as a governor was Elizabeth "Betsy" Duke, a former bank executive and chairwoman of the American Bankers Association. Duke said she was struck by just how isolating it was to be a Fed governor. "It was the loneliest job I ever had," she recalled.

The social atmosphere was a strained one, but Jerome Powell managed to fit into it smoothly. This was one of his primary skills in life. Powell was charming, smart, and even humble in his way, with a self-effacing humor that was impossible to fake. Everybody called him Jay. He had spent his career inside the corridors of American power, moving back and forth between the institutions of big government and big money. When Jay Powell was around the most powerful people in the world, he knew what to say and how to say it. He grew up in the wealthy suburbs of Washington, D.C., attended Georgetown Law, and then went to work on Wall Street in the investment world. After that, he had a senior position in the U.S. Treasury Department, under the first President George Bush, and then he jumped to a very powerful private equity firm called the Carlyle Group. Carlyle was so rich, and run by a group of Washington insiders who were so powerful, that it spawned a number of conspiracy theories that were surpassed only by the Federal Reserve. After his time at Carlyle, Powell was very wealthy and joined a think tank in Washington. He was nominated to be a Fed governor by Barack Obama as part of a compromise deal. Obama nominated one liberal, a Harvard professor named Jeremy Stein, and one conservative, who was Jay Powell.

Powell arrived at the Fed in May 2012, just as the FOMC was entering a period of tense debate. Ben Bernanke was pushing for a new, much larger round of quantitative easing, but he was facing an unprecedented amount of dissent within the committee. Debates inside the FOMC that summer revealed a remarkable level of skepticism, and outright opposition, to Bernanke's plan. During the meeting in late July, about half of the voting FOMC meeting members expressed concerns about quantitative easing. Bernanke began to push hard against this opposition because economic growth remained weak, and the unemployment rate remained high, almost four years after the crash of 2008. This long period of anemic growth was entirely expected and predictable because of the big debt overhang that remained from the housing bubble, but Bernanke felt pressure to act and to keep the Federal Reserve at the center of efforts to boost the American economy. To achieve this, Bernanke pushed the Fed to use tools that were once considered experimental, even radical, but were now the only tools at the Fed's disposal.

The Fed had already employed two of its most powerful tools by the time Powell arrived. The first was "forward guidance," whereby the Fed guaranteed that it would keep rates low, encouraging more lending and speculation. In January, the Fed had signaled it would keep rates at zero for nearly three more years, an extraordinary escalation of the guidance. The second tool was "Operation Twist," a bond-buying program similar to quantitative easing, but with one important difference. Operation Twist didn't pump more cash into the banking system, but only sought to encourage more lending by pushing down the interest rates on long-term Treasury bonds.* The Fed had launched a new Operation Twist operation in late 2011 and extended it in 2012.

But as summer rolled around, Bernanke needed something more. He turned to the final, most powerful, and most controversial tool: quantitative easing. Bernanke began to push for a larger, longer-lasting round of quantitative easing, arguing that maybe this new round would accomplish what the previous round had not. Quantitative easing had now become a normal tool of monetary policy and had even earned its own shorthand description at the Fed and on Wall Street, where people referred to it simply as QE. But even as it was normalized, internal dissent against QE was growing inside the FOMC. Bernanke faced resistance from Fed governors and multiple regional bank presidents. This growing dispute put pressure on Jay Powell to figure out where he stood and to figure it out quickly. A series of FOMC votes in July, August, and September would determine the future course of the Fed and the financial system.

Powell began to work closely with Betsy Duke, a vocal critic of

---

*The way this worked is that the Fed bought long-term Treasury bonds and then simultaneously sold an equal amount of short-term Treasurys into the market. This maneuver was the "twist." The Fed was taking long-term bills out of the market, which lowered the interest rate of those bills by increasing demand for them. But the fact that it was selling an equal value of short-term bills ensured that it wasn't increasing the total supply of new cash in the banking system. Every dollar the Fed added through a long-term T-bill purchase, it took away with a short-term T-bill sale. The goal was to dissuade investors from saving money in a 10-year Treasury bond while not flooding the banking system with cash.

quantitative easing. Both Powell and Duke had come to the Fed from the world of private banking and finance, so they shared a certain sensibility and a technical understanding about the way the Fed influenced the real world of hedge funds and banks. It seemed to be this knowledge that made them skeptical about another round of QE. Duke expressed her concerns repeatedly and forcefully during several FOMC meetings. She was worried that more QE would just build up more risk in the financial system, without doing all that much to help the real economy. She was also deeply worried that the Fed didn't seem to have an exit plan. Quantitative easing was easy to execute, but difficult to reverse. And reversing QE became more difficult the larger the program became. Duke's concerns were amplified by two regional bank presidents: Richard Fisher from Dallas, and Jeffrey Lacker from Richmond. Fisher thought QE encouraged risky speculation and asset bubbles. Lacker feared that more QE would make it harder for the Fed to ever raise interest rates again.

Jay Powell had an outsize influence in this debate because he was a governor. Bernanke focused his energy on lobbying the governors to get behind his plan in a way that safely neutralized any objections that might come from cantankerous regional bank presidents. "That was the way the Bernanke Fed worked," Betsy Duke recalled. "You didn't have dissent from any of the governors. . . . Bernanke viewed it as a particularly big deal. He said he didn't want dissents."

When Bernanke lobbied the Fed governors, the lobbying was aimed at a particular goal. The goal was to build unanimous support among the governors for something called "Option B." When the FOMC members gather for their official meeting, they generally consider three policy options before voting on one. The options are labeled "A," "B," and "C" and arranged like Goldilocks's porridge, ranging from hottest to coldest in their effect on the money supply. Option A was usually the most aggressive, like a round of QE that would be worth $1.5 trillion, while Option C would be extremely conservative, like doing no QE at all. Option B was always structured to be just right. Bernanke spent his time between meetings formulating an Option B that satisfied the governors and guaranteed their votes when the meeting came around. "The objective, always, for the meeting, is to come out with Option B," Duke said. Bernanke was willing to accept one dissenting vote from a regional bank president, but not much more than that.

In his very first meeting at the FOMC, Powell was diplomatic and warm. He voted for Option B. But Powell also signaled that his thinking would hew more closely to Betsy Duke's than to Ben Bernanke's. Powell opened his remarks with something that would become a habit of his: He talked about what his friends and contacts were saying in the private sector. He often surveyed his contacts with precision and rigor; in one meeting he broke down their responses by percentage, like a Gallup opinion poll. During his first meeting in May, Powell said that QE should be reserved as a backup tool, something to be used "as a defensive weapon going forward." He indicated that the weapon was probably not needed now. His industry contacts said that growth was slow, but he wasn't convinced the slowdown would last into 2013. This critique was hardly as sharp as others that were expressed against QE during the meetings, but it signaled that Powell's support could not be taken for granted.

Bernanke lobbied the governors between meetings, an easy job because their offices were a short walk down the hallway from his own. He lobbied them as a politician might do, building support for his cause and seeking to isolate opponents who might hinder it. The FOMC discussions were open, and transcribed for history, but Bernanke's private meetings were not. This allowed people to speak freely. Betsy Duke very much enjoyed these meetings, even when she disagreed with Bernanke. He was a great listener. When Bernanke tried to persuade the Fed governors, he did so respectfully and intelligently. He presented them studies, and he read the studies that they provided in response. He called them unexpectedly. He traded emails and debated. The process wasn't necessarily contentious. Duke, for one, enjoyed the back and forth.

Duke and her colleagues were not an easy sell on QE. "Everyone seemed to agree that you had declining benefits," she recalled. And those tiny benefits came with large risks down the road. "The concerns were, how do you exit? How do you stop?"

One of Bernanke's secret weapons in the lobbying effort was his vice chairwoman, Janet Yellen, the former president of the San Francisco Fed. Yellen was an assertive and convincing surrogate for Bernanke, and she championed an expansive use of the Fed's power. Betsy Duke had become close with Yellen early on. They talked over a private dinner, and commiserated about the strange isolation and stress of being a Fed governor. Yellen joked that she could have keeled over dead in her office at the Eccles Building and no one would have found her body for days. Yellen was friendly, even jovial, when she pressed her views. But she was not in any way ambiguous.

"Janet was the strongest advocate for unlimited" quantitative easing, Duke recalled. "Janet would be very forceful. She is very confident, very strong in promoting the point of view." Yellen and Bernanke were convincing, and their argument rested on a simple point. In the face of uncertainty, the Fed had to err on the side of action. Bernanke pushed this view to Duke, along with other wavering FOMC members like the regional bank presidents Sandra Pianalto of Cleveland, Dennis Lockhart of Atlanta, and Narayana Kocherlakota of Minneapolis.

All of this lobbying meant that the key policy decision making was essentially finished by the time the regional bank presidents traveled to Washington to vote. The regional presidents seemed to sense this fact, and they tailored their criticisms to affect future votes, or give cover to Fed governors who might want to break ranks. Richard Fisher, the Dallas Fed president, had grown adept at this art. During the FOMC meeting in late July, he gave a long, impassioned speech against Bernanke's push into deeper and deeper interventions. Fisher didn't just argue on the philosophical merits of the Fed's ZIRP policies. He presented a specific, detailed case study illustrating how the policies were already causing dangerous distortions in the economy.

Fisher said that he had recently spoken with the chief financial officer of Texas Instruments, who explained how the company was managing money in the age of ZIRP. The company had just borrowed $1.5 billion in cheap debt, but it didn't plan to use the cash to build a factory, invest in research, or hire workers. Instead, the company used the money to buy back shares of its own stock. This made sense because the stocks paid a dividend of 2.5 percent, while the debt only cost between 0.45 percent and 1.6 percent to borrow. It was a finely played maneuver of financial engineering that increased the company's debt, drove up its stock price, and gave a handsome reward to shareholders. Fisher drove home the point by relating his conversation with the CFO. "He said— and I have his permission to quote—'I'm not going to use it to create a single job,'" Fisher reported. "And I think this is the issue. We work under the assumption that lowering the cost of capital and providing cheap money encourage businesses to lever up and to use that levering up to expand [capital investment] and job creation, which is part of our mandate. I don't believe that's happening."

Fisher was describing, specifically, how ZIRP was already building up systemic risk in the economy without creating a single job. Bernanke rarely responded directly to such statements, but in this case he made an exception.

"Thank you," Bernanke said. "President Fisher, I know we put a lot of value on anecdotal reports around this table, and often to great credit. But I do want to urge you not to overweight the macroeconomic opinions of private-sector people who are not trained in economics."

With this comment, Bernanke seemed to have inflicted upon Fisher the most humiliating wound possible in the culture of the FOMC. He had exposed Richard Fisher as being unsophisticated. Neither Fisher nor, presumably, the CFO of Texas Instruments had earned a PhD in economics. This put them at a supposed disadvantage when it came to comprehending the effect of programs like quantitative easing. The Fed's leadership sometimes acted as if only the army of trained economists at the Fed, up to and including its chairman, could understand the design and the effects of the Fed's actions. The implied superiority of economists was a very real force at the Fed, on display at every FOMC meeting, when PhD-trained staff gave long and minutely detailed presentations about the policy choices at hand. The Fed historian Peter Conti-Brown showed how this dynamic helped consolidate power into the hands of trained economists at the Fed like Bernanke and his staff: "Without a PhD in economics, according to one former governor, 'the Fed's staff will run technical rings around you,'" Conti-Brown wrote in his 2017 book, *The Power and the Independence of the Federal Reserve*. This power was also directed against critics like Powell and Duke, who came from the world of banking rather than academia.

During the July meeting, Jay Powell took a measured approach. He bluntly acknowledged that QE would stoke economic growth primarily by first stoking asset prices. "I suspect that the channels that we're using now, which principally are asset prices, may not be working at all as well as our models say," Powell said. QE was building up risks in the economy, he continued, but the risks were probably manageable. Still, he didn't think another round of QE was necessary. "And for me, I think that the bar for another large LSAP is high and not yet met," he said, using an alternative acronym for QE (LSAP stands for "large-scale asset purchase," and people at the Fed use it interchangeably with QE).

Bernanke did believe the bar had been met, but by late July he still could not push the FOMC to agree with him. The Option B approved at that meeting was a lukewarm statement that didn't commit to another round of QE. Bernanke had a chance to change this in late August, when he was invited to speak at the prestigious Jackson Hole retreat. He had used that venue to build support for quantitative easing in 2010. Now he would do it again.

The weather was beautiful as the elite economists and central bankers arrived at Jackson Hole, and Bernanke's speech was seen as the main event. But Bernanke had cause to feel gloomy. The attendees were hardly more friendly to Bernanke's plan for more QE than were the members of the FOMC. Even at Jackson Hole, there was deep dispute about what the Fed was doing. Some economists argued that QE wasn't even achieving its primary goal of lowering long-term rates. Others argued that it had done that, but wasn't creating any meaningful gains for the economy. The dour-looking and influential Harvard economist Martin Feldstein spent a lot of his time at Jackson Hole walking around and badmouthing Bernanke's policies to any media outlet that would listen. The networks were eager to hear Feldstein's views because he was an advisor to the Republican presidential candidate Mitt Romney. In an interview with Fox Business, Feldstein said that the U.S. economy was in a deep hole, but pointed out that low interest rates and cheap lending would do nothing to fix the real problems that afflicted the country. "I don't think there's much the Fed *can* do," Feldstein said in a quote to *The Wall Street Journal* that was even more direct: "The Fed is at a point where another round of quantitative easing would be a mistake."

Bernanke's speech that year was presented as an assessment of the Fed's actions since 2008. It carried a neutral title: "Monetary Policy Since the Onset of the Crisis." Bernanke purported to weigh the benefits and the costs of policies like quantitative easing, forward guidance, and Operation Twist. He seemed to be very careful not to use common English or to talk about what the Fed was doing in a way that might accidentally be understood by anyone without an advanced degree in economics. To give just a flavor, when Bernanke described the way that QE affected markets, he said: "One mechanism through which such purchases are believed to affect the economy is the so-called portfolio balance channel . . . The key premise underlying this channel is that, for a variety of reasons, different classes of financial assets are not perfect substitutes in investors' portfolios."

Bernanke's very dense speech outlined the potential benefits and the potential drawbacks of QE. This approach helped his campaign to build more support for QE precisely because the benefits and costs were so hard to measure. One economist's asset bubble was another's healthy market. His speech meandered through this ambiguous terrain until Bernanke uttered one line that would truly move markets. "Overall, however, a balanced reading of the evidence supports the conclusion that central bank securities purchases have provided meaningful support to the economic recovery while mitigating deflationary risks," he said.

This was the statement that would be carried at the top of *The Wall Street Journal*'s story on Jackson Hole. Bernanke was saying that QE worked. He was also saying that the Fed would "not rule out the further use of such policies." It was a clear signal to Wall Street that the traders ought to hitch up their horses and get ready to ride.

Bernanke's speech overrode the deep divisions on display inside the FOMC by fueling the so-called announcement effect. This happens when the very hint of a new action from the Fed changes what investors expect, which then makes the market prices start to change. Bernanke had benefited from this effect in 2010, when he fed the expectation that another round of QE was on the way, causing some stock and bond prices to rise. This meant that *not* initiating another round of QE would cause prices to fall, putting a very heavy burden on any FOMC member who might vote no.

If Bernanke was slowly squeezing his own FOMC into a narrow set of choices, he justified what he was doing by pointing to two very large economic threats—one foreign and one domestic—that he believed justified his plan. The foreign threat came from Europe. The domestic threat came from Congress.

In Europe, the financial crisis of 2008 had never really ended. The debt overhang in Europe was simply astounding. Just three European banks had taken on so much debt before 2008 that their balance sheets amounted to 17 percent of the entire world's GDP. Europe was crippled for years. European banks and governments owed their debt in dollars, so the European Central Bank couldn't just create more dollars to bail them out as the Fed had done in the United States. The Fed had been working hard to stop the bleeding, extending the "swap lines" that flooded Europe with dollars. But there was only so much the swap lines could do. By 2012, Europe was at risk of entering a "doom loop," whereby failed government loans would damage the banks, which in turn would suffer huge losses and drag down growth, making it even harder for the governments to pay off further debt. As always, this threatened the United States because a massive European downturn would hurt demand for U.S. goods.

The second threat, the domestic threat, was even more urgent. The Tea Party movement had effectively neutralized Congress. The only acceptable public policy plan, in the eyes of Tea Party leaders, was to cut taxes, cut government spending, and reduce government regulation. In the summer of 2011, the Tea Party pushed its crusade into new terrain, threatening to default on the federal government's debt if the Obama administration and the Democratic-controlled Senate did not adopt Tea Party policies. This fight was centered on what was once a routine vote to pay the government's bills, a vote known as "raising the debt ceiling." The term was misleading—the vote wasn't to increase overall spending and debt, but just to finance the spending to which the government was already committed. This nuance was meaningless to the Tea Party, which would not vote to pay. Standard & Poor's downgraded U.S. government debt, an asset that was once considered a riskless bet. A debt default loomed for the first time in American history. This catastrophe was only averted when the White House and the Tea Party reached a very strange compromise. Congress agreed to pay its bills, but only if a time bomb was installed in the federal budget. The time bomb was a series of automatic spending cuts that were so draconian and irresponsible that even many Republicans couldn't live with them. The theory was that the insanity of the cuts would force Congress and the White House to agree to a new, better compromise before the date of detonation. This date, as it happened, was set for January 1, 2013.

Bernanke called the looming budget cuts—which totaled about $500 billion—the "fiscal cliff." The cuts amounted to about 3 or 4 percent of all economic growth in the United States. Economists feared such cuts would push the country immediately into recession.

In the face of these dangers, Bernanke believed that the Fed needed to have the courage to act. And he was helping ensure that the FOMC had no choice but to act. In the days after the Jackson Hole speech, public perceptions began to harden that more QE was coming. And the Wall Street traders began to focus their attention on the Fed's next meeting, in September, when they expected this QE to be announced.

Before that happened, the measure would need to be passed by the FOMC, preferably with no more than one dissent. Bernanke had used dense economic language to promote QE publicly. Now his team would use the same approach internally, with the FOMC. The Fed's economists were already working on a presentation, steeped in numbers and full of charts, to present at the next meeting. The presentation told a story about QE that was very hopeful, and also almost entirely wrong.

On September 12, the members of the FOMC gathered in Washington, D.C., for their regular policy meeting. Bernanke had prepared the ground for another round of quantitative easing, but the scope and shape of the new program were still unclear. Bernanke and Yellen were pushing for an open-ended program. Early versions of the much-polished Option B called for a QE plan that had no set end date. The open-ended nature of the plan was meant to be a compromise with those who objected to it. The idea was that the Fed could readjust or even end the program if it proved to be unnecessary.

There was a sense of inevitability inside the room. Bernanke's speech at Jackson Hole had built up expectations on Wall Street that a new round of quantitative easing would be announced the following day. But it wasn't enough for the FOMC to vote based on a sense of inevitability; the entire rationale for having the committee was that its members would vote on policies after a dispassionate debate. The meeting opened with a long presentation from two Fed staff economists that seemed designed to settle any doubts about the new round. The study was framed as a scientifically rigorous forecast of what another round of quantitative easing might do, and how long it would last. It used rigorous academic language and was full of precise measurements and graphs. But this presentation, for all its detail, was catastrophically wrong in virtually every important prediction that it made. Revealingly, the grave mistakes all pointed in the same direction. And it was a direction that would help Bernanke push his case.

The presentation was written by Seth Carpenter and Michelle Ezer. Carpenter presented their findings to the FOMC. He was a relatively young economist, but his PhD from Princeton and years of working as a Fed researcher gave him a firm command of complex issues. His demeanor, and his vocabulary, exuded expertise and cool competence. The jargon he employed was almost numbingly intimidating, as when he pointed out, at the beginning of his presentation, that "the staff analysis starts from a term structure model that embeds Treasury and MBS supply factors as determinants of the yield curve."

In spite of the jargon, the main points were simple enough.

The forecast predicted that short-term interest rates would remain pinned at zero throughout 2013 and 2014, as the new round of QE was rolled out. But, after that, the forecast predicted that the rates would start to climb again, rising until they reached historically normal levels around the year 2017. Things would get fully back to normal by about 2018, when short-term rates would return to roughly 4.5 percent or higher.

This was magical thinking. In reality, the Fed Funds rate stayed at 0.4 percent until the end of 2016. By the middle of 2018 the rate had only risen to less than 2 percent, or half the rate that was forecast.

This same pattern of error held true for other key metrics, like the average rate on a 30-year home loan. This was forecast to drop at first but then rise steadily until 2020, when the rates would be above 6 percent. In reality, home-loan rates rose during 2013 but then stalled out, and fell steadily until 2015, when they hit 3.6 percent. The rate never hit the 6 percent that was forecast and was only 3.5 percent by early 2020.

The gravest errors had to do with the Fed's balance sheet, which reflected just how many bonds the Fed would buy and, conversely, how many new dollars it would inject into the financial system. Carpenter and Ezer focused on the value of the account used by the Fed traders in New York. The Fed predicted that its holdings would expand quickly during 2013 and then level off at around $3.5 trillion after the Fed was done buying bonds. After that, the balance sheet would start to shrink, gradually, as the Fed sold off all the assets it bought, falling to under $2 trillion by 2019.

In reality, the value of assets in the Fed account exploded far faster and far more than the Fed expected, hitting $4.2 trillion by 2016. The account remained at that high level, virtually unchanged, until February 2018. In other words, the SOMA account became about twice as large as the Fed expected it to, and it never shrank in the way the Fed had forecast.

There was a final, important error in Carpenter's presentation. It assumed that the rate of price inflation would fall during 2012, but then start to rise again, continuing to rise steadily through 2015. At that point, it would level off and hover around 2 percent, which happened to be the level the Fed was targeting with its policies. This never happened. The inflation rate lagged below the Fed target of 2 percent for most of the period between 2012 and 2020. The rate was still 1.9 percent by December 2019.

This last error carried profound consequences. The rate of price inflation was basically the only external brake that could be applied to the ZIRP policies. If consumer prices started to rise, then external pressure would build for the Fed to raise interest rates, and undo quantitative easing. But if that didn't happen, the Fed would keep interest rates at zero and keep buying bonds.

Even as Carpenter walked through his presentation, he peppered his commentary with caveats and warnings. He tried to explain that the forecasts were merely educated guesses. The forecast was based on theoretical models, and those models were based on certain assumptions about the way the world worked. "But there is layering, model upon model, to try to get these effects," he said after the presentation.

When asked about the presentation, years later, Seth Carpenter was almost sheepish about it. "I certainly get mocked for it," he said with a laugh. The reasons for the Fed's errors were systemic, and they illuminated how the Fed used its unrivaled research capacity. When trying to figure out the future, Carpenter relied on a macroeconomic model called the FRB/US model. That model assumed that economic conditions would, over time, revert to the historically normal state. Interest rates, inflation, and unemployment would all tend to go back to the levels where they had been over the previous decade. "The shortcoming of most macro models is that the vast majority of them make the assumption that over time conditions will revert to a prevailing 'norm,'" Carpenter said.

When taken together, the mistakes made it seem as if a new round of QE would be an emergency action that would quickly boost growth and create jobs, and which could then be repealed so everything could return to normal. If that was true, then quantitative easing would be a tool like others used by the Fed, like interest-rate cuts, that could be imposed and then quickly withdrawn as conditions changed. The truth turned out to be the opposite. The distortions from quantitative easing were deep and long-lasting, and the program, once employed, was essentially never-ending.

These forecasting errors were not an isolated incident. Central banks around the world consistently misled themselves about the effects of quantitative easing. The banks overestimated QE's positive impact on

overall economic output, when compared against studies conducted by
outside researchers, according to a 2020 study by the National Bureau of
Economic Research. And central bank researchers who reported larger
effects from quantitative easing tended to advance faster in their careers,
the study found. This could have been due to the fact that the researchers reported to the very central bank leaders who were pushing for the
programs.

The forecast helped Bernanke make the argument that the FOMC
was only making a limited and flexible commitment. But other committee members were still strikingly critical of the plan. Dennis Lockhart,
president of the Atlanta Fed, was clearly torn about it. "I have some
reservations about going down the path of a new [QE]," he said. "This
time around it seems to me that we face a more conventional problem
of inadequate demand, and I am not convinced that lowering general
market rates will stimulate much credit expansion and spending."

Sandra Pianalto, president of the Cleveland Fed, said that another
round of quantitative easing would not help as much as the earlier
rounds, and that it would be hard to end once it started.

These arguments were tame compared to the arguments of the
nonvoting members like Richard Fisher and Esther George, who had
replaced Tom Hoenig as the president of the Kansas City Fed. They
argued that the plan would be ineffective, that exiting it would be difficult, and that the Fed was building up longer-term risks that were difficult to measure let alone mitigate.

Bernanke's answer to these concerns was the same as it had been
since the financial crisis. The Fed had to have the courage to act. Congress was clearly sitting on the sidelines. Growth was slow. The benefit
of quantitative easing might be small, but if the Fed had the power to
gain even small advantages, then it had an obligation to do so. "We want
to persuade our colleagues, and that's certainly laudable," he said. "But
the fact is that nobody really knows precisely what is holding back the
economy, what the correct responses are, or how our tools will work."

Bernanke admitted that another round of quantitative easing was essentially "a shot in the proverbial dark." But he believed there were risks to not taking the shot. And, just as important, they all needed to support his shot in the dark once it was made. "I think, really, it's going to be very important for us to pull together, in a sense, to support whatever efforts that we make," he said. The vote that day was a familiar one. In spite of their concerns, eleven of the FOMC members voted for the plan. Only one voted against it. The single dissenting vote, this time, came from Jeffrey Lacker, the Richmond Fed president. Lacker's dissent didn't really matter. It could be explained away as the stubborn action of a cranky regional bank president. What did matter was the fact that Fed governors like Betsy Duke and Jay Powell supported the plan.

Duke had been won over because Option B was crafted in a way that gave the Fed flexibility. The option didn't set an end date or a specific amount of bond purchases, which gave the FOMC the freedom to either intensify the program or reduce it, depending on the state of the economy. "I genuinely believed that it was a temporary program and that our balance sheet would go back [to normal]," she later recalled.

Almost immediately, she was proven wrong.

When the Fed announced that its QE program would be open-ended, Wall Street investors interpreted the ambiguity as a signal that the Fed was planning to go big. Within three months of launching the plan, the Fed's fundamental mistake was apparent. By January, the average dealer on Wall Street expected the Fed to keep purchasing assets through the end of 2013, buying about $1 trillion in securities during the year. In reality, the Fed was only planning to purchase about $500 billion that year, and planned to make the purchases only through June.

This was particularly frustrating for Betsy Duke. She had voted for the program only because she believed that it would be limited. Now the market was expecting something far bigger. "We got comfortable with a five-hundred-billion-dollar program, but nobody in the markets ever knew it was a five-hundred-billion program. It immediately went to one trillion, one point one trillion," Duke recalled later. If the Fed stuck with its original plan, it would be a disappointment, and markets might fall.

This imposed a choice on the FOMC. The committee could either expand the program or tell the investors that they were mistaken. "It's either going to be, we end up with a program we never intended, because we don't want to disappoint markets, or markets end up disappointed at the size of the program. One of those was going to happen," Duke said. She knew that some members of the FOMC, such as Janet Yellen, would be fine with a $1 trillion third round of quantitative easing. But Duke was not.

Neither, it became clear, was Jay Powell. During the FOMC's January 2013 meeting, Powell abandoned his tone of moderation. Instead, he delivered a warning about the dangers and distortions of quantitative easing that was blunt, and even horrifying in its way. Powell said that the Fed was potentially creating an asset bubble in the markets for debt like corporate bonds and leveraged loans. And the correction, when it came, could be deeply damaging. "Many fixed-income securities are now trading well above fundamental value, and the eventual correction could be large and dynamic," he said. The language was restrained but the message was not. Powell was clearly saying that the Fed might be laying the foundation for another financial crash (or a "large and dynamic" event, as he put it).

This was around the time when Duke and Powell joined together to push back against Bernanke. They were joined by the former Harvard professor Jeremy Stein, who became a Fed governor along with Powell. Duke was particularly impressed with Powell's approach to the problem. After the FOMC meetings, she would reread his comments and think about his critiques. The three governors began to meet and compare notes. They occasionally met for lunch in the Martin Building, an auxiliary Fed building just behind the Eccles Building, which had a cafeteria and private dining rooms. They united around a common goal: to force the Fed to stick with the program it had originally envisioned. This meant that they wanted to start winding down the asset purchases sometime around June. Bernanke knew about this mini-insurrection, and he soon started describing Duke, Powell, and Stein as "the Three Amigos." They posed a political problem for him. If they were to dissent in unison, it could bring an end to the program.

During the March meeting, Powell presented the findings from his own personal survey of seventy-five investment managers. Many worked for exactly the kinds of institutions that were being pushed by the ZIRP policies to make riskier and riskier investments: pension funds, insurance companies, and endowments. Sixty-four percent of them said the Fed was incentivizing people to make investments that didn't make sense. Seventy-four percent were worried that the Fed would not be able to easily exit the quantitative easing program even if it wanted to. Eighty-four percent said the Fed was inflating the value of assets like corporate junk debt. They generally supported the Fed's efforts to have an accommodative policy, but they doubted the effectiveness of quantitative easing.

Powell doubted it as well.

"I think we need to regain control of this," he said during the meeting. The Fed was purchasing $85 billion in assets every month. In January 2013, Fed staff had estimated that the new round of QE would ultimately add $750 billion to the bank's balance sheet. But by March, even $750 billion was starting to look like a conservative estimate if the Fed didn't pull back or end the purchases.

Bernanke met with Stein and Powell. He continued negotiating with Duke. The three governors were unwavering. They wanted the FOMC to impose discipline on the program and cut back purchases. Stein gave public speeches about the inherent risks of quantitative easing. Both Powell and Duke continued to pressure Bernanke during FOMC meetings. Eventually, Bernanke reached a compromise with the Three Amigos. After the meeting in June, Bernanke would announce that the Fed might start slowing down its new QE program. The goal was to clearly tell Wall Street traders that the QE program wasn't going to surpass $1 trillion, and it certainly wasn't going to last forever, as some traders seemed to believe. Duke and Powell agreed to this compromise.

After the June meeting, Bernanke walked to the press room to deliver the news. Duke and the other governors often gathered in a conference room in the Eccles Building to watch as his comments were carried live on CNBC. Bernanke was the first Fed chairman to give regularly scheduled press conferences. He began the practice in April 2011, to help quell the political backlash that followed quantitative easing. "After the blowback that greeted our introduction of QE2 in November 2010 . . . we needed to do more than ever to explain our policies clearly and effectively," he later wrote in his memoir. The tactic was remarkably effective. Carola Binder, the economist who studied media coverage of the Fed, found that most outlets never covered FOMC meetings, unless Bernanke held a news conference. When that happened, the cameras put the focus on Bernanke himself, allowing him to shape the message.

In the press room that June, Bernanke stood on a stage under bright lights that had been set up for the benefit of TV cameras. He went directly to a single chair set behind a lectern, where he sat down, opened a folder, and removed some papers that he placed on the lectern in front of him.

"Good afternoon," he began, looking up to address several rows of journalists who sat behind rectangular tables arranged in rows extending back to the rear of the room. The journalists were a well-dressed crowd with deadly serious glowers on their faces. Most had a laptop open on the table in front of them. The stories they were already typing, and the questions they asked, were instantly transmitted to eager crowds of financial traders staring at television sets across the world.

Bernanke started with a prepared statement, and in the midst of it he said that quantitative easing was essentially temporary. The Fed would likely taper off its purchases if growth remained strong, and would consider ending the program around June 2014. Bernanke soft-pedaled the announcement as much as he could, emphasizing that the Fed would still keep interest rates near zero.

Bernanke's first question came from Steve Liesman, a bulldog of a reporter with CNBC. Liesman zeroed in immediately on the idea that the Fed would be scaling back QE.

"I hate to use my question to ask you to clarify something, but when you said 'gradually reduce purchases,' beginning later this year and ending it next year when the unemployment rate hits seven percent—what is that? Is that a decision by the FOMC?"

Bernanke equivocated. "Obviously there's no change, there's no change in policy involved here. There's simply a clarification, helping people to think about where policy will evolve."

Bernanke's language remained vague and open-ended, but even as he was talking, traders on Wall Street were executing orders based on what he said. They had heard one thing above all else. Quantitative easing would be reduced, and it would probably be reduced sooner rather than later.

What happened next was often described as a kind of market shock, or an unforeseen spasm of volatility. But it was, in fact, an entirely measured reaction to the idea that the Fed would slow down QE. This reaction became known as the "Taper Tantrum."

The Taper Tantrum was the first of multiple market shocks that would illustrate the profound fragility that ZIRP and QE had embedded in the financial system. It is helpful to understand this by thinking of the financial system as a seesaw. On one end of the seesaw there are risky investments, like stocks or corporate debt. On the other end of the seesaw there are very safe investments, like 10-year Treasury bonds. Money travels back and forth, from end to end, on the seesaw depending on how bold investors feel. Since 2010, the Fed had been pushing money away from the safe end of the seesaw, where the 10-year Treasury bonds sat. This was the whole point of QE, to force investors to push their money over to the risky end of the seesaw because the Fed was keeping interest rates low on 10-year Treasury bonds by purchasing so many of them.* When Bernanke indicated that the Fed would be buying fewer 10-year Treasury bonds, the money started to move back over to the safe end of the seesaw, and away from the risky assets. This is when the seesaw tips, and it would do so with increasing velocity as the Fed's interventions became more extreme.

The most obvious symptom of the Taper Tantrum was a sudden decline in stock market values. The Dow Jones Industrial Average fell by 1.35 percent almost immediately on the chairman's remarks. But the stock market was actually a sideshow. The real danger showed up in the market for 10-year Treasury bonds, a bedrock of the global financial system. The interest rates on 10-year Treasurys shot up the day of Bernanke's announcement by 0.126 percent. That might not sound like much, but in the world of ultrasafe Treasury bonds it was a massive and jarring movement. The rate would jump over half a percentage point, from 2.2 percent the day before Bernanke's press conference to 2.73 within weeks. This movement didn't register as a financial crisis, or even a market crash, for most Americans. But it felt like the beginnings of a crisis inside Wall Street. Everybody could see what would happen if the money started rushing to the safe side of the seesaw and left the risky investments to survive with less cash. The balance of risk was changing quickly. Rising yields on Treasurys meant that Wall Street might have a savings account again, and investors didn't need to keep their money out on the risky side of the yield curve.

When this fact was apparent, investors turned around and looked at all the risky junk they'd bought, like leveraged loans and corporate junk bonds. They could now dump those investments and put their

---

*Interest rates fall on Treasury bonds when the Fed buys them because the Fed is increasing demand for those bills. When demand is high, a borrower has to pay less money in interest to get a loan, hence rates fall.

money somewhere safer. This was what started happening in late June and early July. And it happened in the kinds of arcane markets where the Fed's QE money flowed. Real estate investment trusts (REITs) began force-selling their holdings as mortgage rates adjusted. Money fled from corporate bonds, and indebted companies saw their interest rates rise.

Even within hours of the press conference, Betsy Duke was watching the Taper Tantrum play out on the television set in her office. She also had a Bloomberg computer terminal providing real-time financial data. Her heart sank as she watched the Treasury rates spike. It reflected an almost instantaneous wiping out of all the work the Fed had just done. So many billions had been pumped into the banking system to push down Treasury rates, and now the declines were disappearing. "At that point, it forced the Fed to be even *more* committed to continuing on," she said. "The continuing of the purchases—there just kind of wasn't any choice at that point. They had to continue, and had to bring reassurance to the market that they were going to continue."

The plan to taper was abandoned.

The new round of quantitative easing had started as a small commitment in 2012. It was sold as an insurance policy and a contingency plan that could be withdrawn. In January 2013, an internal FOMC memo described the QE plan as a program that would end in June 2013 and would add $750 billion to the Fed's balance sheet. Instead, the program continued through September. Then it continued into December. It was only then that the Fed started to even diminish the size of its monthly purchases, and it did not end them. The quantitative easing program continued through June 2014, and then into October 2014. Finally, the Fed stopped making purchases that month.

The $750 billion program ended as a $1.6 trillion program.

The program's quick withdrawal, which had been forecast in the presentation by Seth Carpenter, never materialized. The Fed would not even attempt to start shrinking its holdings until October 2017, and even then the effort was halting and largely unsuccessful. Ben Bernanke and the FOMC had fundamentally redrawn the economic landscape and the rules of monetary policy.

Betsy Duke announced in July 2013 that she was leaving the Fed board. Her resignation had nothing to do with the policy disagreements over quantitative easing. She had been on the job for five years, commuting between Washington, D.C., and her home in Virginia Beach. She was ready to move on to new things. At one of her final meetings, in June, she said that she wanted to cast a dissenting vote. The quantitative easing policy had gone on for too long and had grown too large. But she voted along with the majority.

"The time to oppose it would have been at the beginning," she said.

The Fed was locked into the asset purchases and the program was creating new levels of debt across corporate America, while also inflating asset prices. This wasn't an unintended consequence of QE. It was the goal.

One of the Fed's own economists, David Reifschneider, clearly explained during an FOMC meeting in 2012 that ZIRP policies boosted growth through three channels: cost of capital, wealth effects, and the exchange rate. Translated, this meant that QE made debt cheaper, stoked asset prices, and devalued the dollar (which could boost exports). At the same meeting, economist William English said QE would boost asset prices, and adding more QE would boost them higher. In March 2013, the Fed economist Nellie Liang told the FOMC that low interest rates were already inflating asset prices, possibly stoking bubbles. This wasn't a forecast based on models, but an assessment based on the Fed's unparalleled market surveillance. But some of the most dire and most prescient warnings came from Jay Powell.

"While financial conditions are a net positive, there's also reason to be concerned about the growing market distortions created by our continuing asset purchases," Powell had said at the January FOMC meeting.

He warned that the Fed was wrong to presume that it could clean up the mess after a bubble burst. "In any case, we ought to have a low level of confidence that we can regulate or manage our way around the kind of large, dynamic market event that becomes increasingly likely, thanks to our policy."

Powell was concerned about one market in particular: the market for exotic, risky corporate debt. This was the kind of debt that private equity firms and hedge funds used to buy other companies. The debt, sometime in the form of "leveraged loans," was packaged and resold, just as home loans had been during the 2000s. Back then, home loans were packaged into something called a collateralized debt obligation, or CDO. In 2013, corporate debt was being resold as something called a collateralized loan obligation, or CLO.

When Powell talked about leverage loans and buyouts, he was describing his own life experience. He had spent a good part of his career engineering exactly the kinds of risky debt that he was now warning about. As it happened, Powell's experience in the private equity world would become directly intertwined with his experience at the Federal Reserve.

CHAPTER 8

THE FIXER

(1971–2014)

When Jay Powell was a senior in high school, his classmates included a future congressman and Panama's future ambassador to the United States. Other students from Georgetown Preparatory School became U.S. senators, lobbyists, federal judges, and senior corporate executives. Two future Supreme Court judges, Neil Gorsuch and Brett Kavanaugh, graduated from Georgetown Prep in the mid-1980s.

The Georgetown Prep campus was near Powell's childhood home in Chevy Chase, a suburb of Washington. The streets of Chevy Chase were lined with majestic oak trees, and the stately houses were set back behind wide, lush lawns. Powell was one of six children in a large Catholic family. He was named after his father, a prominent corporate attorney who had argued in front of the Supreme Court. Powell's mother, Patricia, earned her master's degree in liberal arts from George Washington University and was a well-known volunteer around Chevy Chase who also worked part-time for the Republican National Committee. The family belonged to the Chevy Chase Club, along with an exclusive dining establishment in Washington called the Sulgrave Club. Every morning, during high school, Jay Powell was dropped off at Georgetown Prep's isolated campus, just off the busy Rockville Pike. After entering the campus, a long, winding road took students past a golf course, tennis courts, and a guard shack to the main cluster of academic buildings centered around a grassy quadrangle. It looked like an Ivy League college campus. The curriculum at Georgetown Prep was rigorous, but a lot of the real education happened between classes, and it taught lessons that were impossible to replicate elsewhere. At Georgetown Prep, a person learned how to be around the most powerful people in the world. The savvy students would have picked up on a million unspoken cues, and subtle rules of etiquette, that govern interactions of the very rich and influential. It is difficult to even quantify this code of conduct. A person needs to live it.

As an adult, Jay Powell knew how to operate at the center of things. He would spend almost his entire career at a very specific spot at the pinnacle of American power: the intersection of public government and private money. He occupied the offices that connect the worlds of Washington and Wall Street. He was a fixer who helped things operate smoothly between big capital and big government, and he developed a very good reputation in this rarefied world. Powell was a man of discretion and good judgment. He was solid. But he was never a prime mover in the halls of power, never an elected official or a CEO. He was impeccable at his job. While never famous, he was nonetheless deeply respected in the circles that really mattered. It was fitting that when Powell was eventually appointed chairman of the Fed, in 2018, his selection generated almost no controversy. He was seen, above all things, as being an effective operator. In a 2017 interview with *The Washington Post*, an investment manager named Michael Farr said of Powell: "He's neither a hawk nor dove," using the terms that defined a Fed governor's stance on fighting inflation. Powell had been a Federal Reserve governor for roughly five years at that point, and had engaged in some of the thorniest, most complicated debates about Fed policy. And yet Farr and others saw Powell as a man with no fixed belief system, just a desire to get things done. "He's a pragmatist who will pursue an economic good and turn a deaf ear to politics," Farr said.

Powell never turned a deaf ear to politics. His ear was sensitive and his judgment was keen. His career path was the path of a person who listened closely and who learned lessons at every step along the way. He would often be described as a "lawyer," because he had earned a law degree. But his career was far more varied than that.

After he graduated high school in 1971, Powell enrolled at Princeton. After graduation, he became a legislative staffer on Capitol Hill and then went to law school at Georgetown University, earning his degree and then clerking with a federal appeals court judge in New York. Powell followed his father's footsteps and became a corporate attorney, joining the firm Davis Polk & Wardwell. In 1984, however, at the age of thirty-one, Powell made a consequential move. He left the world of law and joined the world of investment banking. Powell was hired at a firm called Dillon, Read & Co. This was where he'd begin his long path toward great wealth in the world of corporate debt.

When journalists describe Dillon, Read & Co., they almost inevitably use terms like *white shoe*, *elite*, and *exclusive*. The company had been around, in one form or another, since the 1800s. Partners at Dillon, Read were the relentlessly effective servants of big money. When two big companies wanted to merge, for example, they asked Dillon, Read to handle the details. When a city needed to borrow money by issuing bonds, its politicians asked Dillon, Read to package the debt and sell it to banks. Deals like this generated millions of dollars in fees for the firm's partners.

It might seem odd that a lawyer like Powell would join an investment firm. But the transition from corporate law to high finance is common because lawyers can handle the thorny, wildly complicated contracts that make big-money deals possible. A background in law trained someone like Jay Powell in a key skill set necessary for success at Dillon, Read: discretion. "The corporate culture was very private," recalled Catherine Austin Fitts, a managing director at the firm during Powell's tenure there. The reasons for discretion were strategic. When a publicly traded company started talks to merge with another one, secrecy was key. If a Dillon, Read partner leaked details of the deal, it might open the door for someone to illegally trade on the inside information. Big companies worked with Dillon, Read because they trusted its partners to stay quiet, maybe for months at a stretch, as they helped negotiate the deal.

The other key attribute to success at Dillon, Read was loyalty. The company built long-lasting relationships with its clients that endured years, if not decades. Fitts said that the partners at Dillon, Read were like members of the Hanseatic League, a guild of merchants who operated in northern Europe during the 1300s. "Their tagline was 'Serious business with long-term partners,' which is a perfect description of Dillon, Read," Fitts said. "They went about their things very quietly. Discretion was everything. And relationships. They really prized long-term relationships."

Dillon, Read focused on deals that were profitable, but not flashy. The firm dealt with energy companies, manufacturers, and city infrastructure departments. This was tedious, highly profitable work that required a certain creativity in realms of life that people believed to be lethal to creative minds, like accounting, bond repayment scheduling, and the writing of loan covenants. If a person operated effectively in this space, the payouts were enormous. By all indications, Powell thrived in the environment.

Powell would have learned, at Dillon, Read, about the granular mechanics of issuing corporate debt. This form of debt came to play a central role in American economic life during the decade of quantitative easing and ZIRP. When Powell warned, in 2013, that loan values were being inflated and might crash, he was talking about corporate debt. His warnings reflected his deep knowledge about a corner of the financial world that was once dominated by elite firms like Dillon, Read. Because he helped create and sell corporate debt for so many years, Powell would have understood that the debt was structured in a strange way that eventually made it a profound danger to the global financial system.

There are two basic kinds of corporate debt: a corporate bond and a leveraged loan. These things sound complicated, but they're not. A corporate bond is, in many ways, like any typical bank loan. A company might borrow $1 million by issuing a bond, and the bond will carry an interest rate of 5 percent. The bond has a life span, like a 30-year home loan, at the end of which it must all be paid back. But this is where the similarities end. Corporate bonds have a strange structure that's different from credit card debt or a car loan. With a corporate bond, the company only makes interest payments during the life span of the loan, and then pays off the entire debt on the day the loan expires. So the loan doesn't get gradually paid down over the years, like a mortgage. The open secret about corporate bonds is that the companies almost never intend to actually pay them off. Instead, they usually "roll" the loan, meaning they hire a bank to sell the debt before it comes due and then replace it with a new loan. The bonds expire, but the debt survives and is rolled into a new bond that the company will later sell and roll again. Companies continually roll over corporate debt for years. This is what leaves them exposed to risk. If interest rates are rising when it comes time to roll the loan, companies can be in deep trouble. They face two bad choices: They can pay off the entire debt at one time, or they can roll over the debt into a bond that has a higher interest rate, and is therefore more expensive.

In spite of this risk, there is a vigorous market where corporate bonds are bought and sold. The bonds are standardized, and regulated by the Securities and Exchange Commission, just like shares of stock. The price of a bond can go up and down, just like a stock. (A bond price is usually expressed in terms of how likely the borrower is to repay. A good bond might be trading at 95 cents on the dollar, meaning there is an expectation that the bond will be paid back nearly in full.) People buy bonds—even very risky bonds—because it's a great way to make steady money if you can stomach some risk. The interest payments are regular, providing great cash flow for whoever owns the bond. The riskier a bond is, the higher the interest rate it pays to compensate for the danger that the borrower might default. A big, safe borrower like Walmart pays a low rate while smaller companies with a lot of debt pay a high rate. The riskiest corporate bonds are the ones called junk bonds.

The other type of corporate debt is called a leveraged loan. This is like a corporate bond in some ways: A leveraged loan is bought and sold, and it carries an interest rate that reflects its risk. The key difference is that leveraged loans are more tailored. They tend to be extended directly from a bank to a company, and they aren't standardized in the same way bonds are.

Firms like Dillon, Read used corporate bonds and leveraged loans as rocket fuel to propel corporate takeovers, mergers, and acquisitions. Powell thrived in this business. When he was in his mid-thirties, he looked like the kind of guy you would trust to operate a secret multimillion-dollar corporate takeover deal. He had the type of baritone voice that telegraphed confidence and authority, with a narrow face and dimpled chin that blended handsomeness and bland reliability. The only jarring thing about him was the shock of white hair that rose up right at his part, like a stripe. Powell did well at Dillon, Read, but his education in corporate debt was interrupted before he could earn the kind of fortune that drew corporate lawyers to Wall Street. In 1988, the company's chairman, Nicholas F. Brady, was recruited by Ronald Reagan to become secretary of the Treasury. After George H. W. Bush was elected president, and Brady's job security was ensured, Powell left Dillon, Read to join Brady at the Treasury. There is no more telling sign of Powell's success during his early years in private equity. "He clearly had Brady's trust, if he went to Treasury," Fitts said. "Brady was no fool."

Brady's trust in Powell would be validated almost immediately after Powell arrived in Washington, D.C. A scandal erupted inside the Treasury Department involving criminal fraud, risky derivatives contracts, and a too-big-to-fail Wall Street investment house. Powell was called upon to help fix the mess, and it provided him with the next phase of his education in the ways of power in Washington.

The problem started inside the large bureaucracy that Powell oversaw. He was assistant Treasury secretary for domestic finance, a job that put him in charge of issuing the government's debt. His division was the one that actually issued U.S. Treasury bonds. In some ways the job was mundane and predictable, sort of like running a printing press. The U.S. debt system was well established and well run, so Powell's job was like that of a station manager who had to make sure the trains moved smoothly through a busy station. His department worked closely with the New York Federal Reserve Bank, which auctioned off the Treasury bills to the primary dealers on Wall Street.

In February 1991, the traders at the New York Fed reported something odd. There was a small detail that seemed askew on one of their Treasury bond sales. During one of the auctions, the Fed sold Treasurys to two customers: an obscure investment firm called Mercury Asset Management Group and another one called S. G. Warburg Group. The strange thing was that both companies turned out to be different affiliates of the same investment firm. If these two companies were buying Treasury bonds on behalf of their common owner, that would be illegal. The government put strict limits on how many Treasury bonds any single company could buy so that nobody could corner the market. The trades looked fishy, raising suspicion that a big bank might be trying to sneak around the limits by purchasing Treasury bonds through seemingly separate shell companies. The suspicious bids had been submitted by a primary dealer called Salomon Brothers.

A lower-level employee in Powell's department sent a letter to

Salomon, asking what was going on. Did Salomon know that these two customers were actually one customer?

Inside Salomon Brothers, this letter was quickly conveyed to Paul Mozer, the bond trader who oversaw the firm's Treasury bond purchases. Mozer came clean to his bosses very quickly, admitting that he had been running a scam using affiliate companies to buy enough Treasurys that the firm could quietly amass more than the 35 percent of all the Treasury bonds sold in a given auction, the limit imposed by law. The goal was to get so many Treasurys that Salomon could then put the squeeze on other firms that bought the bonds in a secondary market. There was no gray area here. It was a criminal scheme. But Mozer wasn't fired, and Salomon covered up his behavior. The company sent a letter back to the Treasury Department explaining that the suspicious purchases were an innocent mistake. Mozer continued the scheme, cornering the market and squeezing competitors. In May 1991, Salomon used the scam to buy so many Treasury bonds that it controlled 94 percent of the supply. The Treasury Department, meanwhile, seemed entirely content with Salomon's explanation that nothing was amiss. Jay Powell's division kept auctioning off Treasury bonds through the New York Fed, and Salomon kept gaming the market.

Powell's boss, Secretary Nicholas Brady, happened to be good friends with Steve Bell, the managing director of Salomon Brothers' office in Washington, D.C. Bell wasn't a bond trader. He was one of those people who had worked in Washington for years and seemed to know everyone. Bell had become friends with Brady, for example, because Bell was staff director for the U.S. Senate Budget Committee when Brady was appointed briefly to the Senate seat in New Jersey. The two were close, and Bell was a regular guest at Brady's rural estate in Maryland, where the two of them would hunt doves. Bell must have made a great hunting companion. He was whip smart and profane. One of Bell's greatest achievements, back when he was a Senate staffer, was helping the Reagan administration create a novel legislative maneuver called "reconciliation," which allowed the president to pass a budget through the Senate with a bare majority of votes, bypassing the filibuster. Reconciliation was later used to pass Obamacare and the Trump tax cuts, earning Bell a level of notoriety on the Hill, a fact that he advertised decades later with pride. "I talked to somebody a couple of days ago and she said: 'You're the motherfucker that invented reconciliation, aren't you?' Her *exact* words," Bell recounted. Bell's Salomon Brothers office was located in the Willard Hotel, just across the street from the Treasury Building. This meant that Bell was at ground zero when Salomon's criminal behavior exploded into public view.

Salomon's bid-rigging became public after the May 22 auction, when Salomon bought so many Treasurys that it controlled 94 percent of the market. The conduct was simply too egregious to go unnoticed. This time, regulators from the Securities and Exchange Commission and the Federal Reserve didn't take Solomon's word that nothing was amiss. It quickly became clear that the bid-rigging would almost certainly result in criminal charges and massive fines. But even more dangerous for Salomon was the chance that the Department of the Treasury might revoke Salomon's designation as a primary dealer. Without that designation, the firm would go bankrupt. "It was an existential threat," Bell said.

There was one person who helped ensure that this threat was not realized, Bell believed, and it was Jay Powell.

When the bid-rigging was exposed, Salomon's CEO stepped down and was replaced by one of the firm's biggest stakeholders, the Omaha investor Warren Buffett. Bell and the team at Salomon believed that Buffett's reputation could help save the firm. Buffett immediately admitted that the firm was guilty and prohibited Bell's team from hiring the kind of high-priced D.C. legal firm that might be able to wage a war against the SEC and the Treasury. Buffett came to Washington, set up shop in Bell's office kitchen, and got on the phone to start negotiating with the Treasury Department over Salomon's survival. The person on the other end of the phone line was Jay Powell, Bell recalled. Buffett delivered a simple message: He would help clean up Salomon, but he needed the Treasury to show forbearance. "Buffett said: 'I will take on this task, but not if you make it impossible for us to survive,'" Bell said.

Nicholas Brady still suspended Salomon's status as a primary dealer, a death sentence in Bell's eyes. He believed that if the company was allowed to die, it would take down other Wall Street firms with it, and his message was simple: "What if you knock down the biggest tree, and it collapses, and knocks down a lot of other trees in the forest?" Bell said. Jay Powell would have understood this argument because of his background on Wall Street. "I think he knew that there would be some substantial disruption of global financial markets, given the huge position that Salomon had in derivatives and other instruments," Bell said. And while Bell knew very little about Powell, he knew that Powell's advice would carry enormous weight with Brady, because Brady had hired him. Brady "needed *his guy*. The guy brought to Treasury with him," Bell said. "Jay knew markets well. He had been with Brady earlier. He had the trust of the secretary."

Warren Buffett called Brady directly to plead Salomon's case, and the Treasury Department soon reversed its decision and reinstated Salomon's designation as a primary dealer. Bell would always credit Jay Powell with the victory, and with keeping Salomon alive. "I know that Jay was critical in informing Secretary Brady's decision," Bell said. The ruling gave Buffett time to pursue his cleanup plan for the company.

But the bigger problem that worried powerful members of Congress was the regulatory fiasco that had allowed Salomon to cheat in the first place, and to continue cheating even after its trades first raised suspicion. The House of Representatives held a public hearing on the matter in September. In Washington, such hearings are the equivalent of a ritualistic beating, giving lawmakers a chance to publicly express their fury. It was revealing, who the Treasury Department sent to testify. While the SEC had sent its chairman and the New York Fed sent its president, Nick Brady sent Powell to testify on his behalf. Powell was the designated target for incoming fire. He arrived at the hearing wearing a gray suit, white shirt, and gray tie. He spoke in long paragraphs as chilly and rehearsed as a court filing. And he was brutalized by the lawmakers. Press accounts of the hearing used words like *assailed* and *interrogated*. But Powell never seemed to get agitated. The Treasury had failed to detect Salomon's scheme and allowed it to continue. But Powell managed to explain everything in such a bloodless way that it seemed to drain the passion of his inquisitors. After the hearings, Powell oversaw the writing of a lengthy report on the scandal, and the role of regulators who enabled it. Ultimately, very little was changed. The Treasury Department amended the way Treasury auctions were conducted, moving to the "Dutch auction" style, which was seen as harder to game. Mozer was convicted and sent to prison. Salomon's CEO, John Gutfreund, was fined $100,000.

Powell was promoted. He became undersecretary of the Treasury at the age of thirty-nine. His tenure in that role was cut short, however, when George H. W. Bush lost his reelection bid. Powell wasn't out of work for long. His background at Dillon, Read, combined with his years of service at the Treasury, made Jay Powell an ideal candidate for one of the most rarefied jobs in the world, the one that would make him extraordinarily wealthy. He was hired to become a partner at the Carlyle Group.

Leveraging the connections and influence of Washington insiders was the core of the Carlyle Group's extremely successful business strategy. The company was cofounded in 1987 by David Rubenstein, a former staffer to Jimmy Carter, who said the company's location in the nation's capital was what gave it an advantage over the other 250 private equity firms that were in business then, most of them in New York. Carlyle specialized in buying and selling businesses that relied on government spending, and it hired former government officials to help. Carlyle partners included James Baker III, a former Treasury secretary, and Frank Carlucci, a former defense secretary. President emeritus George H. W. Bush was an advisor to the firm. In 2001 alone, Carlyle hired the former chairman of the Securities and Exchange Commission, the former chairman of the Federal Communications Commission, and the former chief investment officer of the World Bank. These people helped steer deals to Carlyle, and Carlyle helped these people monetize their granular knowledge and personal connections in the industries they once regulated.

The Carlyle Group, like other private equity firms, went out and raised money from wealthy people and institutional investors, like pension funds, that put big chunks of money into a pool of cash that Carlyle would use to buy companies. The basic goal was to "invest, improve, and sell" those smaller companies. Carlyle typically held on to a company for about five years and then sold it, ideally for a profit. Debt was key to this business model. The pool of investment money was always supercharged by leveraged loans and corporate bonds. Carlyle would put up some of its own cash, then borrow much more to fund the deal. Importantly, the debt was loaded onto the company that Carlyle bought. Then that company had to work hard to pay off the loan. It was like being able to buy a house that earned cash and paid off its own mortgage.

The key quality for a successful partner at Carlyle was to be connected. The ideal Carlyle partner had to know the right people in government agencies. They also had to know the right bankers who could arrange and syndicate massive amounts of leveraged loans. And they had to know talented people to bring in and help run the companies they bought in order to get them ready, in a matter of years, to sell.

Powell joined Carlyle in 1997, when he was in his mid-forties. His office was on the second floor of Carlyle's headquarters building on Pennsylvania Avenue, not too far from the White House. The Carlyle offices were hardly lavish by the standards of private equity. Wall Street firms often decorated their spaces with hardwood finishes and fine art hanging on the wall. The aesthetic at Carlyle was utilitarian. The company hung prints instead of original paintings, and the partners met in stripped-down conference rooms that could have been found in any law firm or insurance office. "Our offices were so boring and plain that it was a joke," recalled Christopher Ullman, a former Carlyle partner and managing director. The partners kept their focus on the marketplace. And the marketplace returned the favor. A parade of banks came to Carlyle to advertise companies that were for sale.

It was the job of people like Powell to sift through the offerings, like flipping through the pages of a catalog, seeking out deals with the most potential. In 2002, one deal caught his attention. An industrial conglomerate called Rexnord, based in Milwaukee, was looking for a new owner. Rexnord made expensive high-precision equipment that was used in heavy industry, like specialty ball bearings and conveyor belts. The company had been owned by a string of investors since the late 1980s, each one loading the firm with more debt and then handing it off to the next, hoping to reap a profit. Even after this treadmill of debt and resale, the firm remained attractive. It produced the thing that private equity partners valued above all—a steady cash flow. This meant the company was in a good position to pay down the debt that would be loaded on to it.

Powell eventually decided that Rexnord was worth the risk. He put together a team to manage the acquisition, and helped arrange the financing to make it happen. Carlyle would invest $359.5 million of its own money, from its buyout fund. Using this cash as a down payment, Powell helped secure two loans, worth a total of $585 million, to pay for the rest of the purchase price. This acquisition would mark the pinnacle of Jay Powell's private equity career. It also provided him with a firsthand education in the uses, and risks, of corporate debt.

Rexnord's headquarters were located in an unremarkable two-story brick building next to a big parking lot in west-central Milwaukee. Just behind the main office building was one of the company's factories and a tall smokestack that had CHAIN BELT stenciled down its side in white lettering, a nod to the company's original name, which dated back to the late 1800s (the name Rexnord was born about a hundred years later, after one of many mergers). The facility was surrounded by working-class neighborhoods of modest houses.

Tom Jansen started working at Rexnord in the 1980s, in the accounting department. After several promotions over many years, he became the chief financial officer, a job title that understated his level of responsibility. Many CFOs are in charge of a company's financial affairs. But Jansen was also in charge of shaping and reshaping the entire firm as it repeatedly changed hands starting in the late '80s. Jansen's work was grueling. At one point he quit, but was lured back within a year or so. There was something exciting about being Rexnord's CFO in a world of private equity. The company had become a case study in the debt-fueled model of American capitalism under private equity. One of the early buyout kings, named Jeffrey Steiner, bought Rexnord with junk bond debt, cut costs at the firm, then sold it off in the mid-1990s in a deal that paid him $6.3 million. Rexnord continued to change hands after that. After one acquisition, the new owners fired the entire management team above Jansen with one decree. He was asked to help rebuild the company, and in doing so became close with the next CEO, named Robert Hitt.

In 2002, the various corporate divisions of Rexnord were once again being split up and sold for parts by the firm's latest private equity owner, a company based in London. Jansen and Hitt created a "road show" that advertised the virtues of Rexnord as a corporate property. They hired investment bankers to spread the word among private equity owners, and soon they were making their pitch to a parade of speculators who traveled to Milwaukee. "There's a whole variety of people that come to kick the tires. There's bottom feeders—that you can tell right away," Jansen recalled. The bottom feeders wanted to buy Rexnord, strip it down, and sell off the pieces for a quick profit. The bottom feeders made Jay Powell and the team from Carlyle stand out. The Carlyle team was cool, calm, and exuded the kind of confidence that comes from big money. When Jansen got up to give his presentation, he explained that Rexnord's products could be found in just about every factory, oil refinery, and mining operation in the country, even if nobody knew what the company did. "You don't know what a 'Rexnord' is—there's no such thing," Jansen liked to joke. But there was real money in Rexnord's product lines of highly engineered conveyor belts and specialized ball bearings that were used in airplanes. "It made things that people needed to make the world move," Jansen explained. Rexnord's business model was like the one used by razor-blade companies. The razor was cheap; the replacement blades were expensive, and very profitable. Rexnord made its real money selling replacement parts when the vitally important conveyor belts broke down, or the expensive ball bearings wore out. The company's annual sales were reliable, at about $755 million a year. It earned more than $113 million a year in profit before taxes and interest payments.

Jay Powell and his team were sold. To Jansen's surprise, Powell turned the tables and started pitching the Rexnord team on the benefits of being owned by the Carlyle Group. "Their pitch was—we want to help you. We want to help you grow," Jansen recalled. The team from Carlyle promised that they wouldn't micromanage. Carlyle would place its people on Rexnord's board of directors, where they would steer the company, but they'd give the local management team autonomy.

The deal was closed in September 2002, funded mostly by corporate debt that was loaded onto Rexnord's balance sheet. Rexnord's debt level instantly jumped from $413 million to $581 million and its annual interest payments on debt rose from $24 million in 2002 to $45 million in 2004. Rexnord would pay more money in interest costs than it earned in profit during every full year that Carlyle owned it.

The debt put pressure on Rexnord. In early 2003, Rexnord

employees in Milwaukee agreed to take an average pay cut of $3 an hour, along with other concessions, to convince the management team not to move seventy jobs to North Carolina. The Milwaukee employees were unionized, and so moving those jobs to a nonunionized southern state might have saved Rexnord money. But Jansen said the Carlyle team was sensitive about the headlines such an action might create. "They were very, very aware that if cuts had to be made, we had to make them with respect. Treat people with respect. They did not want any bad publicity at all over this stuff," he recalled.

After Powell joined Rexnord's board of directors, he often traveled to Milwaukee to meet with Jansen and the rest of the management team, holding long meetings about the company's strategy, budget, and operations. They didn't gather for these meetings at Rexnord's actual headquarters, near the factory. Instead, they rented conference rooms at places like the Pfister Hotel, a century-old building downtown, with a four-story-tall atrium lined with marble columns and domed with a glass ceiling. Roughly twice a year, the board gathered for a multiday strategy session at the Doral Country Club in Miami (the club was later bought by the Trump Organization). The resort was a good place to think, with spacious patios near the pool and golf course, just outside the sprawling hotel complex that looked like a Southern Gothic mansion. Visitors could rent meeting rooms in the hotel that were encircled with wall-sized windows, looking out onto the rolling greens and palm trees. This was where the board would strategize about optimizing Rexnord's strategy and increasing its cash flow, boosting profits and paying down debt. The part about paying down debt was key. This was what made the private equity business something like a self-starting perpetual-motion machine. Rexnord employees were working hard to pay down debt that Carlyle used to buy the company, and as they did so they increased the value of Carlyle's ownership stake by making the debt disappear. If all went smoothly, Carlyle would be able to sell the firm in a matter of years.

Unfortunately, the deal started to go sideways almost immediately. The economy slowed down in 2003 and the weakness killed demand for Rexnord's parts as factories, mines, and refineries cut back on production. Carlyle had nearly $1 billion in cash and debt riding on the deal. Jansen wasn't entirely sure that the bet was going to pay off. And he had to deliver this bad news directly to Powell and the other directors. Jansen was surprised by their reaction. Nobody was pounding their fists on tables. Powell, in particular, just asked a lot of questions. "I think Jay was probably the guy that had the most pointed questions. I guess I would classify him as a deep thinker," Jansen said. When Powell was told that Rexnord was starting to founder, he only had one primary question: What's your plan? Jansen and Hitt spent long days in meetings at the Miami resort hashing one out.

During their off hours, the board members and executives played golf. Jansen felt that he really got to know Jay Powell on the golf course. Golf can be so frustrating that it pushes people to near hysteria. A perfectly good shot, right down the middle of the fairway, can be followed immediately, inexplicably, by a shank that sends a ball on a heartbreaking angle out into the long grass. Powell didn't seem to get cocky when his shots were perfect, and didn't get bitter when he shanked it. This sounds like a trivial thing, but it was telling. A person can't fake that kind of behavior for hours at a time. "It was just like golfing with a buddy," Jansen recalled. Like many people who worked with Powell, Jansen felt a kinship with him. "I don't think he's a midwesterner," Jansen said. "But he seemed like it."

Jansen took his cues from Powell, who didn't panic when the market sank. Rexnord eliminated about 385 jobs, from its workforce of 5,285 employees, to lower costs and help pay the interest costs of $45 million in 2004. But orders rebounded that year, and with lower overhead, Rexnord's profits jumped. Powell's confidence in the management team had been justified.

But it wasn't enough for Rexnord to simply survive from year to

year, boosting its sales and cutting costs. That didn't deliver the kind
of profits that Carlyle's general partners sought from their investments.
Private equity firms sought double digits, usually after selling a company
within five years or so. These were hard numbers to achieve by inventing
new products or breaking into new markets. The more common tactic
was to take on more debt and buy more companies. This loaded more
debt onto the existing firm, but instantly added new product lines and
customers while providing a quick way to cut costs when the firms were
merged. Thomas Hoenig would have described this as a "misallocation
of resources." When it's easier to borrow money, companies use the debt
for mergers or private equity takeovers. These activities benefit the people with access to capital, but they rarely spark innovation, create new
jobs, or give pay raises to working people.

In early 2005, Rexnord still carried more than $507 million in debt
and paid twice as much money on interest costs than it earned in profit.
But Jay Powell, and the company's board of directors, decided that
there was room for Rexnord to borrow more. A corporate takeover target caught their eye; it was another old-line manufacturing firm based
in Milwaukee, called Falk Corporation. Falk was more than a century
old and made industrial components like gear drives and couplings.
Rexnord's executive team engineered a deal to borrow $312 million in
the form of a leveraged loan, which was loaded onto Rexnord's balance
sheet, pushing the company's annual interest payments from $44 mil-
lion to $62 million. Rexnord's total debt jumped from $507 million to
$754 million. Still, this acquisition made Rexnord more attractive to an
outside buyer. The company had diversified its product line, expanded
its footprint, and still enjoyed a steady flow of cash from operations. It
was time for the Carlyle Group to cash out its position.

First, Rexnord toyed with the idea of going public and offering
shares for sale on Wall Street. But there wasn't strong enough interest and Rexnord didn't follow through. The real opportunity came in
the form of another private equity firm, called Apollo Management LP.

Apollo wasn't afraid of Rexnord's heavy debt burden, because Apollo believed that Rexnord could borrow even more. It devised a plan to purchase Rexnord just as Carlyle had done, by syndicating new leveraged loans and loading them onto Rexnord. Apollo's ambition on this front was remarkable. The company raised $1.825 billion, more than twice what Carlyle had paid just four years earlier.

The payoff to Jay Powell and his team was immense. People at Carlyle would talk about the Rexnord deal years later. It is difficult to determine just how much profit Powell earned from the sale, because Carlyle does not disclose such figures. But Apollo's purchase price was more than $900 million higher than Carlyle's. Under Carlyle's investment rules, 80 percent of the profits would have gone to the limited partner investors who put up money for the buyouts and 20 percent to Carlyle. Of the Carlyle money, 45 percent went to the corporate "mothership," as they called it, and 55 percent would go to Jay Powell's team. Tom Jansen, Rexnord's CFO in Milwaukee, also cashed out with the Apollo deal. He'd been through multiple ownership changes by that point, and figured he would get off the merry-go-round.

The Rexnord buyout in 2006 was the kind of deal that changed a person's life. Jay Powell's father had been wealthy by most people's standards, owning a house in Chevy Chase, sending his kids to private school, and belonging to a country club. But the kind of wealth that Powell obtained during his career—wealth estimated at between $20 million and $55 million by 2018—put him in a different economic realm. He ended up leaving Carlyle after the Rexnord deal. Powell would dabble in private equity, on and off, for a few years. Then he joined a think tank in Washington, D.C., before he was nominated to be a Fed governor.

Rexnord itself didn't fare as well. The company Powell left behind was crippled with debt. Its total debt burden rose from $753 million to $2 billion in one year. Its annual interest-rate payments rose from $44 million in 2005 to $105 million in 2007. The company would pay more money in interest than it earned in profit every year for more than a decade. Rexnord had become a company that was emblematic of the private equity world. It was no longer a company that used debt to pursue its goals. It was now a company whose goal was to service its debt.

Between 2011 and 2020, the debt-heavy world of Rexnord would intersect with the Fed's world of ZIRP. Leveraged loans and corporate bonds were the exclusive tools of a boutique industry when Jay Powell used them to buy Rexnord. The decade of ZIRP would change that. It turned these debt instruments into a retail item, sold through emporiums to the investing masses. One of those emporiums was Credit Suisse bank, which built a thriving division that sold leveraged loans. Rexnord, as heavily indebted as it was, would become a gold mine for the deal makers at Credit Suisse, who underwrote multiple, massive debt deals for Rexnord. These transactions were part of a new American economy, powered by the flood of money that the Fed began to release in 2010.

One person who helped underwrite and arrange Rexnord's revolving series of loans was named Robert Hetu. He was a managing director at Credit Suisse who helped underwrite the loans that allowed Apollo Management to buy Rexnord, so Hetu was no stranger to big borrowing. He had seen a lot during his years on Wall Street. But he had never seen anything like the debt markets after quantitative easing began. There was so much cash flowing into the banking system that no one knew what to do with it. But predictably, Credit Suisse and others did figure something out. It was called the CLO assembly line, and it helped create the largest amount of corporate debt in U.S. history.

CHAPTER 9

THE RISK MACHINE

(2010–2015)

Some of the most profitable products created by Rexnord were not created on the company's factory floors. They were created hundreds of miles away, in a stately skyscraper with vaulted archways over its entryways, located at the corner of Madison Avenue and Twenty-Fifth Street in the heart of Manhattan, New York City. This is where Robert Hetu arrived very early in the morning on most workdays, so he could get a jump on his day as a managing director at Credit Suisse. He worked in the division that created and sold leverage loans, many of them originating from Rexnord's headquarters in Milwaukee. Rexnord might have been an obscure company that occupied old factories in shabby neighborhoods, but it provided a fountain of prosperous work for the debt engineers on Wall Street.

Hetu's office overlooked Madison Square Park, but everyone was working too hard by the middle of the morning to enjoy the view. The private offices for managing directors like Hetu were arranged around a central pen of cubicles, staffed by an overworked team of junior analysts and associates. Hetu had been one of these associates, years earlier, and had grown accustomed to the grinding pressure of the job. It was a seven-days-a-week endeavor, and not in the metaphorical sense that the job was always hanging over you. The junior employees were at work literally every day, sometimes for years on end, making frantic phone calls on Sunday afternoons to finalize the details on a bond issue or leveraged loan. Even after Hetu was promoted to managing director, he arrived at the office around seven in the morning and left at seven in the evening, giving him a couple of hours to see his kids before they went to bed, which was when he started working the phones again.

Hetu took a vacation once, to a luxury resort in Shangri-La, China, where he joined his family in a tour van to see the countryside and ended up on his cell phone in meetings with a lawyer; he remembered the van stopping to let a bunch of pigs cross the road while he negotiated over the phone. "That's the lifestyle. You get rewarded for it, but there's a price to it," Hetu recalled.

The incentive to live this life was obvious. A single managing director at Credit Suisse could generate tens of millions of dollars' worth of fees in a year for the bank and take home a cut of the money. There was never a shortage of fees to earn, because the world of corporate debt was an ever-turning wheel of new loans that replaced old loans as the debt was rolled over again and again. When Apollo bought Rexnord, for example, it borrowed the money through leveraged loans that it rolled over repeatedly. Each refinancing generated fees for Credit Suisse. The benefit to Rexnord was keeping its debt afloat at relatively low interest rates. This was why people like Hetu were on the phone all the time, usually with lawyers. Hetu helped Rexnord refinance $1 billion in debt in March 2012, and the contract for the deal was 344 pages long. Virtually all of the paragraphs in those 344 pages were produced under heavy scrutiny, negotiation, and anxiety. A successful debt contract contained a multitude of components that had to fit together snugly, immune from legal challenge, in such a way that it would entice outside investors to buy the debt. Selling the debt was crucial for the business model to work. Credit Suisse arranged the leveraged loans, but never meant to keep a lot of them. "They're not in the storage business, they're in the moving business," Hetu said.

The moving business was usually brisk. Hetu and his team arranged debt deals, then syndicated the loans and sold them to institutional investors like pension funds. This was still something of a niche business in 2006 when Apollo bought Rexnord. The big investors, like pension funds or insurance companies, shied away from buying leveraged loans because they were considered somewhat opaque and risky. This changed in 2010, when the Federal Reserve began its second round of quantitative easing and kept interest rates pinned at zero. When the Fed pumped trillions of dollars into the banking system, and harshly disciplined anybody who tried to save it, the cash was forced toward the offices of Credit Suisse. Hetu saw the change clearly. There was so much cash, and so few places for that cash to go. "With more capital that's available, then you've got to find product," Hetu said.

The product, in this case, was a company like Rexnord that was willing to take on more debt. In America the supply of such companies seemed almost limitless. If entrepreneurial optimism was America's greatest resource, then the leveraged loan market was harvesting it, providing debt to anyone who could dream up a way to spend it. There was, however, a natural limit to this system, and it was in the banking system's tolerance for risk. Credit Suisse was in the moving business. It didn't want to keep leveraged loans on its books as much as it wanted to reap the fees from selling the loans. Credit Suisse needed a supply of outside buyers if it wanted to expand its business.

When the tidal wave of QE cash arrived on Wall Street, it created a new opening for banks like Credit Suisse, an opening that would expand their leveraged loan business to an unprecedented scale. This would be made possible by something called the collateralized loan obligation, or CLO for short.

———————

This name, CLO, might sound familiar to big fans of the 2008 financial crisis. In 2008, the market imploded thanks to an exotic debt product called the collateralized debt obligation, or CDO. The CDO was a package of home loans (or derivatives contracts based on home loans) stacked together and sold to investors. The CDO made the housing crash possible by creating a seamless assembly line that allowed mortgage brokers to create risky subprime home loans that were quickly packaged and sold to investors, which in turn allowed the mortgage brokers to extend yet more new loans. At that time, the lowly CLO was the undernoticed stepchild of the debt markets. There were only about $300 billion worth of CLOs during the Global Financial Crisis of 2008, while in 2006 alone about $1.1 trillion of new CDOs were issued. But the important thing about CLOs was that they didn't suffer nearly the losses that CDOs suffered. When Wall Street emerged from the rubble of the crash, around 2010, CLOs gained a reputation as relatively safe investments.

Credit Suisse was a leading producer of CLOs. It issued eleven between 2010 and the first half of 2014, worth a total of $6.7 billion, making it the third-largest CLO dealer in the country. Robert Hetu found himself at the epicenter of this new debt assembly machine. He and his team had deep expertise in arranging new leveraged loans, which they could then sell to CLO managers. The barrier to making new leveraged loans had been broken down.

But there was another Credit Suisse executive who was crucial to breaking down that barrier. That's because it wasn't just the size and volume of the CLO machine that made it so important—it was also the way the deals were structured. Leveraged loans were once the domain of private equity firms like Carlyle and Apollo, which were comfortable with the complicated and nonstandardized terms set out in a 344-page debt deal. The CLO made leveraged loans an off-the-shelf chain-store product. And that was thanks to people like John Popp, the head of Credit Suisse's CLO unit.

Popp looks like a trustworthy guy. He wears the pin-striped suit uniform of any good banker, has close-cut gray hair and a cherubic smile that highlights high cheekbones. In May 2012, Popp put out a document that was basically an invitation for people to pour their retirement savings into CLOs. The document was called a "white paper," and it was published by Credit Suisse's Credit Investment Group. The white paper addressed a vexing problem faced by conservative institutional investors: How were they supposed to earn a yield on their pools of cash when the Fed kept interest rates pinned at zero? This was a matter of survival for pension funds and insurance companies. In a 0 percent world these companies were suddenly underfunded. They had been counting on interest rates to pay them a certain amount of money every year, because that's how things had been for decades. Popp was sensitive to this problem. His paper began with a question, posed somewhat plaintively: "What can investors do when real yields on 10-year Treasuries [sic] are negative?" Luckily, Popp had a solution to the dilemma. His paper politely suggested that institutional investors consider investing in a type of debt that was once seen as too arcane, and opaque, like leveraged loans. If investors were willing to take on a little more risk, they could explore the middle-tier varieties of corporate debt, which paid about 4.4 percent in interest, compared to a yield of 1.2 percent interest on the safest kinds of corporate debt. The riskiest corporate loans yielded around 5.6 percent.

The pension funds had been settling on a low return from safe corporate bonds because those bonds were standardized, like a Model T Ford. The bonds were regulated by the SEC and traded on exchanges. People understood them. Leveraged loans, however, were very complicated contracts with terms that could vary widely, and weren't overseen by a regulator in the same manner as stocks and bonds. The CLO solved this problem. It would standardize leverage loans in ways that made the pension funds feel safe.

The key innovation of CLOs was how they standardized the

leveraged loans inside them. A CLO divided its loans into three big chunks, divided by risk. The riskiness of the three groups was determined by where the owners stood in line when it came time to collect the interest payments made by all the borrowers. The first group was the safest and rated with a AAA label. People who owned these AAA loans were the ones to be paid first by the borrowers, and the owners would be the first in line to get their money back if the underlying loans went bust. These AAA investors could sleep easy, but their chunks of the CLO paid the small interest rates, because they were so safe. Investors who had a higher appetite for risk could buy the next chunk of the CLO, which was the second-riskiest group, called the mezzanine group. People who owned these loans got paid second, and they stood in line behind the AAA people to collect their money if the loans went bad, meaning that they might not get all their money back. Because of this risk, they got paid a higher interest rate. Finally, there was the third and riskiest chunk of the CLO, called the equity chunk. Equity owners got paid last, and if the loans failed they might be wiped out entirely.

This meant that a pension fund could order CLO chunks like someone ordering a meal at McDonald's, picking between the AAA, mezzanine, and equity slices of the package. This opened a new pipeline for Robert Hetu and his team of leveraged loan makers. The proliferation of CLOs, at Credit Suisse and elsewhere, created the steady buyer they had been looking for. Rexnord's debt was chopped up and distributed into a wide variety of funds that were offered by Popp's division. The buyers came storming into Credit Suisse's CLO shop, desperately searching for yield. The Rexnord debt—which was still rated as junk debt, meaning the big credit-rating agencies believed the debt was so risky that it was below investment grade—was sliced and split like cord wood and then stacked into a wide variety of funds that were sold to investors. Rexnord debt ended up in Credit Suisse's offerings with names like the Credit Suisse High Yield Bond Fund, the Credit Suisse Asset Management Income Fund, and the Credit Suisse Floating Rate High Income Fund.

All of these funds contained debt from numerous corporations that, like Rexnord, had taken out heavy loads of leveraged loans and issued corporate bonds. The majority of CLOs were owned by big institutional investors like insurance companies, mutual funds, and banks. Rexnord's debt, for example, ended up in the portfolio of state employee pension funds that paid the retirement incomes of government workers in South Carolina, Pennsylvania, and Kentucky. Rexnord debt was even snapped up by the giant investment firm Franklin Templeton, which managed mutual funds and retirement accounts. The CLOs helped create more leveraged loans than ever, while disbursing them more broadly than ever throughout the financial system.

These loans had one key attribute that made them safe for investors, but more risky for the borrowers, like Rexnord. Leveraged loans very often carried variable rates, meaning that the interest rate on the loan could change before the loan was due. This protected investors if rates went up, because it shifted more of the risk onto the borrower. If rates rose, the borrower's interest payments increased significantly. None of this seemed like a problem during the years of ZIRP because rates were kept so low.

Credit Suisse helped Rexnord roll its debt multiple times, keeping the company one step ahead of the day when it needed to repay the full amount. The rates remained low for Rexnord, and Credit Suisse earned fees on each refinancing. This was the case all across Wall Street. Global investment banking fees rose steadily as QE money was pouring into the financial system, hitting a monthly peak of $11.1 billion in June 2014, surpassing the previous record of $10.7 billion, set in the summer of 2007, right before the crash.

It was around this time, in 2014, that a junk bond analyst named Vicki Bryan noticed a pivotal change in the market for corporate debt. The old rules of junk debt and leveraged loans didn't seem to apply anymore. "The market became disjointed, completely, from economic reality," Bryan recalled. Her job, as a junk bond analyst, was to hunt for fraud or incompetence at the companies that borrowed junk debt and then warn her clients about it. Her entire business model relied on the fact that when analysts released important information, it affected the market. When Bryan exposed wrongdoing at a company, her clients who owned that company's risky debt could sell it, or at least demand a higher interest rate for the risk of owning it.

That's how Bryan worked until the dawn of ZIRP, which fundamentally altered the dynamics of corporate debt markets. Around 2014 or 2015, Bryan noticed that she could bring new revelations to the market, but it didn't seem to matter anymore. "It's been a result of what the Fed started to do in 2010, and continued to do later," she said. "You've got an artificial bottom, and the higher part of that bottom is set by the Fed. So you can't lose in this market. And if you can't lose, it's not really a market," Bryan said.

All that money, believing that it could not lose, began to pour into the new market for leveraged loans and CLOs. At the end of 2010, there had been a little less than $300 billion worth of CLOs in the United States. By the end of 2014 there were $400 billion. By 2018 there would be $617 billion.

This created a lot of work for people like Robert Hetu, at Credit Suisse. There was just too much cash chasing every leveraged loan that the banks could sell. Hetu could see what this was doing. More loans were getting sold, and investors were willing to accept more risk with each passing year.

Hetu described this situation as being caught in a vise. On the one side, there was pressure from investors, like pension funds, clamoring for loans. On the other side there were the private equity companies, like the Carlyle Group, which were the best source for these new loans. The private equity firms had leverage, and they began to use it to their benefit.

A typical leveraged loan was born when a private equity firm like the Carlyle Group landed a deal to buy a company like Rexnord. The private equity companies were the original fountain of eternal debt, and were known as "sponsors" of the loans on Wall Street. After Carlyle sponsored a deal, it approached a bank like Credit Suisse and offered the bank a chance to fund the deal by arranging a group of investors to contribute the money. Hetu was this middleman at the bank, and he was often dependent on the sponsors for his flow of leveraged loans. Over time, the sponsors became more demanding. They knew banks were desperate to secure more leveraged loans. The sponsors sometimes flexed their muscle in irritating ways, like insisting that they could choose which law firm Credit Suisse hired to oversee a deal. Hetu didn't like that the sponsors were dictating which lawyer he could use, and he suspected that the sponsor-selected lawyers would probably be sympathetic to the sponsor when they looked over the paperwork. But what could he do? The companies like Carlyle had the upper hand.

The sponsors exerted their bargaining power in more important and worrisome ways. They started to offer leveraged loans for sale that had very loose covenants, meaning the contract terms that protected investors. A typical covenant might dictate that a borrower like Rexnord couldn't immediately go out and take on more debt that made it harder to pay back its earlier loans. Or a covenant might say that a borrower needed to get permission from their lender before selling off assets. These kinds of covenants had always been common. But the leveraged loan sponsors started insisting that they be cut. Eventually, the sponsors got so bold that they started sending lists of detailed loan terms, maybe twenty pages long, insisting that they be included in the deal, Hetu recalled. These terms gave the borrowers more flexibility, and stripped out covenants that protected the investors. This became so common that Wall Street came up with a nickname for loans with the covenants stripped out, calling them Cov-lite loans.

It became Hetu's job to take the Cov-lite loans out to the market and see if anyone would buy them. He would sometimes insist to the sponsor that if he couldn't find a buyer, he would add covenants back in to protect investors. But he didn't need to. There was always a buyer. A $1 billion loan would have $2 billion worth of takers. This happened repeatedly. The demand for Cov-lite loans was intense, which only encouraged the deal sponsors to insist upon them more. There was just too much money looking for yield for investors to demand high standards.

"It's tough. You see what people agree to and you're like: 'Oh my god. Do you realize what you're agreeing to?'" Hetu said. "These deals get more and more aggressive by the day because the market, again, is supplied with a lot of cash. The CLOs have to put money to work. There's a limited number of deals that are coming to market. They all love it. They buy it."

Hetu was aware of the risks inherent in the leveraged loan business, he also knew that there were benefits. The loans went to companies across the country and gave them credit that they could use to expand, hire workers, or invent new products. And bundling the loans into CLOs could help mitigate the risks for investors by diversifying their exposure and limiting their losses if a handful of loans went bad. The institutional investors who bought the CLOs were sophisticated, and they knew what they were doing when they bought into the Cov-lite market.

The Cov-lite loan, once an exotic debt instrument, became the industry standard. In 2010, they accounted for less than 10 percent of the leveraged loan market. By 2013, they were over 50 percent, and by 2019 they accounted for 85 percent of all leveraged loans. Even though the looser covenants took away protections for investors, demand for such loans still grew stronger and the competition to issue them grew more intense. Carlyle and other private equity firms, like Apollo, Bain Capital, and KKR, even started their own loan divisions to meet demand, creating and managing CLOs of their own rather than rely on banks like Credit Suisse. The appetite for CLOs was large in part because the debt packages had performed so well during the crisis of 2008, retaining their value as other credit products cratered.

Bankers and private equity firms weren't the only companies competing to issue corporate debt. They were joined by a once-obscure type of investment firm called a business development corporation, or BDC, which had been created by Congress in the 1980s. The BDCs got a tax break to lend money to small businesses that were so risky they couldn't get a traditional bank loan. The BDCs bunched these loans together and sold them to investors, who could buy pieces of a BDC on the public stock exchange. BDCs had operated in a quiet corner of finance for decades, issuing loans to midsize bakeries, medical device makers, or food companies. Most of the loans carried superhigh interest rates. After 2010, the amount of money under management by BDCs exploded. There were about forty BDCs managing $27 billion of risky debt in 2010. By 2014, there were seventy-seven of them, managing $82 billion. By 2018, some ninety-five BDCs were managing $101 billion in assets.

The rush to extend, package, and sell corporate debt was unstoppable. Corporate borrowing rose to record levels in the United States. At the end of 2010, the total debt of nonfinancial companies was $6 trillion. That became $7 trillion by the end of 2013, almost $9 trillion by the end of 2017, and $10 trillion by 2019.

The rise in corporate debt embedded a deep set of risks within the American financial system. The risk was double-sided, with borrowers on one side and lenders on the other. The lenders, or investors, held more risk because of all those covenants that were discarded over the years. If borrowers defaulted, the investors were less protected than ever before. As for the borrowers, they faced a different kind of risk. When all those companies took on loans or issued bonds, they committed themselves to surviving on the roll. They depended on the ability to roll over the debt at a decent price, before it expired and they had to pay off the full amount. This worked fine, as long as the Fed helped to suppress interest rates and keep the financial system afloat on new money. But if the money was withdrawn, or interest rates crept higher, the cascading effects would be shattering. Companies would have to pay off the debt or accept much higher interest costs. Defaults would spell more losses for investors.

Hetu watched this all unfold, and he noticed the same thing that Vicki Bryan noticed. No one in the world of CLOs or leveraged loans seemed to think they could lose. A twenty-seven-year-old CLO loan manager in 2018 would have been only seventeen years old during the financial crisis. "There are portfolio managers in CLOs today that were kids in 2009. [They] don't have the experience of dealing with a very tough cycle," Hetu said. Investors were buying loans that they knew were crummy, but they operated on the belief that they could sell them when they needed to. "Well, the problem is when things don't go well . . . the markets freeze and you can't sell."

It would be easy, years later, to point fingers at the Wall Street deal makers who built and financed these towers of risky corporate debt. But the financiers were only doing what the Federal Reserve gave them the incentive to do. None of this should have been surprising to senior leaders at the Fed. In 2013, while the FOMC was overseeing its largest round of quantitative easing yet, the Dallas Fed president Richard Fisher explicitly pointed out that the policy would primarily benefit private equity firms, like Jay Powell's former employer the Carlyle Group. Fisher challenged the theory that this would create the "wealth effect" Bernanke hoped for, as higher asset prices translated into more pay and more jobs for working people.

"It has, I believe, had a wealth effect, but principally for the rich and the quick—the Buffetts, the KKRs, the Carlyles, the Goldman Sachses, the Powells, maybe the Fishers—those who can borrow money for nothing and drive bonds and stocks and property higher in price, and profit goes to their pocket," Fisher said during the meeting. He argued that this was not going to create jobs, or boost wages, to nearly the degree the Fed hoped it would.

That, of course, would depend largely on how the companies spent all that borrowed money. Rexnord, for example, borrowed billions of dollars through multiple rounds of debt financings underwritten by Credit Suisse. What happened at Rexnord would illustrate exactly how much the cheap debt would shape the fate of most workers.

CHAPTER 10

THE ZIRP REGIME

(2014–2018)

When Jay Powell sat on Rexnord's board of directors, and helped manage the company on behalf of the Carlyle Group, the executive team held their important meetings at hotels and country clubs, rather than at the company's headquarters building near the factory in west central Milwaukee. By 2014, the separation between Rexnord's leadership team and the rest of its workforce was made concrete, and permanent. The executive team moved into a newly refurbished office building in downtown Milwaukee, near a riverside pedestrian park. It was in one of those up-and-coming areas where once-empty storefronts were being repopulated with wine bars, microbreweries, and Mexican takeout joints. During lunch break, the Rexnord executives could stroll along the winding pedestrian path across the street, overlooking the Menomonee River, which snakes through downtown. The new offices were a self-contained environment, elevated above the middle layers of management and the thousands of employees who worked at Rexnord's global network of factories.

These factories were seen as assets, and the executive team's job was to earn as much profit as possible from those assets. The effort was led by Rexnord's relatively new CEO, Todd A. Adams. He had joined Rexnord as a finance guy back in 2004, when he was still in his early thirties. During his first years at the company, Adams worked under Jay Powell, giving Adams the chance to observe firsthand how the Carlyle Group earned hundreds of millions of dollars by owning the company for less than five years. Adams quickly advanced to higher and higher positions within Rexnord until he became CEO in 2009. It is no coincidence that Rexnord's new chief executive had a background in finance, rather than in engineering or manufacturing. After Carlyle sold the company to Apollo, Rexnord was swamped with debt, and managing that debt became one of the company's top priorities. In 2010, the first full year Adams was CEO, Rexnord's debt burden was $2.1 billion and it paid $184 million in interest payments alone. The company lost $5.6 million that year, during the depths of the Great Recession, having lost $394 million the year before. Rexnord wouldn't turn a profit until 2012, and it paid millions of dollars in interest costs each year. But Adams wasn't deterred. Apollo still owned Rexnord, and in the world of private equity, there was more to running a business than turning a profit or being debt-free. Rexnord had become Apollo's strategic vehicle to generate periodic windfalls through financial engineering. Right after Apollo bought the company, for example, it loaded Rexnord down with $660 million in new debt, which was used to buy an industrial plumbing firm called Zurn Industries. This expanded Rexnord's reach into new markets, and created a new pathway for even more debt-fueled acquisitions. One of Adams's main jobs was to help shape Rexnord into a commodity that could be sold outright or at least monetized along the way.

When Todd Adams talked publicly about managing Rexnord, he talked about the company's unique management philosophy, which they called the Rexnord Business System, or RBS. They even drew up a logo for the thing. During one promotional video about Rexnord,

Adams stood before the camera and talked up the virtues of RBS. "Any business can win once. Winning every day, and in every market, requires a repeatable process," Adams said. With his bald head and square shoulders, Adams looked a bit older than his age. He wore a dark suit with a white shirt and no tie, affecting the benign look of middle management everywhere. He said that the source of Rexnord's strength was the wisdom and process encoded in RBS. And it was true that Rexnord's managers and employees were trained in the mantras and techniques of this management theory, but RBS didn't really explain what drove Rexnord. What happened on the factory floor was, in a very real sense, almost incidental to the company's overarching strategy.

Financial engineering was key to Rexnord's strategy. Rexnord, like any corporation, responded to the environment in which it operated. And that economic environment, starting in 2012, was dominated by the influence of ZIRP. The abundance of cheap debt, the corresponding rise in asset prices, and the desperate search for yield pushed companies toward a certain set of broad strategies. The management team's biggest maneuvers had to do with leveraged loans and rising stock prices, rather than conveyor belts or ball bearings. The idea of spending money to research new products faded away in the glow of new debt offerings. Rexnord was an early pioneer on this terrain, having been owned by private equity firms since the 1980s, with their debt-driven profit models. But the company soon became a typical example of what was happening across corporate America as all the cheap money came flooding into the system through quantitative easing and ZIRP. This strategy would prove to be wildly profitable for company owners and executives. Todd Adams, for example, earned a respectable $2.5 million in 2010, his first full year after becoming CEO. But this was just the beginning. In 2012, a good year for him, Adams earned $8.7 million, thanks to a generous allotment of stock options the year the company went public. Not every year was so great. But Adams was consistently paid more than $1 million a year and he earned $12 million in one particularly good year.

But the gamble of ZIRP was not that it would make people like Todd Adams rich. The gamble was that it would help people like Rexnord's employee John Feltner. He believed, at one point, that a job at Rexnord might provide him a narrow pathway to a stable middle-class life. All the financial engineering encouraged by ZIRP was supposed to make that belief come true.

When John Feltner got the chance to interview for a factory job at Rexnord, he jumped in his car and drove for more than fifteen hours, overnight, to make sure he arrived at the interview on time. His big chance came in 2013, when Rexnord's factory in Indianapolis was hiring a machine operator. Feltner was born and raised there, but was living in Dallas when he got the call. He had moved to Dallas after being laid off from a previous factory job. A position at Rexnord, with the high pay it offered, was worth extraordinary efforts.

This was the thing about John Feltner. He was always game. He was willing to do what was needed to help feed his family. Feltner was a well-educated guy, and he was educated in the complex mechanics of modern industrial production. He had an associate's degree from ITT Technical Institute and had worked various jobs as an engineer, at one point designing the complex piping systems used inside refineries. Then he moved into factory work. Feltner knew how to work hard, and the fact that he and his wife had three children tended to focus his mind on the task at hand. Unfortunately, Feltner's adult life happened to coincide with the epochal collapse of America's manufacturing sector. This meant that his career was punctuated by wildly destabilizing layoffs and dislocations. When Feltner was growing up in Indianapolis, during the 1970s, the eastern part of town was a busy hive of factories and distribution centers. The appetite for labor seemed bottomless. There was an old joke in town that a person could get fired in the morning and have a new job after lunch. But one factory after another was closing. If someone was fired in the morning, they might very well be kicked out of the middle class for good. Feltner had earned about $60,000 a year as an engineer designing pipe systems when he was young. When he got a factory job at the auto parts maker Navistar, he earned between $80,000 and $90,000 a year. He got laid off from that job in 2007, which was what prompted him to move to Dallas to work for an insurance company. He didn't make as much money in Dallas, but Feltner was always willing to obey the new rules of American economic life. When he was knocked over, he got back up. When one job disappeared, he trained himself to get a new one. "Reinventing yourself—you use a little bit of everything from the past," Feltner said. "I always call it, like, modeling Play-Doh. You change, and now you're something else."

That's why Feltner was willing to drive fifteen hours overnight to get an interview at Rexnord. It was one of the last opportunities he might get at a stable working life. The Rexnord plant was located on the far western part of town, just north of the airport. The building was enormous, the size of a city block, and surrounded a crowded parking lot full of cars. Feltner arrived on time for the 7:00 a.m. interview. When he sat down, the guy from Rexnord made small talk and asked Feltner how long the commute had taken him that morning. "I thought he was serious, and I said, 'Fifteen hours,'" Feltner recalled. "And he said, 'Excuse me?' I said, 'Bud, I don't know if you realize this, but I live in Dallas, Texas.'"

During the interview, Feltner said that he'd be willing to pack up everything and report for work the following Monday. But he didn't get the job. The managers were worried he didn't have enough experience. He got called in again, however, for another interview. He went through the whole process a second time only to be told again that he lacked experience. This time, Feltner pushed back. He is a big guy, with a burly frame and a big tattoo covering his left shoulder. He has an intimidating goatee and wears very large and somewhat scary-looking rings on his fingers. But when Feltner talks, he isn't brusque or tough. He is persuasive and surprisingly even-tempered. Feltner told the Rexnord interviewer that his character mattered more than experience. "I said, 'I come to work every single day. If you want a guy who's going to come in and work, and I can learn anything . . . well, then I'm your man. Hire me.'"

Feltner was hired. He was put in charge of an enormous fabricating machine called a Johnford mill, which he came to believe might be the oldest and worst-maintained machine in the entire factory. He came to know it intimately, and seven years later could remember its designated number, like the phone number of an old friend; it was machine number 5898. The Rexnord factory made highly specialized and heavily engineered ball bearings that were used in airplanes, cement factories, and manufacturing plants. A single Rexnord ball bearing might cost about $1,800. This value was created in a relatively tough environment. Feltner's workstation was cold in the winter and hot in the summer. During the hot months, he'd wear a T-shirt, shorts, and steel-toed boots. But there were perks. Feltner joined the local United Steel Workers unit at Rexnord and eventually ran for election to be a union official. He won, and he gained a measure of power in helping shape his working conditions.

Feltner and his wife, Nina, moved the family back to the Indianapolis area. They settled in a suburban development east of the city, in the little town of Greenfield, where they rented a tidy home in a newly built cluster of houses beside a giant cornfield. Feltner and Nina had stuck together through the long season of instability and hardship. Now they were back in their hometown, with health insurance and a reliable income from a unionized job. Feltner had fought hard for this privilege.

The house that John and Nina were renting was near the corner of Mozart and Silver Spoon Drives. Almost as soon as he started work, the Feltners started saving money to buy it.

From the view of Rexnord's headquarters office in Milwaukee, the ball-bearing factory in Indianapolis was seen as a single asset within a network of assets owned by the company, all of them arrayed on a complex and ever-shifting game board. CEO Tom Adams and his team had to figure out how these game pieces might be moved in ways that generated the most profit for the company's owners. Apollo Management still owned about 24 percent of the company, while another 23 percent of stock was split between T. Rowe Price Associates and JPMorgan Chase. Other chunks of the company's shares had been broken apart in an initial public offering and sold on Wall Street. The sale of that stock raised $426.3 million in cash, but very little of that money went to the company itself. Apollo took $15 million off the top as a management fee and $300 million was used to pay down debt. In 2013, the company announced another public offering, this time aimed at raising $1.36 billion. Unfortunately, as the *Milwaukee Journal Sentinel* reported, "The offering would not raise proceeds for Rexnord."

The dilemma faced by Adams and his team was not so different from that of any corporate leader. They had to maximize profits, increase the return to owners, and demonstrate that the company had a pathway to major growth in the coming years. There were many different ways of doing this. Rexnord could try to invent new products, try to branch out into new industries, or reinvest in its factories to improve the quality of the products it already made. But when searching for big profits, Rexnord's leaders could focus on two things in particular: the booming market for the company's debt, and the booming market for the company's publicly traded stock. This was where the real money was churning.

The debt markets seemed like the most pressing concern. Every decision that Adams and his team made had to be considered within the context of Rexnord's debt load. In 2014, the company still owed $2 billion in debt. It paid $109 million in interest payments that year, while earning only $30 million in profit. Rexnord's leaders spent a lot of their time working with Hetu and Credit Suisse to roll and refinance the debt on a constant basis. Rexnord's debt was still rated as junk, and it paid more money on interest costs than it earned in profit every year until 2020. Paying down the debt would take years, and the process would require bitter compromises and painful costs. This wasn't the stuff of an exciting corporate strategy.

There were more energizing opportunities presented by the rising stock market. One of the strange realities of the ZIRP era was that even though overall economic growth was anemic, the growth in asset prices was spectacular. This created the opportunity for executives like Adams to exploit a once-obscure financial tactic that allowed them to cash in on the inflation of company stock. This tactic was something called a stock repurchase, or stock buyback. This was a strategy that Rexnord began to pursue, along with the rest of corporate America.

Stock buybacks were made legal in 1982, and they are exactly what they sound like. A company uses cash to buy shares of its own stock. The basic appeal of a buyback was obvious for the people who already owned the company's stock. When shares are purchased, they get taken off the market, which decreases the total amount of shares in existence. This can boost the price of remaining shares because there are less of them to buy. Stock buybacks also help juice an important metric by which many CEOs get paid, called "earnings per share," which measures how much profit a company earns per share of stock. Take away more shares, and the earnings per share go higher. In this way, stock buybacks are a great way to meet the earnings-per-share target without doing things like winning new customers, innovating new products, or improving operations. Also, maybe most obviously, the share buybacks give money to people who already own the stock, which can include the company's executive team.

In spite of all these benefits to executives and shareholders, stock buybacks remained relatively rare through much of the 1990s. There were compelling reasons to avoid them. Buybacks almost always increase a company's indebtedness, which weakens it.* This tendency was only amplified when companies borrowed cash to make a buyback. But the strategy became almost unavoidable when debt was so cheap and stocks were rising so fast.

The most boring-seeming companies in America became financial engineers, borrowing cash, buying their own stock, pumping up their share price, and often justifying higher pay packages for their executives. The actual business these companies engaged in became less and less important to their management teams. What mattered more was access to debt markets and rising share prices. McDonald's, for example, borrowed $21 billion in bonds and notes, according to an extensive investigation in *Forbes* magazine, between 2014 and 2019. The company used the cash to help finance $35 billion in stock buybacks. It also paid out $19 billion in dividend payments, directly to its owners, giving the owners more than $50 billion during a period when the company earned only $31 billion in profit. Yum! Brands, the fast-food conglomerate that operates chains like Taco Bell and KFC, borrowed $5.2 billion to help pay for $7.2 billion in stock buybacks and dividend payments.

The buybacks made these companies more vulnerable to an economic downturn by increasing their debt loads and reducing their equity. Between 2014 and 2020, for example, Yum! Brands boosted its net debt from $2.8 billion to $10 billion. This meant that its debt went from 42 percent of its total sales to 178 percent.

Rexnord was considering a stock buyback in 2015, but the company was so deeply in debt that it would have effectively been buying its own shares with borrowed money. During most eras of American economic life, this would not have made sense. The company owed $1.9 billion

---

*This almost always happens because a company's debt level, or its leverage, is determined by the level of its debt compared to its equity and its assets. A stock buyback uses an asset (cash) to reduce a company's equity (by removing stock from the market) and therefore increases its leverage ratio.

and it paid $88 million on interest costs in 2015, which was more than the $84 million it earned in profit.

Nonetheless, in 2015 Rexnord's board of directors authorized Adams and his team to buy back $200 million in stock. In 2016, the company bought back $40 million of its own stock. In 2020, the company expanded its buyback authorization, and bought back another $81 million in stock. As was the case with many companies, Rexnord's CEO enjoyed a financial windfall during this period. In 2016, he was paid $1.5 million but the following year he was paid $12 million, mostly in stock awards, and in 2018 he would earn $6 million.

The Federal Reserve was encouraging this kind of activity, and it knew that it was encouraging it. But Rexnord's stock buybacks were seen, by the Fed, as a means to an end. It was okay if CEOs used debt to help engineer multimillion-dollar paydays, as long as the prosperity was eventually dispersed through the "wealth effect" to neighborhoods like the Feltners', near Silver Spoon Drive.

Feltner was a longtime union guy, and he believed that work life was dictated by rules and contracts. The labor union and management sat down and negotiated the rules, agreed to them in writing, and then both parties had to abide by them. He was a stickler for this stuff. But Feltner believed that the rules were increasingly tilted against employees.

One big change had come years earlier, in 2012, when the local union negotiated a new contract. Managers said at the time that the factory might get closed down, so if employees wanted to keep their jobs, they needed to work for less pay, or give up some of their benefits. The union reached a compromise. It agreed to a two-tiered pay scale under which new hires would earn about $5 or $6 less each hour than existing employees. Feltner was offended when he learned about it. He chastised the union for agreeing to it. "They've already split our local in half. They're going to divide and conquer," Feltner said.

When it came time to renegotiate the labor contract, the union pushed to get rid of the two-tiered system. Surprisingly, management agreed. But this was actually troubling to the union. Management had given up too easily. Maybe they did it because they knew the factory was closing.

In May 2016, Rexnord made an announcement that made clear the rules would be changing once again. Unfortunately, the announcement wasn't written in a way that anybody could understand, except for the very small group of people who worked in corporate finance. Rexnord announced new "change of control" policies, regarding the way that pay and benefits would be administered if the company were taken over. In the world of mergers and finance, this was an advertisement that all but declared: "We are for sale."

Todd Adams and his team were doing things that would make Rexnord more attractive to an outside buyer. The company was still deeply indebted, but it had been slowly rotating off some of its loans, beating down its debt from $2.4 billion in 2012 to $1.9 billion in 2016. But Adams had also launched another important initiative, one that had a far bigger impact on the lives of Feltner and his coworkers. This initiative had a rather bloodless name; it was called the Supply Chain Optimization and Footprint Repositioning plan, or SCOFR, as the insiders began to call it. Under the SCOFR plan, Rexnord would evaluate its entire game board of assets, evaluating how each one might be moved, improved, or liquidated in a way to benefit the company's stockholders and burnish its financial statements. The SCOFR plan called for an elimination of about 20 percent of Rexnord's manufacturing footprint. Factories in high-paying parts of the world, like Indianapolis, could be moved to low-paying parts of the world, like Mexico.

In total, the first two phases of the SCOFR would save about $40 million a year in costs for Rexnord. This wasn't transformational. Rexnord paid $91 million in interest payments in 2016 alone. But the savings would be attractive to outsiders. They boosted the company's profit margin, even if they didn't lessen its debt.

When the team implementing the SCOFR plan evaluated Rexnord's ball-bearings plant in Indianapolis, they saw an opportunity.

Looking back, Rexnord employees would say that the first suspicious thing they noticed was that the company installed new security cameras in the Indianapolis factory. The cameras went up over a weekend. It seemed odd. Curious employees were told that it was just a security measure.

Feltner was in the factory when employees were told to gather for an announcement. Again, there was a strange detail about this. Half of the employees were asked to go to a loading dock at the back of the building, and half were asked to go to a spot in front of the building. They didn't know why the company would want to split everyone up.

Feltner joined his half of the coworkers and they stood around while a Rexnord manager got up in front of them to give a short, unsentimental speech. Rexnord had decided to close the ball-bearings factory and move its production to Monterrey, Mexico. The union later learned that employees in Mexico would earn about $3 an hour and that closing the American plant would save Rexnord roughly $15 million a year. The impact of this news was immediate and severe for Feltner and his coworkers. They didn't live in a world where someone could move fluidly from one well-paying job to the next. Getting laid off was more akin to falling over the side of a cliff. They had been on a relatively high plateau, and the odds that they would ever be that high again seemed very small. Feltner had fought hard to join Rexnord, and he had fought hard for a reason. He knew how rare and valuable the job was. With one meeting, the three hundred jobs at Feltner's factory disappeared. "It rocks your world. It really does. People were pissed. You just had your entire life shit on," Feltner said.

The employees did what they could to fight the decision. They gave interviews to the local television news cameras. They even tried to pressure political leaders to do something, but that was a long shot. Labor unions had once been political power brokers in American life, but now they were just a marginal interest group that garnered scattered media attention. But there did seem to be one reason for hope: 2016 was a presidential election year. The Republican candidate, Donald Trump, was campaigning in a strange way for a Republican. Trump was the first major party presidential nominee in decades to argue—passionately, belligerently, profanely, and repeatedly—that it was more important to keep jobs inside the United States than it was to earn maximum profits for shareholders. Trump had latched on to another, larger case of layoffs in Indianapolis: A company called Carrier announced it was closing its Indianapolis plant, eliminating about 1,400 jobs, and moving 700 of them to Mexico. Trump made Carrier the villain of his campaign speeches and promised to punish Carrier or any company that moved jobs overseas by imposing taxes or tariffs on it.

Feltner supported Trump and his running mate, Mike Pence, who was the governor of Indiana. If any political team could do something about the layoffs, it seemed like it was Trump and Pence. Trump's Democratic opponent, Hillary Clinton, did not inspire such hope. She had long advocated for an economic system defined by global trade agreements that smoothed the way for transferring jobs into markets where labor was cheaper. Feltner and his coworkers hoped, desperately, that more media attention might entice Trump to intervene more aggressively on their behalf. In December, as Christmas approached, the Rexnord employees held a church service with their fellow union members from the Carrier plant. They convened at the Mount Olive Ministries church, in an industrial area south of the Rexnord plant, near a large parking lot for the airport. Before the services began, the attendees arranged a big sign composed of holiday lights, near the altar, that read, "SAVE ALL THE JOBS." The local television cameras were invited inside while the employees sang "O Come, All Ye Faithful." Employees stood up and gave short speeches with the gloomy, funereal tone of the prayers given in hospice. They were praying to God, but also praying to Trump or anyone else who might listen. Nothing really came of it. Trump won the election, Christmas came and went, and Rexnord moved ahead efficiently with operation SCOFR. Trump attended a press conference at the Carrier plant, falsely overstating how many jobs would be saved there, and then got into a Twitter dispute with one of the labor union leaders. Trump's interest in the jobs in Indianapolis dissipated quickly.

Rexnord gradually disassembled production at the Indianapolis plant and prepared its new facility in Monterrey. The company offered Feltner and his coworkers extra pay and severance if they stayed on the job until the factory was entirely closed down that summer. They would be asked to help train the workforce in Mexico who would be taking over their work. Employees who helped in the training would get a $4-per-hour increase in pay. Feltner's one act of defiance, his rebellion, was refusing to sign up. "There's absolutely no way I'm going to train this guy to take my job," he said. This was the victory Feltner could claim when the plant finally closed for good in 2017 and he went back on the job market.

Todd Adams never managed to find a buyer for Rexnord or any of its major divisions. But the executive team did manage to keep whittling away at the company's debt, driving it down from $1.9 billion in 2016 to $1.4 billion in 2018. And the profit margins were improving as the company imposed more rounds of SCOFR. Rexnord closed seven facilities in its water-management division alone between 2017 and 2020.

It appeared that Rexnord's board of directors was pleased with Adams's performance. He earned $1.5 million in 2016, when the Indianapolis plant closure was announced. In 2017, when the plant was closed, Adams was paid $12 million, largely in stock benefits. The financial data company Wallmine, which tracked public data of stock sales and awards, estimated Adams's net worth to be at least $40 million by 2020.

Moody's credit rating agency steadily raised Rexnord's debt ratings over the years, as the company cut costs. But in 2020, the debt was still rated as junk.

John Feltner did his "Play-Doh" routine again, whereby he reshaped his working life. After his last day at Rexnord, Feltner kicked around looking for a job that might pay something similar to what he made. He eventually got a decent one doing maintenance at a grocery store, then a job as a temporary maintenance contractor. He and Nina put their plans on hold to buy the house near Silver Spoon Drive. The interruption was stressful, but Feltner wasn't deterred by it. He and Nina still aimed to eventually build up enough savings to buy their house and put their kids through college. Each of Feltner's jobs paid less than the one before it, but both he and Nina were willing to work hard. They would make it. Although it was painful, expensive, and destabilizing to be laid off, Feltner had grown accustomed to it. "I call that the new normal. It's something you get used to."

Jay Powell had earned his personal fortune from Rexnord in the way Powell did most things—discreetly, and efficiently.

It appears that when Rexnord's layoffs made the national news in 2016 and 2017, there wasn't any public mention of the role Jay Powell played in the company's fortunes. His ownership of Rexnord was a decade in the past, but there was a straight line between Powell's stewardship of the company and its later travails. When Powell flipped Rexnord, the company was dropped into a deep well of debt from which it never emerged. This reality shaped everything that happened afterward, including the birth of SCOFR and the closing of the Indianapolis plant. But Rexnord was long in Powell's past.

During 2016, Powell and the Fed governors were focused intently on difficult internal debates. They were trying, with little success, to figure out how the Fed might control and contain the side effects of its monetary experiments. Powell had warned in 2013 that the market for leveraged loans and other debt assets was overheating because of the Fed's interventions. By the end of 2016, corporate debt had increased by

25 percent, to $8.5 trillion. It was proving to be extremely difficult for the Fed to withdraw its interventions before the debt markets became even more overheated.

Powell was at a social function in Washington one night when he bumped into someone who might have been able to offer him some insight into the Fed's dilemma. It was a chance encounter when Powell met the former president of the Kansas City Fed, Tom Hoenig. The two men shared some polite conversation, but didn't talk too much about monetary policy, as Hoenig would later remember it. Their conversation was short.

Hoenig also had other things on his mind at the time. He had returned to Washington, D.C., after retiring from the Fed, to take another job in government service. He had been lured back to become vice chairman of the regulatory agency charged with maintaining stability in the U.S. banking system, the FDIC. It had been years since Hoenig had warned that quantitative easing and ZIRP would cause a massive misallocation of resources, increase financial risk, and primarily benefit the rich, who owned assets. Now, as a bank regulator, Hoenig had a front-row seat to watch it happen. He also had the responsibility to help clean up the damage if those risks ever again spilled into the open.

CHAPTER 11

THE HOENIG RULE

(2012–2016)

After Thomas Hoenig left the Federal Reserve, he was not rewarded with a relaxing retirement. Instead, he was invited to move from Kansas City to Washington, D.C., so he could take one of the most difficult and thankless jobs in that city. He would help run the government agency that tried to keep the financial system stable, even amid rising debt and risky investments. To make matters worse, he arrived in town with a highly detailed plan to break up the big banks.

It started back when Hoenig was still president of the Kansas City Fed. He got a phone call from a U.S. Senate staffer who worked for Mitch McConnell, the Republican majority leader. The staffer asked Hoenig if he knew anyone who might be interested in becoming a commissioner for the Federal Deposit Insurance Corporation, or FDIC. Hoenig said he would think about it. The staffer later called back and asked if maybe Hoenig himself might be interested. "I said, 'Well, there's always a chance I might be interested,'" Hoenig recalled. During one of his regular trips to Washington, Hoenig stopped at the Capitol Building for an official job interview with McConnell's staff. Hoenig said he would take the job, but wouldn't join a political party. After decades of working at the Fed, Hoenig wanted to stay within the ranks of an independent agency to remain outside party politics. This worked for McConnell's staff. Hoenig was nominated and approved by the Senate.

The FDIC seemed like a perfect fit for Hoenig. The agency was created during the Great Depression with a sweeping mandate to regulate banks and protect the banking system. The agency is best known for insuring the bank accounts of everyday people—if a bank fails, the FDIC will cover the losses of anyone who has money at that bank up to $250,000 (the average U.S. family had about $40,000 in total savings in 2016). The agency also examined the banks' books to make sure they had enough money to meet their obligations. The agency played a central role in determining the shape and structure of America's banking system, and therefore its entire social system.

Hoenig took the job in part because there was urgent work to do regarding America's big banks, even years after the financial crisis had ended. One of the strange side effects of the Global Financial Crisis was that it entrenched the power of the big banks that helped create it. The banks that were too big to fail in 2008 were now bigger and even less able to fail. The top banks controlled far more of the nation's assets than they had ever controlled before, and the federal government seemed intent on keeping things that way. This was something Hoenig had been talking about for years. The number of community banks in America was falling by the thousands while the assets held by a small group of very large banks got larger. The industry was becoming more consolidated than any time in modern history. At exactly the same moment, the Fed was encouraging these banks to take on more risk. The risk was also spreading into the "shadow banking" system, where hedge funds and private equity firms were taking on bank-like functions of lending huge amounts of money.

Everybody knew where Tom Hoenig stood on this issue, and he didn't surprise anyone when he arrived in Washington in 2012. Almost immediately, he went on a speaking tour. He accepted gigs to speak at high-end banking and regulation seminars around the capital. Back in 2006, Hoenig had shocked a group of bankers into silence after he spoke at their gathering in Tucson, Arizona. He seemed to be making a cottage industry of doing the same thing in Washington. His speeches for the FDIC followed a broad theme. He argued for the need to re-shape the banking industry with an eye toward simplicity rather than complexity. When speaking to a crowd of bank regulators, Hoenig said they should tear up the very complicated rules they'd been negotiating for years (called the Basel III accord). When he spoke to a group of bank lobbyists and journalists, he told them the banks should be broken up rather than regulated, and monitored under the new Dodd-Frank Act, which was roughly 850 pages long.

This approach was considered radical in the political environment of 2012, but Hoenig wasn't irrational to pursue it. He had been selected for his job by one of the most powerful Republicans in the country, and his selection had been approved by the sitting Democratic president, Barack Obama. During the entire process, Hoenig's views were well known and transparent. He didn't just advocate breaking up the big banks. He had written a detailed blueprint on how to do it when he was still president of the Kansas City Fed. When Hoenig arrived at the FDIC, he believed there was a real chance for reform. Hoenig was the number two official at the FDIC. The chairman, Martin Gruen-berg, was a longtime Democratic staffer who seemed open to the idea of constraining the bigger banks.

But very early on, the warning signs were evident. During Hoenig's confirmation hearing, a Republican senator named Bob Corker men-tioned that Hoenig's nomination was already causing tension. Corker was supportive of Hoenig's appointment, but Corker said he had been getting phone calls from "some of the larger institutions" that were aware of Hoenig's earlier comments about too-big-to-fail banks. "Some of them are concerned," Corker said.

——————

Hoenig was called before a Senate hearing, in May 2012, to outline his plan to break up the big banks. Corker was nonetheless enthusiastic about the plan. He called it the "Hoenig rule."

If there was enthusiasm for the Hoenig rule, even among conservatives, it was fueled by the unsatisfying series of compromises on bank regulation that had been put in place after the crash of 2008. The banks had been allowed to remain as they were, but would be subjected to new rules that would modify their behavior. This was in stark contrast to what the government had done during the Depression, which was the most recent comparable bank crisis. The Roosevelt administration and Congress had passed laws that redrew the shape of banks in a way that constrained their powers and the risks that they could pose. The Obama administration took a different approach. It is true that Congress passed bank reform laws, and even created a new regulatory agency, called the Consumer Financial Protection Bureau, that had a real impact. But rather than restructure the banking system, the government chose to create a hyperdense web of new rules that would be layered over the big banks, allowing them to remain big but subjecting them to scrutiny and micromanagement. It was the regime spelled out in the hundreds of pages of the Dodd-Frank law in the United States and the international banking agreement called the Basel III accord.

Hoenig argued that this was a losing game. He said that bank rules needed to be simple in their aims, easy to understand, and straightforward to enforce. He argued that the banks should be broken up again as they had been under the New Deal. Banks should once again be divided up by their function, with commercial banks handling insured customer deposits, while other banks did riskier things like trade derivatives contracts. This division would help ensure that taxpayers were on the hook only to insure deposits at commercial banks (which would still be covered by FDIC insurance), instead of extending that safety net to megabanks that held deposits and also engaged in riskier speculation.

Once the banks were broken up, Hoenig believed, they needed to live by simple rules that determined how much capital they should keep on hand in case of an emergency.

The key idea behind the Hoenig rule was breaking the riskier parts of banking away from the economically vital parts (like making business loans), so that the riskier banks could fail without taking down the rest of the system if they made bad bets. The financial columnist Allan Sloan, who wrote for *Fortune* and *The Washington Post*, published a widely read column after Hoenig's Senate hearing that said the Hoenig rule is exactly what Wall Street needed. "It's so simple, it's brilliant," Sloan wrote. "It's a smart separation of high-risk from low-risk activities."

With this support, Hoenig kept pushing. In September 2012, he was invited to speak at the exclusive Exchequer Club in Washington, an event attended by bank lobbyists, bank regulators, and the financial press. A certain etiquette was usually recognized at events like this, and Hoenig respected it, to a degree. His speech was laden with technical language and the bloodless prose of a good financial bureaucrat. But what he said was still shocking, and rarely spoken on the high-end financial speaking circuit. He began by saying the financial reforms of 2009 and 2010 hadn't gone nearly far enough. The banking system was still a threat to the American economy, and it needed to be broken up, even if most people thought the era of bank reform was behind them.

But the need to reform banks went beyond the need for financial stability. Hoenig said that the reform was a necessary thing to restore trust in the banking system. "That trust can be reestablished, and accountability can be put back into the system, so that the banking industry can win without the rest of us losing," Hoenig said. Even during this speech, to a banking crowd, Hoenig talked about the Hoenig rule in a way that was bigger than just financial regulation. He believed that the rule would stabilize banks, but he also argued that it would accomplish something beyond that. Restructuring the banking system was a crucial step toward repairing some of the deeper scars that had been left behind from the crash of 2008. It would repair the kind of damage that Hoenig had seen firsthand when he was invited to talk to Tea Party groups in Kansas, or when he met his old war buddy Jon McKeon for lunch. The financial crash had drained the reservoir of Americans' faith in their own governing institutions. If that faith wasn't restored, the results could be wildly destabilizing. "How can we possibly convince Americans that the fiscal steps will be equitable when we bailed out the largest banks and yet they remain—larger, more powerful, and insulated from the market's discipline?" he asked during the talk at the Exchequer Club.

There was bipartisan support for this view. Corker wasn't the only senator who expressed enthusiasm for Hoenig's ideas. Hoenig had lunch twice with Senator Elizabeth Warren of Massachusetts, a Democrat whose entire career was built on tougher regulation for Wall Street. Warren supported Hoenig's ideas vocally, as did the Democratic senator from Ohio, Sherrod Brown.

Hoenig believed his plan was viable. "When I showed up, I thought maybe I could convince people that it was an option," he said. His education to the contrary came quickly.

Hoenig made the rounds on Capitol Hill, visiting senators who could play an important role in pushing any bank reforms. After sitting down with one senator, Hoenig was on his way out of the office when he saw a prominent banking lobbyist walking in to meet the same senator right after him. "I was coming out of one door—and I recognized him—and he was going in the other door," Hoenig said. He wasn't surprised. He knew that bank lobbyists would be making the rounds as well. "That's their right. I don't have an objection. I just kind of laughed at it."

The bank lobbyists were numerous, persistent, and engaged on Capitol Hill. They had their own think tank, called the Bank Policy Institute, that churned out high-quality studies and white papers to promote the bankers' point of view. This made it hard to break through.

"Lookit. A senator only has so much time," Hoenig recalled. "So they have to try and stay up on the issues and so forth. If you have fifteen lobbyists for the industry, and two lobbyists for the public-interest groups, or the agency that is proposing to tighten up on the [regulatory] standard, who's going to present the arguments most?"

Hoenig visited the senators, and the senators smiled politely, and the bank lobbyists came in right behind him. He eventually realized that the Hoenig rule was a dead letter. It was never going to happen. The course had been chosen in 2010 when Congress passed Dodd-Frank, which had been a bitter political fight. "Congress was tired of working on this issue," Hoenig recalled. "I fully understand it. Dodd-Frank was a huge lift to get done . . . But they made a decision to go in that direction, rather than to go the way of breaking up [the banks]."

The very complexity of Dodd-Frank, while vexing for the banks, became helpful to the biggest institutions. The law spawned about four hundred new rules, and each rule became a small regulatory quagmire of battles as it passed through a long process to become finalized by agencies like the FDIC. This gave the banks numerous chances along the way to dispute every detail of the rules. One rule, on the regulation of derivatives, received 15,000 public comments. Some agencies were so overwhelmed that they missed deadlines to put the law into effect. By 2013, only about one third of the law's rules had been implemented. The banking lobby didn't let up. It spent about $1.5 billion on registered lobbyists alone between 2010 and 2013, a figure that didn't include the money that went into public campaigns or think-tank papers.

The Dodd-Frank system tried to manage the risk inside big banks while allowing them to grow bigger. One of the key ways it did this was through something called a "stress test," a procedure championed by Obama's Treasury secretary, Timothy Geithner. The stress tests required banks to pretend that they were facing a crisis, and then to explain, in writing, why they would survive it. To pass a stress test, the banks had to prove that they had enough capital on hand* to cover losses during a hypothetical crisis. But this just opened a lot of debate over what counted as capital and even what counted as a crisis. It became a never-ending negotiation that hinged on speculative arguments about how well the value of an asset—like a CLO—might hold up under hypothetical market conditions. A second, lesser-known procedure was something called a "living will," which was essentially a document that the banks produced to prove that they could indeed fail without bringing the entire financial system down with them. They had to prove that they could die without a bailout. This also turned into a tedious negotiation, and Tom Hoenig was in the middle of it.

In 2013, the big banks submitted their living wills, which ran to thousands of pages, to both the FDIC and the Federal Reserve. Hoenig and others at the FDIC were not impressed. The banks were telling a story in their living wills, and it wasn't convincing. Hoenig argued that the banks needed to redo the documents with more detail, explaining precisely how they'd be able to close down without government bailouts. The regulators gave the banks more time to do this, and the process dragged out for years. The banks submitted new living wills, and those wills were again rejected in August 2014. In July 2015, the banks resubmitted their plans. In April 2016, the living wills were rejected once again. The process continued on.

One group of people who seemed to have zero faith in the living wills were the Wall Street traders. In these circles, there seemed to be no pretense at all that living wills were anything more than political theater. The Democratic chairman of the FDIC, Martin Gruenberg, launched a public campaign in 2012 to convince people that the FDIC would actually let the banks fail. Nobody seemed to believe him. When asked about

---

*To be specific, the banks had to have enough "ownership capital funding," as the regulators called it, meaning capital that was provided by owners or shareholders, which is permanent to the bank and can be used to absorb losses. Loans don't count as this kind of capital because loans have to be paid back.

this prospect, Cornelius Hurley, director of the Center for Finance, Law, and Policy at Boston University, told *American Banker* magazine that "markets are convinced that in the next crisis the [too-big-to-fail banks] will be bailed out just as they were in the last one."

There was a reason that the banks fought so hard for the living wills to be accepted. If the wills were rejected, the FDIC could require the banks to do something that they had resisted doing for years—put more capital aside to cover losses in a time of crisis.

This was the issue that Hoenig began to focus on when he realized the banks were not going to be broken up. If the big banks were getting bigger, regulators could at least insist that they put aside enough money to withstand big losses in a downturn. This problem had supposedly been dealt with by the passage of the Basel III accord, the international agreement on bank regulations named after the city in Switzerland. Like Dodd-Frank, Basel III tried to use complexity as a way to make banks safer without breaking them up or restructuring them. Basel did this by creating an accounting system under which the banks could report how much hard capital they had on hand, compared to the amount of assets on their books. The banks had to show that they had enough reserve capital to cushion the blow when asset values crashed during a downturn. This seemed simple enough. But Basel let the banks use a "risk-weighted" formula to determine the value of their assets for regulatory purposes. Under that formula, a bank might be able to say that it didn't need to hold any capital against the debt of nations like Greece, because government debt was considered so safe. It was such decisions that made Basel unworkable, in Hoenig's view, and that made the banking system appear safter than it was.

"Risk-based capital measures are highly complex. *Highly* complex. There's no one that understands them. Even the companies themselves— at least the CEOs of those companies—often do not understand what goes into it," Hoenig said. "They give you a sense of safety that isn't real."

Hoenig tried to cut through Basel's complexity in a very public way. He created something called the Global Capital Index, which the FDIC started publishing regularly. The index was really just a glorified spreadsheet, but it told a shocking story. One row of numbers showed how much capital the banks had on hand under the Basel III standards. Usually, these numbers were reassuring. JPMorgan Chase, for example, reported in 2013 that its capital ratio under Basel III was an impressively fat 11.94 percent. But Hoenig's spreadsheet went on to show how much capital the banks had on hand under a more traditionally used measure, called a leverage ratio, which didn't use Basel's risk-weighting. Under that standard, JPMorgan had only a 6.22 percent cushion. When you applied international accounting standards, things were even worse, with a mere 4.22 percent cushion.

Hoenig used the Global Capital Index as a type of perpetual irritant, reminding everyone that the banks probably didn't have enough money on hand to face another major downturn. When Hoenig argued for tougher capital requirements, he was joined by influential allies like Sheila Bair, the former Republican chairwoman of the FDIC. Somewhat surprisingly, Hoenig and Bair ended up on the winning side of the argument. The United States created its own capital requirements that were more strict than those laid out by the Basel III accord.

Still, by 2016, Hoenig believed the U.S. banking system was fragile and susceptible to crashes that would necessitate more bailouts. Hoenig believed that the banks needed a cushion of about 10 percent of their total assets. He used a metric for bank reserves called "tangible capital," meaning hard capital that the bank could use to pay for losses. In 2007, before the banking crisis, banks had tangible capital worth about 3 percent of their total assets. By 2016, the tougher U.S. standards pushed that ratio up to about 5.5 percent, a meaningful increase that made U.S. banks safer than European banks, which enjoy a looser standard under Basel. The reason Hoenig was still worried was that losses had surpassed 5 percent at many banks in the 2008 crash. And banks didn't need to lose all of their capital to need a bailout. If a bank lost just 3 percent, investors might question how much more the bank could lose before it failed. At that point, they might pull their money out, which could lead to a panic. Hoenig spent much of his time in debates over this issue, sending letters to senators and arguing that having more capital on hand didn't cripple a bank, as many argued, but made it stronger.

These kinds of fights defined Tom Hoenig's career as vice chairman of the FDIC. He argued that the banks needed to be limited in their reach, required to hold more capital, and less assured of a taxpayer-backed safety net. Hoenig was praised in various corners, from Senator Elizabeth Warren on the left to the *Wall Street Journal* editorial page on the right, but his views never gained much traction in Washington.

As hard as Hoenig fought, he was still fighting a rearguard effort. As the FDIC worked to constrain the banks, the Federal Reserve was pushing in the opposite direction.

Between 2007 and 2017, the Fed's balance sheet nearly quintupled, meaning it printed about five times as many dollars during that period as it printed in the first hundred years of its existence. All those dollars were forced into a zero-interest-rate world, where anybody was punished for saving money. It was impossible to trace the path of each QE dollar released in the flood of $3.5 trillion. The dollars were like drops of water added into a swimming pool, merging instantly with the broader whole. But the level of the pool could be measured. The McKinsey Global Institute, for example, determined that the Fed's policies created a subsidy for corporate borrowers worth about $310 billion between 2007 and 2012 alone, by pushing more money into corporate bonds. During the same period, households that tried to save money were penalized about $360 billion through lost earnings on interest rates. Pension funds and insurance companies lost about $270 billion during that time, and that was just the beginning of the ZIRP era.

This money flowed out into the system, and it pushed all the major financial institutions to search for yield. Many Wall Street traders saw clearly what was happening, and they developed a nickname for it: the "everything bubble."

The Fed's policies created such an intense and broad-based search for yield that the risks were building up all over the place.

The search for yield pushed money into corporate debt and stocks.

By the end of 2018, the U.S. market for CLOs was about $600 billion, double the level a decade earlier. Banks in the United States held about $110 billion. The banks believed that their investments were ultrasafe because they bought only the safest tranches, rated AAA. The high demand kept corporate debt cheap so that more and more companies were induced to borrow.

The demand for loans reduced the scrutiny that was applied to them. Predictably, many corporate borrowers were overly optimistic when it came to estimating how much money they would earn. Fully 90 percent of all the new corporate loans extended in 2016 would fall short of their earnings target, according to a survey taken later by the ratings agency Standard & Poor's. Companies had estimated that their debt would only equal about triple the amount of their profit (before taxes and other costs). It ended up equaling about six times as much. The optimistic assumptions were overlooked. The money had to go somewhere.

Quantitative easing was designed and initiated with the specific goal of inflating stock market prices. The plan worked. The value of stocks rose steadily during the decade after 2010, in spite of the weak overall economic growth, the broad-based wage stagnation, and the host of international financial problems that the Fed cited as justification for its interventions. The value of the Dow Jones Industrial Average rose by 77 percent between 2010 and 2016. One hedge-fund trader, who was a bit more caustic by nature, described the frothy stock market of 2016 as being like the crowded deck of the *Titanic* as it sank. The deck wasn't getting crowded because it was a great place to be. It was getting crowded because people had nowhere better to go.

The search for yield pushed money into the oil industry.

The money needed to find assets, and there was a gusher of assets pouring out of the ground in newly developed oil fields in Texas and North Dakota. The new oil-drilling technology called hydraulic fracturing, or fracking, opened a wild new frontier for the energy business. There was no limit to the optimism that sprang from entrepreneurs who pitched their fracking dreams to Wall Street. Money went flooding into fracking country in the form of cheap corporate debt. By one estimate, oil industry debt tripled between 2005 and 2015, rising to $200 billion. In 2017 alone the fracking industry borrowed $60 billion.

In a theme of this era, scrutiny and skepticism were in short supply. The frackers presented a case for their borrowing that was optimistic to the point of delusion. This optimism centered on just how much oil each well would produce, which in turn would determine how quickly they could pay down their loans. Fully two thirds of the production estimates made by leading fracking companies in Texas and North Dakota between 2014 and 2017 were inflated, promising more oil than was ultimately delivered, according to an in-depth investigation by *The Wall Street Journal*. The estimates were, on average, about 10 percent too high.

It didn't take a forensic accountant to realize this. The frackers lost money in a large and very public way. Between mid-2012 and mid-2017, the biggest fracking exploration and production companies had a collective negative cash flow of $9 billion every quarter. And still the money flowed to them in the form of corporate bonds and leveraged loans. Ares Capital, one of the new breed of business-development companies that bundled and sold corporate junk debt, arranged loans for companies throughout the oil belt. The debt was extended to obscure companies with shaky financials to which traditional banks avoided lending. They borrowed millions of dollars at interest rates of about 10 or 11 percent.

Wall Street investors didn't give the frackers money because the investors were stupid or because they believed wholeheartedly in the future production promises. They invested because the Fed was incentivizing them to invest. Thousands of wells were drilled across the country.

The search for yield pushed money into commercial real estate.

In 2013, a bond analyst named John Flynn was preparing for a wave of mortgage-debt failure. He called this apocalyptic moment "the Wall of Maturities." The wall he referred to was the moment when billions of dollars in commercial real estate bonds, extended during the real estate bubble of 2006, were set to mature. This would be a moment of reckoning for the commercial real estate industry, spelling doom for irresponsible developers who borrowed money to build shopping malls, office parks, and factories when they had no realistic way of repaying the loans. This debt had been packaged up and sold as something called commercial mortgage-backed securities, or CMBSs. Flynn had worked around CMBSs for most of his career. He created and sold them, he rated them for a ratings agency, and he eventually started his own company to advise investors about them. This was why he knew about the Wall of Maturities. Between 2005 and 2008, billions of dollars' worth of CMBSs had been created with absolutely horrible underwriting standards. It was a lot like the home-loan bubble, but it hadn't imploded yet. This would happen on a rolling basis between 2014 and 2016 as bonds came due and either had to be repaid or rolled over.

But a strange thing happened: nothing. There was no wall. There was no carnage. Only a tiny handful of CMBS bonds went belly-up. Flynn was caught up short. "I wasn't the only one in the market expecting this, right?" Flynn recalled. "I know shops that hired forty people to handle the onslaught . . . of maturity defaults. But it never happened."

This nagged at Flynn. He knew that the underlying loans in the CMBS market were rotten. And not only were these loans not defaulting—lenders were packaging and selling *new* batches of CMBS bonds. Flynn went to his brother's cabin in Minnesota where he could do research, unbothered. He downloaded the very dense CMBS prospectuses, which describe the loans inside a CMBS. He read the very detailed financial information about the borrowers, including how many units were for lease in a given office building. All this detail, added together, measured the profitability of the underlying commercial real estate property.

Then Flynn looked to a separate database that tracked actual cash flows for commercial properties, going back years. He downloaded this data and compared it to the information inside the CMBS prospectuses. These data sets were the opposite of user-friendly. "That's why I took so much brain damage to get it," Flynn said. "I was constantly cutting and pasting and inputting into new Excel sheets and combining that with the . . . prospectus information." Eventually, he was able to build a database that compared the actual profitability of commercial properties with the profitability that the banks advertised in their CMBS prospectuses.

"My jaw dropped," he said. The numbers were being inflated. Banks were reporting profits in their CMBS loans that were consistently higher than the profit figures Flynn obtained through independent databases. The profit figures were inflated by as much as 30 percent, or even 65 percent, depending on the CMBS bond. Flynn could think of no explanation for this inflation other than fraud. He contacted lawyers, spent months polishing his data, and then filed a whistleblower lawsuit with the Securities and Exchange Commission in 2019 that accused fourteen large lenders of intentionally fudging the numbers to make the loans look healthier than they really were. Flynn's findings were later supported by two researchers at the University of Texas, who studied about 40,000 commercial real estate loans, worth a total of $650 billion, originated between 2013 and 2019. The income figures on nearly a third of those loans were inflated by 5 percent or more. This meant that the properties didn't earn as much money as the lender promised they did, even when the economy was doing well. If the economy ever stalled, these properties would be more vulnerable to the downturn.

Roughly $76 billion in CMBS bonds was issued in 2018, and another $96.7 billion was issued in 2019. By 2020, the CMBS market was estimated to be worth about $1.4 trillion.

If Flynn was right, then the banks were fraudulently boosting the income numbers buried inside the CMBS prospectuses. But the problem was bigger than the dishonest behavior of banks. The problem reflected the same thing that was happening with fracking bonds and corporate debt. Investors were desperate to find yield, so they didn't want to ask questions. And the investors were so desperate because the Fed was forcing them to be desperate.

"It's a self-perpetuating cycle where they lower the interest rates, so you offer a minuscule yield on a secured note and investors have to gobble it up. No matter the underlying details, they have to gobble it up," Flynn said. "And in fact they're incentivized not to look. Because they don't want to know what's under there."

The search for yield pushed money into the debt of developing nations.

When the McKinsey Global Institute tried to track the flow of dollars created by quantitative easing, it discovered that billions of those dollars flowed to developing nations like Mexico, Poland, and Turkey. These countries were considered a bigger credit risk than the United States, so they had to pay higher interest rates to attract lenders. Turkey borrowed six times as much money by issuing bonds between 2009 and 2012 than it did between 2005 and 2008. That nation's president, Recep Tayyip Erdogan, used the borrowed money to finance a building spree, solidifying his power and helping push economic growth to an annual rate of 7 percent by 2018. The borrowed money helped construct new shopping malls next to old shopping malls in Istanbul. New condominiums, a new bridge, and a new skyscraper called the Sapphire were erected. Construction contractors borrowed roughly $56 billion thanks to bonds denominated in foreign currency.

Even if the shopping malls remained largely empty, they still got built. The borrowed money created jobs. But the borrowing left nations like Turkey enormously vulnerable to any changes in the debt markets. When Ben Bernanke said in 2013 that the Fed might taper its quantitative easing program, the market adjusted immediately, and investors started to sell off riskier government debt. About $4.2 billion of Turkish bonds were sold in the following three months. About $2.4 billion fled Poland. When foreign investors dumped their bonds, it damaged these nations by causing the value of their currencies to decline. The value of currencies in Turkey, Brazil, Mexico, and Poland fell by about 4 or 5 percent during the Taper Tantrum of 2013. Currency values are affected by a lot of different factors, of course (Turkey and Brazil were already suffering some devaluation), but the link to the Fed's policy was unmistakable. When the Fed reversed course and said it would not taper after all, the value of currencies like the lira and the peso jumped by 2 percent. The demand for bonds in the developing world strengthened, and the borrowing resumed.

Finally, the world's central banks went further to push the search for yield, turning the very concept of yield upside down.

Maybe the strangest creature that evolved during the era of ZIRP was the negative-interest-rate bond. The term *negative interest rate* should be oxymoronic. It means that an investor *pays* money to the borrower for the honor of lending to them.

The experiment in offering negative-rate debt began in Europe after the financial crisis. Virtually no debt in the world offered negative rates until about 2012. The first bonds with a penalty rate were presented as an emergency measure. Countries like Sweden entered the market gingerly with bonds that cost money to own each year. Sweden didn't charge much money at first. In 2015 the Swedish central bank, the Riksbank, dropped its interest rate to −0.1 percent. Other countries, like Germany and Denmark, did the same, as did the European Central Bank.

The idea was that negative rates would have the same effect as quantitative easing. Instead of incentivizing investors to reach for risky yields, the central banks of Europe literally punished investors, financially speaking, who saved money. The negative bonds were supposed to have a quick effect, and disappear. But then a very strange thing happened. Investors started lining up to buy these bonds. By 2016, they accounted for 29 percent of all global debt. About $7 trillion worth of bonds carried negative rates.

The bond market is often considered to be the sober older sibling of stock markets. And in 2016, this sober older market was sending out flashing red warning lights, indicating that things were not normal. Bond investors were so desperate to find a safe haven for their cash that they were willing to pay a fee to governments like those of Germany and Denmark to safeguard it. When *The New York Times* reported on negative-interest bonds, in 2016, the paper interviewed Kathy A. Jones, a chief strategist at Charles Schwab. "It's all upside down," Jones told the newspaper. "Negative interest is hard to even think about. Our whole financial system is built the other way, on positive interest rates. This is mind-boggling."

This was happening as Tom Hoenig was bogged down in long disputes over living wills and stress tests and capital reserves. Hoenig's office at FDIC headquarters was large, sparsely decorated, and bathed in sunlight during the afternoon hours. There was a large wooden desk where he conducted his work, and next to that a spacious sitting area with chairs to receive visitors. In August 2016, Hoenig seemed contemplative and sanguine. But he also seemed to possess absolutely no illusions about the limit of his accomplishments during four years in Washington. After all the fights and attempts at reform, the financial system remained too fragile to absorb a major shock, and the banks were still too big to fail.

Now that the Fed had reshaped the financial markets, how could it ever withdraw its support? The world had reorganized itself in ways that would be painful to undo. "Think about it," Hoenig said. "You had seven years of basically zero-interest rates. Now, what happens in an economic system over seven years? The entire market system develops a new equilibrium—around a zero rate.

"An entire economic system. Around a zero rate. Not only in the U.S. but globally. It's massive. Now, think of the adjustment process to a *new* equilibrium at a higher rate. Do you think it's costless? Do you think that no one will suffer? Do you think there won't be winners and losers? No way. You have taken your economy and your economic system and you've moved it to an artificially low zero rate. You've had people making investments on that basis, people *not* making investments on that basis, people speculating in new activities, people speculating on derivatives around that, and now you're going to adjust it back?

"Well, good luck. It isn't going to be costless."

CHAPTER 12

TOTALLY NORMAL

(2014–2019)

During most of Jay Powell's career as a Fed governor, the central bank was working hard to try to make things normal again. This effort had been under way, in stops and starts, since at least early 2010. Back then, FOMC members believed that the Fed's extraordinary interventions would be temporary. They even coined a term for reversing the ZIRP and QE programs: "normalization." At least as far back as January 2010, the Fed was debating how to normalize. Credible arguments were made that the process would be completed by 2015, meaning that the Fed would have sold off the assets it purchased through quantitative easing, and would have drained virtually all the excess cash reserves out of the banking system. This never happened. Instead, the bank decided to simply rearrange the definition of *normal*.

Jay Powell entered this debate from a position that was quite close to Tom Hoenig's. Both gave voice to the idea that the Fed was a highly imperfect engine to drive economic growth in America. Hoenig's critiques drew from his decades of experience at the Fed. Powell's critiques drew on his decades of experience in private equity, and he used hard data and interviews with his industry contacts to make his critiques of QE both specific and alarming. Both men warned about the ways that the Fed was stoking asset bubbles as it chased relatively small gains in the labor market. But this was where the similarities ended between Jay Powell and Tom Hoenig. Powell, for all his critiques, never cast a dissenting vote. And Powell, unlike Hoenig, started to soften his criticism, and he ultimately came to embrace the policies he once criticized inside the FOMC's closed meetings. When this happened, Powell's star began to rise.

Powell's growing clout within the Fed was made clear as early as January 28, 2014, when the FOMC members gathered in Washington, D.C., for Ben Bernanke's final meeting as the chairman. Bernanke was leaving the bank on good terms. His service had been like wartime service, and he was best known for the dramatic bailouts and rescue packages he oversaw in 2008. When Bernanke's last meeting began, it opened with sustained applause. The clapping came to a close when Bernanke's vice chairman, William Dudley, said, "We thought we'd just do this for a couple of hours," drawing laughter from the committee.

What followed next was something akin to a royal ceremony, with all its orchestrated pomp and circumstance. On cue, the Fed governor Jeremy Stein nominated Janet Yellen to become the chairwoman starting the day after Bernanke left, at the end of the month. This was just a ritual: The U.S. Senate had already approved Yellen for the job at the start of the month. But the formal vote was part of the Fed's internal process.

"I would like to nominate Janet Yellen," Stein said.

"Is there a second?" asked the governor Daniel Tarullo.

It was Jay Powell who formalized Yellen's chairmanship role.

"I second that nomination," Powell said. Yellen was approved.

Yellen's tenure at the top of the Fed was remarkable in many ways. She was the first woman to hold the role, and she commanded nearly universal respect from her colleagues. Her intelligence was unmistakable. She had the tactical ability to quickly absorb the complex information relayed by the Fed economists at the beginning of each meeting, along with a deep knowledge of the Fed, the U.S. Department of the Treasury, and the White House. But the constraints placed on Yellen's tenure were also remarkable. She would serve only four years at the helm of the Fed, and she would spend a great deal of that time trying to unwind the extraordinary interventions that she had advocated during the Bernanke era.

During Yellen's first year on the job, the FOMC was debating a central question: Should the Fed even try to normalize? The unemployment rate was falling. The economy was growing, even if that growth was slow. So why not just keep printing money indefinitely? Why not even expand the quantitative easing regime and promise to keep interest rates at zero indefinitely? The Fed could create money out of thin air, which seemed harmless and free from cost.

There was one big and compelling reason that many economists cited when they argued that the Fed should not normalize at all. This reason was the mysterious and near total absence of price inflation. The Fed's conservative critics warned constantly about price inflation, and there was good reason for it. That's how things had always worked. Printing more money devalued money and caused prices to rise. But the defining characteristic of the ZIRP era was not inflation. It was the surprising and scary specter of *deflation*. Deflation is the state of constantly falling prices, and it's a suffocating death spiral for any economy. People don't buy things when they know the price will fall. Companies don't make things when they know those things won't fetch a good price. The shadow of deflation was now hanging over everything. The Fed poured more money into the world's economic bathtub, but there was a deflationary hole at the bottom, which no one could quite understand, causing all that money to drain away without causing prices to rise. Nobody was more surprised by this than the Fed. For three years running, the Fed had consistently overshot its predictions of how high inflation would be.

Experts grappled with this puzzle and pondered what might cause it. Even by 2020, nobody was really certain. The prestigious Brookings Institution held a daylong seminar on the topic that year, attended by Janet Yellen and other leading economists, and the final verdict of the day's discussion might as well have been: *Who knows?* Globalization probably had something to do with it. There were more workers working for less money, making cheaper products, and generating more cash savings. The Fed's own past successes probably also played a role, because they kept expectations of future inflation low, which calmed the bankers in a way that in turn really did keep inflation down. One important thing about this, from the Fed's perspective, was that the absence of price inflation disguised the extravagant inflation occurring in assets. As long as prices didn't rise, the Fed had license to keep intervening aggressively by printing more money, which stoked asset prices yet further.

Jay Powell, in 2014, was determined to highlight the costs of the Fed's actions. He, as much as anybody inside the FOMC, was pushing for the Fed to normalize. In June, when members of the FOMC gathered to debate, he presented a clear case for normalization.

"After almost six years of highly accommodative policy, the risks are out there and continue to build," Powell began. He said that he wasn't worried about a financial "meltdown at the core of the system," as had happened in 2008 when the big banks collapsed. He believed that the banks were better capitalized and regulated than they were in the past. What worried him more was the prospect of "a sharp correction amplified by the liquidity mismatch in the markets that would damage or halt the progress of what is still a weak economy." He was saying that a lot of traders and hedge funds had built up risky positions using a ton of debt. If markets fell—because inflated asset prices started to reflect their real value—then these hedge funds would start selling off whatever they could to pay their debts. But in such a scenario, not many people would be buying much of anything. This is what economists might call a "liquidity mismatch." The Fed was laying the groundwork for a market crash, and the possibility only grew more likely with each passing month of ZIRP and QE.

If this wasn't enough for the Fed to pull back, there was another important reason. By keeping interest rates at zero, and keeping the banking system so flush with cash, the Fed was leaving itself with little room to maneuver if the economy did start to sink into recession.

His speech was remarkable for its clarity. But it was remarkable for another reason. It appears to be the last speech of its kind that Powell delivered during an FOMC meeting. Not too long after that, his attitude appeared to change.

Roughly seven months after delivering his warning, Jay Powell gave a speech at Catholic University in Washington, D.C., aimed at disarming the central bank's critics. By February 2015, when he gave the speech, there was growing opposition to the Fed in conservative and far-right circles. The movement was led by libertarian figures like Ron Paul, a former congressman and presidential candidate. Paul was pushing a movement to audit the Fed, giving the public a chance to better scrutinize and govern the central bank. Paul's followers were animated by the long-held fears of hyperinflation and currency devaluation.

Powell said that the increasingly vocal criticisms of the Fed were misguided. "In fact, the Fed's actions were effective, necessary, appropriate, and very much in keeping with the traditional role of the Fed and other central banks," he said. The Fed's conduct, in other words, was entirely normal.

He went out of his way, during that speech, to defend the very policies that he had been warning about internally since he had become a Fed governor. He said that "unconventional policies," such as quantitative easing, were largely responsible for America's economic growth, and that the critics of those programs had been proven wrong. "After I joined the Federal Reserve Board in May 2012, I too expressed doubts about the efficacy and risks of further asset purchases," Powell said. "But let's let the data speak: The evidence so far is clear that the benefits of these policies have been substantial, and that the risks have not materialized."

Powell did not mention that he had warned, in June, that the risks of quantitative easing were not only materializing but growing, and could lead to corporate defaults and a financial market crash. His reversal was noted by his colleagues at the FOMC who had previously argued alongside him. "There was a shift, and I think it's noteworthy," said Richard Fisher, the Dallas Fed president. Fisher had been raising concerns about QE for years, and he believed that Powell played an important role in giving those concerns more weight. It mattered that Powell's office was just down the hall from Yellen's. "He was important because he was a governor," Fisher said.

Fisher was not aware of any study or new data set released between June and February that would justify a reversal of Powell's judgment about QE or ZIRP. "There was no condition in 2015 that would have indicated, or necessitated, easing off that argument," Fisher said. More likely, he believed, was the effect of being a Fed governor. "The evolution may well have come from being there longer, being surrounded by brilliant staff that has a very academic side to them and bias," Fisher said. "You're living in a cloistered atmosphere. It's a different environment when you're in that hallway. You conform more. I don't think there's anything nefarious about it. I just think it's the social dynamic."

In closed-door meetings, Powell continued to cast doubt on the efficacy of quantitative easing. "I think we've never looked at asset purchases as other than a second-best tool," he said during the FOMC meeting in September 2015. "I think that's been the way it's been talked about since the very beginning—uncertain as to its effect, uncertain as to bad effects, and certainly uncertain as to political economy characteristics," he said. But a review of his comments, which are available only through the end of 2015, indicate that Powell was softening his arguments and his warnings. The language became less vivid and less focused on "large and dynamic" market crashes.

As Powell's rhetoric appeared to cool, the Fed was starting to take concrete actions that addressed the risks he warned about earlier. Janet Yellen moved forward on the plan to hike interest rates and stop quantitative easing. She was pushing to normalize in a real way.

In December 2015, the Fed raised rates for the first time in nine years, boosting them by a tiny fraction, from 0 to a range between 0.25 and 0.5 percent.* The era of living at the zero bound finally appeared to be over. But it wasn't ending quickly. The FOMC members believed they would raise rates all the way to 1.375 percent by the end of 2016, but they only raised them to 0.5 percent.

The Fed had somewhat better luck in ending quantitative easing. The bank had stopped buying bonds at the end of 2014. But it wasn't able to reverse the program, as some had hoped to do. There was still about $2.4 trillion of excess bank reserves sitting in the vaults of the primary dealers on Wall Street, and the Fed still owned $4.5 trillion in bonds that it had purchased through quantitative easing. The ocean of cash on Wall Street was akin to a permanent low interest rate. If the Fed ever wanted to truly tighten the money supply and reduce the pressure to search for yield, then it would need to start drawing this money down.

The Fed was normalizing slowly in part because of the sheer size of the task. Excess bank reserves were about 135,000 percent higher than they had been in 2008. The Fed's balance sheet was about $4.5 trillion, almost five times its level in 2007. Interest rates had been pinned at zero for nearly seven years. Caution was the Fed's guiding principle as it sought to reverse these changes.

*The FOMC hadn't raised rates since June 2006, and hadn't raised rates above the zero bound for the previous seven years, since late 2008.

The American body politic was not moving cautiously in 2016, when Donald Trump was elected president. This was the abrupt, unexpected event that would end Yellen's tenure at the Fed.

One of Trump's primary appeals was that he would work diligently to dismantle whatever was left of America's fiscal policy institutions. He set to work dismantling regulatory agencies like the EPA while passing a tax cut that would become a fiscal fiasco, enlarging the annual federal deficit to $1 trillion a year even when the economy was growing.

Trump's animosity toward most government institutions was transparent. But his attitude toward the Federal Reserve was less clear. During the 2016 campaign, Trump made strange and provocative comments that made it seem like he would support the Fed's efforts at normalization. During a debate with Hillary Clinton, he responded to a comment about the struggling middle class with something that seemed like a non sequitur. He started ranting about the Federal Reserve, and talking about asset bubbles. "Look—we have the worst revival of an economy since the Great Depression. And believe me, we're in a bubble right now," Trump said. "The only thing that looks good is the stock market. But if you raise interest rates, even a little bit, that's going to come crashing down. We are in a big, fat, ugly bubble. . . . And we have a Fed that's doing political things. . . . [T]he Fed is doing political things by keeping interest rates at this level. When they raise interest rates—you're going to see some very bad things happen."

This comment didn't generate much traction on the campaign trail, and Trump rarely mentioned the Fed again. When he became president, however, he had a chance to imprint his influence on the central bank. Janet Yellen's term as Fed chairwoman would expire in early 2018. As the end of Yellen's tenure approached, Trump interviewed a handful of candidates to consider as Fed chairman, including Yellen herself. After meeting with Yellen, Trump said he was impressed.

Jay Powell was hardly considered a front-runner for the job. When financial traders and bank analysts made bets about the next Fed chairman, Powell was seen as a far outside chance. But Trump's Treasury secretary, Steven Mnuchin, changed those odds. Mnuchin came from the investment banking and hedge-fund worlds, which would have given him a good understanding of Powell's previous career at the Carlyle Group. Mnuchin recommended Powell directly to Trump. Powell also impressed Trump during the interviews. There was a view inside the administration that Powell and Yellen would essentially promote the same agenda when it came to monetary policy. What tipped the balance toward Powell was his approach to bank regulation. He was seen as more closely aligned with the Trump administration, which was working to scale back some of the regulation imposed during the Obama years. Trump went with Powell as his nominee. The Senate confirmed Powell quickly.

Powell's selection was seen as a safe choice and a vote for continuity. He was not a dissenter. He would continue the path laid out by both Ben Bernanke and Janet Yellen. The path, in this case, would be the path to continued normalization. The Fed had gotten off to a slow and halting start, in 2015 and 2016, but during 2017 the bank started moving forward in a real way.

Powell was also seen in some quarters as an ally of Donald Trump on one key issue: helping peel away the regulations that were put on big banks. The Dodd-Frank law ensured that banking oversight was still divvied up among multiple agencies, including the FDIC and the Fed. This gave the central bank enormous influence over the rules governing Wall Street. Powell's vice chairman of bank supervision was Randal Quarles, a former Carlyle Group employee who had also worked for Jay Powell at the Treasury during the George H. W. Bush administration. Quarles met with bank lobbyists in the Fed's boardroom in the Eccles Building to hear out their concerns. The Fed softened rules around the stress tests, and eased back parts of the Volcker rule that would have given bank examiners more power to assess how banks valued their assets.

At that time, Tom Hoenig was moving in the opposite direction.

It was unclear, at first, what Trump's victory might mean in terms of banking policy, and for Hoenig's career trajectory. Trump had cast himself as a hero of the working class and criticized big banks. Less than a week after Trump's election, *The Wall Street Journal* ran a brief story reporting that there was speculation Tom Hoenig might even be elevated to chairman of the FDIC. There was also discussion that Hoenig could join the Federal Reserve board of governors, as vice chairman overseeing bank supervision—the job that Randal Quarles would eventually get.

By late 2017, the Trump administration needed to make a decision about Hoenig. His term as FDIC vice chairman was coming to an end. Hoenig said that he was willing to remain in Washington, but only as the FDIC's chairman or the Fed's regulatory chief. "I did make it clear, behind the scenes, that for either of those two positions I would be willing to stay on for a while, but not just to sit there," Hoenig said. He wasn't optimistic about his future in Washington. He'd been antagonizing the big banks since he arrived, and he knew that these many fights had dimmed his chances at promotion. He had even been warned about it. "It was suggested to me, rather indirectly, that I should tone it down if I expected to really have an opportunity to do these other things I might want to do," Hoenig later recalled. "I just ignored it. Because I don't have an interest in changing my views. If that's what it takes, I don't need this stuff."

In January 2018, Hoenig got his answer from the Trump administration. It came in a phone call from a staffer whose name Hoenig couldn't recall later. The staffer thanked him for his hard work. Hoenig was also informed that even if he wanted to stay at the FDIC, he no longer had the option. The White House had nominated a senior banking attorney named Jelena McWilliams to fill Hoenig's seat. McWilliams was going to be the FDIC's chairwoman.

In April 2018, Hoenig left the FDIC and returned to Kansas City. There was no doubt about what his departure would mean for the fortunes of the big banks. Bloomberg News reported the story under the headline "Wall Street's Least Favorite Regulator Is Calling It Quits."

Becoming Fed chairman presented Jay Powell with a remarkable opportunity. He had been pushing the Fed for years to normalize its operations, limiting the downside risks of asset bubbles. Now he had the chance to lead the effort. He could be something like a modern-day Paul Volcker, who ended one period of Fed history and began another, even if it caused volatility on Wall Street. The process was already under way. The Fed had raised interest rates three times in 2017, bringing its target rate to 1.5 percent. Maybe even more important, the Fed finally began to reverse quantitative easing in October, selling off the bonds it had purchased earlier. The Fed promised to keep normalizing steadily during 2018 and beyond, drawing down the size of its balance sheet from $4.5 trillion to somewhere between $3 trillion and $1.5 trillion.

The difficulty of this effort was apparent as soon as Jay Powell took the job. The Fed had barely begun to normalize, but the financial system was already falling apart.

On Monday, February 5, 2018, Jay Powell was welcomed to his first day on the job as the Fed chairman. The stock market plunged. The Dow Jones Industrial Average fell by 1,175 points, its largest single-day drop in history. Just a few days earlier, the average had fallen by 666 points, the largest single-day drop since 2008.

The market turbulence was not a sideshow. It was tied directly to the Fed. As the central bank normalized its operations, it was doing nothing less than rearranging the global economic order, because it was now at the center of it. This reality was described in a 2016 book called *The Only Game in Town* by the influential investor Mohamed A. El-Erian, the CEO of the investment powerhouse PIMCO. When El-Erian talked about the only game in town, he was talking about the world's central banks. They had become the anchor of economic development as democratic institutions were increasingly mired in dysfunction

around the world. The problem with this arrangement was that central banks weren't built for this job. All they could do was create more
money. "Somehow, the world was now depending on the one set of
institutions—central banks—with one of the narrowest sets of instruments at their disposal given the task at hand," El-Erian wrote. "And the
longer such policy was in play, the greater the probability that the costs
and risks would start outweighing the benefits."

When the Fed acted, its actions affected everything. The market
turmoil of 2018 had many faces, and emerged from many places. But
there was a singular, important force that was driving it. What appeared to be a series of unrelated market panics was actually the result
of smart investors reacting, rationally, to what the Fed was doing. These
investors listened to Jay Powell and took him seriously. The age of ZIRP
was coming to an end, even if it was ending gradually. The big money
had to move in different directions to accommodate this new reality.

Powell's leadership on this front was steady from the very beginning.
When he took charge, the FOMC hiked interest rates on a predictable
schedule and at regular intervals. The bank sold off billions of dollars
in bonds each month, sucking the excess cash back out of Wall Street
and easing the very high pressure it had created to search for yield. The
reason to do this, Powell said, was the economy's underlying strength.
During his first speech as Fed chairman, he pointed out that the unemployment rate had hit 4.1 percent, a level so low that it was previously
considered abnormal, an almost certain precursor to price inflation. The
United States had created jobs for ninety consecutive months. The unemployment rate was as low as it had been since 2000, near the peak
of the dot-com bubble. If the Fed couldn't normalize now, then when
could it ever normalize?

In June, the Fed hiked rates again, to a range between 1.75 percent
and 2 percent. This was the highest that short-term rates had been in a
decade, but it was still an early landmark on a long road ahead. If the
Fed wanted to have significant power to cut rates in the future, when it

came time to ward off a crisis, then the bank needed to push rates to 3 or 4 percent.

There was no question that market volatility would intensify as normalization continued. But Powell was careful to tend relationships in Washington that would help him keep a steady hand if things got rough. During Powell's first eight months on the job, he met with fifty-six lawmakers on Capitol Hill, splitting his time almost evenly between Republicans and Democrats. Janet Yellen, by contrast, had visited just thirteen lawmakers during the same period in her tenure. Powell formed connections that would provide him support if the Fed was ever drawn into political disputes.

As Powell built support, he continued the efforts to normalize, with the FOMC continuing to hike rates at regular intervals. The Fed was continuing to reverse QE by selling off roughly $50 billion in bonds every month. During a news conference in late September 2018, Powell signaled that the Fed would keep tightening: "These rates remain low," he said. "This gradual return to normal is helping to sustain this strong economy for the longer-run benefit of all Americans."

In October, Powell once again pressed hard on this point. During a public economics forum, he said that interest rates were a "long way" from being at the neutral level, meaning they were still well below the level at which they neither helped nor hurt economic growth. The implication was that there were many more interest-rate hikes to come.

The markets fell sharply after this, with the Dow dropping 5 percent in just two days. Among the worst-hit stocks were banks and energy companies.

Powell might have quietly forged political alliances in Washington, but there was one relationship that he could not manage: his relationship with Donald Trump. The president began to wade into monetary affairs in the typical Trumpian way, by drawing wide attention to the matter and then getting people arguing about exactly the wrong thing. In this instance, Trump began to publicly pressure Jay Powell into cutting interest rates. This outraged the community of Fed followers who believed the bank should be independent and free from political pressure. Powell suddenly became famous, but he was famous only as a foil to Trump's public tantrums. Powell became another Washington figure representing institutions that Trump sought to deface or destroy. The larger issue—about the need to normalize, the cost of normalizing, and the complicated side effects of normalization—all fell to the shadowy edge of the audience's view. Trump turned monetary policy into a circus, and he was at the center of the ring.

Trump paraded his grievances about Powell in front of the television cameras and on Twitter. His central complaint was that Powell raised rates even as other nations were keeping their rates low. Trump had once complained that the Fed was stoking asset bubbles. Now he took the posture that rates needed to stay near zero, and the Fed should stop selling off $50 billion of bonds each month. "Stop with the 50 B's," Trump proclaimed on Twitter in December. "Feel the market, don't just go by meaningless numbers. Good luck!"

The public dispute between Trump and Powell helped overshadow the slow, chaotic unraveling of the global financial system. By the end of 2018, the reality of normalization was beginning to express itself.

The direct relationship between the Fed's actions and the market volatility was obscured, in part, because there was always a short-term explanation, a new headline of the day, to explain what was happening.

When the value of technology stocks began to fall, for example, the headlines described the increasing political scrutiny on monopolistic tech companies like Facebook and Google. The headlines were accurate; there really was an increasingly powerful movement to regulate technology companies. But a larger force behind the stock market decline was the Fed's normalization. When the Fed diminished its pressure on investors to put their money into stocks, the investors first withdrew their money from the stocks that were most overvalued. These included technology stocks, which had drawn so much attention from investors during the years of ZIRP.

As the global economy started to slow, the headlines described the effect of President Trump's trade war and tariffs against China. These headlines were also accurate. Trump's actions were unpredictable and disruptive, slowing global trade and causing investors to reexamine and even rearrange supply chains. But once again, the larger force was the Fed's normalization, which coincided with similar actions from other central banks. In December 2018, the European Central Bank followed the Fed's lead and ended its own version of quantitative easing. The tightening financial conditions exposed the rot that had formed in global debt markets. China was a particularly instructive example. It was suffering from a debt crisis, and a wave of asset bubbles that its government and central bank helped create over the years. A Fed report from 2018 put it succinctly: "In China, the pace of economic growth has been slowing recently, and years of rapid credit expansion have left lenders more exposed in the event of a slowdown." Private-sector debt in China had nearly doubled since 2008, and amounted to more than twice the level of China's annual economic production. This enormous level of debt "could trigger adverse dynamics," as borrowers found themselves unable to repay in the event of an economic slowdown. The trade war overshadowed a deeper problem in China that had to do with cheap money and high asset prices.

December was the pivotal month. There was a broad global downturn that was scary in the way that it seemed to affect everything. Usually, markets for different assets and different commodities move in different directions. When stock prices fall, for example, gold prices rise as investors rush for a safe haven. This didn't happen in December. Instead, the downturn was broadly synchronized across asset classes in a way that shocked Wall Street traders. Stocks ended the year down about 6 percent. Even high-quality corporate bonds ended down 6 percent. Crude oil prices and other commodities were down about 15 percent.

It was the beginning of a global retreat from risk and a reshaping of the economic system after ZIRP. If the instability continued along this course, it could threaten the global banking system, intensify the global economic slowdown, or even lead to another financial crisis that could cause the unemployment rate to jump quickly.

Jay Powell made a choice, in mid-December, to stand firm in the face of these risks. Normalization would continue. During a press conference on December 19, Powell said that the Fed would continue to reverse the process of quantitative easing by selling bonds "on automatic pilot." He was saying that the Fed would not be deterred by the market turmoil. Financial traders took Powell at his word, and responded rationally. They started dumping their riskier assets.

On Christmas Eve, a normally quiet trading day, the Dow Jones average fell by 653 points, nearly 3 percent. This smelled like panic to the Wall Street types. The Dow was now down about 19 percent since October, just 1 percentage point short of an official "bear" market, meaning a downturn that generally presages a recession. A terrible economic reversal was in the making.

When the full shape and scope of this economic tyrant came into view, it would be only a matter of weeks before Jay Powell surrendered entirely.

On January 25, 2019, a story was leaked to *The Wall Street Journal*. It turned out that the Fed's reversal of quantitative easing might not be as "automatic" as Jay Powell said earlier. In fact, the story said, unnamed senior Fed officials were close to deciding that the Fed would keep more money on its balance sheet than it had originally expected. Markets rose on the news.

After the FOMC meeting that month, Powell emerged to give a news conference. He began his comments with a litany of technical points and data, but he didn't obscure the central message. Normalization was effectively over. The bond sales were over. The interest-rate hikes were over. The tightening was finished. "The case for raising rates has weakened somewhat," Powell said.

Powell's language was colorless, but the traders on Wall Street heard his message clearly—Powell's reversal had been total. The moment coined a term in the investing world: the Powell Pivot. This phrase was just another way to describe the safety net that Wall Street assumed the Fed would provide. They called it a "put," as in a contract to buy a stock at a floor price if it ever sank too low. First there was the Greenspan Put. Then the Bernanke Put. Then the Yellen Put. Now the Powell Put. It had become a de facto policy, the Fed Put, that implied the Fed would create a floor to asset prices.

By February 3, days after this announcement, the values of stocks and bonds were rising in tandem, a rare thing to see.

It soon became clear, however, that simply stopping normalization would not be enough. The world economy was like a big building with bad wiring that was smoldering behind the walls. Some rooms were smoky, some rooms were just hazy, and it seemed that open flames might break out at any moment.

Deflation was a central problem. Demand was weak and industrial production was slowing in Germany and China. Prices were stubbornly low across the European Union. In March, the Fed announced it would be keeping interest rates flat, and Powell acknowledged that the puzzling lack of inflation was a large reason. "I don't feel we have convincingly achieved our two percent mandate in a symmetrical way," he said. "It's one of the major challenges of our time, to have downward pressure on inflation."

By March, shares of stock in banks were falling over worries about the financial system, and the specter of a global recession was becoming more pronounced. The markets sent out a particularly stark warning that month when interest rates on short-term bonds became higher than those on long-term bonds. This is something called an "inverted yield curve" that signals a coming economic downturn. In July, the

European Central Bank announced it would cut interest rates, largely because inflation remained alarmingly low. President Trump tweeted his fury about this development. He believed that the Fed should be leading the way on rate cuts and stimulus, not the ECB.

In July, Powell led the Federal Reserve to something extraordinary. The bank would cut interest rates, even though the economy was growing. The unemployment rate was 3.7 percent, the lowest it had been in about fifty years, and wages had been rising. This was the point in an economic cycle when the Fed normally kept rates higher, giving itself the power to cut them if the U.S. economy began to slow. The rate cuts were described as an insurance policy. The traders on Wall Street suspected that this insurance policy was just the beginning. Futures markets priced in three more rate cuts by the end of the year. Central banks around the world, from Europe to China to Russia, started to ease again. They were the only game in town, and by August the banks were fighting off a global downturn.

If Powell felt like he had control over the situation, that feeling was extinguished on the Tuesday morning of September 17, 2019. The members of the FOMC gathered that day in Washington for their regularly scheduled meeting. But the meeting was overshadowed by urgent reports from the trading desks at the New York Fed. An obscure but vitally important market for overnight loans had seized up. The problem was getting worse. If left unattended, it could lead to a financial crisis, maybe worse than the one in 2008. Very few people outside Wall Street even knew what was going on.

The economy was as strong as it would be for years to come. But the financial system was so fragile it was about to implode.

PART 3

LET THEM EAT ASSETS

CHAPTER 13

THE INVISIBLE BAILOUT

(2019–2020)

At 9:05 on the morning of Friday, September 13, 2019, a group of financial traders and analysts gathered for their regular daily meeting at the New York Federal Reserve Bank. These traders were expected, every weekday, to have a firm grasp of what was happening in global markets so that they could explain it to their boss, Lorie Logan, who oversaw the New York Fed's entire trading floor. Logan was a petite woman with dark hair, cut in a shoulder-length bob. Her features were sharp, and her language had the crisp cadence of an effective bureaucrat. She had an advanced degree in public administration, not economics, but had developed a sharp and finely detailed view of the Fed's financial plumbing system since joining the bank in the late 1990s. On that Friday in September, Logan's mind was on an upcoming trip. She would soon head to Washington for the FOMC's regularly scheduled meeting, which started the following Tuesday. Logan and her team would set up shop at the Eccles Building on Monday to finalize their presentations for the committee. Usually, this would occupy most of Logan's attention. But, on her last day in New York, the analysts delivered a warning during the morning meeting. They were detecting troubling signs in the market. And they believed things might well get worse on Monday, when Logan would be on the road.

The conference room in the New York Fed was located just off the main trading floor, and its doors were open during meetings so people could quietly go in and out. The room was anchored by a large table, with a couch along the wall for staffers to sit with their laptops open and take notes. There was a set of large digital monitors hanging on one wall, one of which provided a live video feed from an eerily identical room in Chicago, in a Fed satellite office near the important Chicago Mercantile Exchange.

After everyone got settled that morning, the New York traders described what had them worried. They had been watching the enormous global market for U.S. dollars, which they referred to simply as "money markets." The money markets tracked the flow of real, actual hard cash as it circulated around the world. There were many parts of this market, including overnight loans that banks used to keep their books straight, along with the billions of dollars borrowed daily by hedge funds to finance their bets. The New York Fed was obsessed with global money markets. The Fed's primary job was to control the price of money, and this price was expressed in the short-term interest rates paid by the banks and hedge funds. The Fed's traders were worried that there might be a cash squeeze looming on the horizon. It was true that the world was awash in cash, perhaps more cash than existed at any point in history. But the traders were seeing market signals indicating that short-term interest rates were rising, and they might continue to do so, maybe sharply. This got Lorie Logan's full attention. Her primary job was to ensure that interest rates did not rise or fall beyond the narrow band dictated by the FOMC. She directed her team to elevate their monitoring of the marketplace, which meant that they would start making calls to financial traders and heighten their surveillance of certain contracts that reflected the short-term price of money.

The Fed itself was directly responsible for the situation. The strain on financial markets was happening as a direct result of the normalization process overseen by Jay Powell. Normalization had been taken off autopilot, and had been essentially halted, but the FOMC had nonetheless withdrawn some of the extraordinary interventions of the Bernanke era. When the Fed reversed quantitative easing, it drained more than $1 trillion of excess cash out of the banking system. Excess bank reserves—meaning the level of cash that banks kept in vaults inside the Fed—had been drawn down from about $2.7 trillion in 2014 to about $1.3 trillion in September 2019. This was still about 76,000 percent more excess bank reserves than existed in 2008. But the reduction was significant.

The problem, in the view of Logan's team, was that even $1.3 trillion in excess reserves might not be enough to keep the banking system working.

The warning signs, Logan's team explained, were coming from the crucially important cash "repo" market. The repo market was part of the bedrock of the financial world, and it was supposed to be a supersafe form of lending. A repo loan was short-term, maybe as short as overnight. It always worked the same way: A borrower would hand over Treasury bills in exchange for cash. Then, the next day or the next week, the borrower would give back the cash in return for the Treasury bills, paying a very tiny fee for the transaction. The whole point of a repo loan was to be able to get cash when you needed it, in exchange for ultrasafe Treasury bills. This was very important for Wall Street firms—they had hard assets like Treasury bills, which were worth a lot, and they needed ways to unlock that value in the form of cash to meet their overnight obligations. Banks were more than happy to do this short-term loan because it was so safe; the banks held on to the Treasury bills as collateral so there really wasn't any risk. If the borrower went belly-up, the bank could sell the Treasurys and recoup the total value of the loan. This is why the repo loan market was a multibillion-dollar market. All kinds of financial institutions used it every day to swap Treasurys for cash, so they had money on hand to do daily business.

On Friday the thirteenth, however, the repo market was sending out flashing signals. There were early signs that big banks like JPMorgan were increasing the very tiny interest rates that they charged for repo loans. Logan's team believed the banks might raise rates because they were growing hesitant to extend repo loans. The banks seemed to feel that they were running too low on cash reserves.

On the following Monday the banks would be running extra low on cash because two things would happen at the same time. First, it was Tax Day for big corporations, which meant that banks would be sending a lot of cash out the door to pay tax bills. Second, this happened to also be the day when a lot of auctions for U.S. Treasury bills were going to settle, meaning that banks had to pay cash for Treasury bills they had earlier agreed to buy. All of this would drain cash from the system and reduce the level of excess reserves.

Logan was persuaded that this might be a problem. If the banks started balking at offering repo loans on Monday, they might charge more money for the loans, pushing repo rates from their current level of about 1.5 percent to elevated levels of 1.8 percent or even 2 percent. This would, in turn, spill out into all corners of the money markets, elevating rates for money everywhere. This was why Logan instructed her staff to heighten their monitoring of repo markets. Logan left work that day focused on her trip to Washington and the upcoming FOMC meeting. Her staff in New York focused all their attention on repo loans.

The events of the following Monday showed that the Fed's New York trading team was essentially flying blind in the age of ZIRP. This meant that the entire leadership team of the Fed, including Jay Powell, was also flying blind. The central bank had transformed the financial landscape by swamping it with money and in doing so had destroyed one monetary regime and replaced it with a new one. But there was no reliable instrument to measure the terrain of the new regime. This fact was made a stark reality on Monday, when the repo market blew up. The resulting market crisis almost became a full-fledged financial crisis, at a moment in history when the markets were supposed to be stable and in good health. The only reason that this didn't happen was that the Fed stepped in, almost instantaneously, and initiated a $400 billion bailout. This bailout was unprecedented, and it benefitted a small group of hedge funds that had essentially hijacked the repo market and used it as a vehicle to make risky bets. The Fed saved them from the consequences of those bets. But maybe the most remarkable part of the bailout is that the Fed did it without much notice. A $400 billion emergency cash injection was no longer news. The Fed described it as a matter of normal maintenance. But that's not how it looked from inside the Fed, as the repo market melted down.

On Monday morning, September 16, Logan and her team arrived at the Eccles Building. As always, they arranged a temporary office in a large conference room on the third floor of the building. They gathered around a table and started to prepare for the series of complex presentations they would give the next day to the FOMC members. This preparation was laborious and could take a long time. But Logan's team barely had time to begin. The chaos erupted before markets even opened. The third-floor conference soon turned into a war room and frantic communications hub. The trading analysts in New York reported that repo rates were spiking.

It wasn't unusual for repo rates to rise by about 0.3 percent in times of stress.* In December 2018, for example, the repo rate spiked dangerously during the market turmoil that prompted Jay Powell to reverse the normalization process. At that time, the rates had jumped alarmingly high, from about 2.5 percent to over 3 percent. Nobody was expecting

---

*Rates in this passage refer to the so-called SOFR repo rate used by the Fed, a commonly cited rate in the market.

that much movement in September, when markets were tranquil, unemployment was low, and the economy was growing.

The New York desk sent an alarming dispatch to Logan's team on Monday morning. Repo rates continued spiking. They would hit 5 percent that day.

Nobody knew what was going on. This was the kind of repo rate that signaled a market panic. But there was no discernable reason for a panic. No bank had gone bust, no nation had just defaulted on its debt, and no major news had come out of a central bank. The analysts in New York were trying to get a handle on why the rates were spiking. Two of Logan's top deputies, Patricia Zobel and Nate Wuerffel, were with her in the conference room in Washington, and they quickly started work on a plan to quell markets if the rates didn't fall. One option seemed obvious: The Fed could start trading in the repo markets itself, offering cheap repo loans in the same way it offered emergency loans to a failing bank. This would be a radical step. The Fed hadn't done repo trades, at least on a significant level, in nearly a decade.

It quickly became clear that the turmoil was not a fluke. The market was deteriorating. Logan quickly elevated the crisis to her boss, John Williams, the newly appointed president of the New York Fed. Williams was an economist who was previously the president of the San Francisco Fed. His background was in economic research, not market operations. He came across as a congenial professor, with a big smile and large round eyeglasses. He had taken over the New York Fed shortly after Jay Powell became Fed chairman, and the two men had developed a close working relationship. On that Monday morning, Williams was down on the second floor of the Eccles Building, in an office that was permanently reserved for the New York Fed president. He, too, was preparing for Tuesday's FOMC meeting. The world was expecting another rate cut from the Fed, following the cut in July. This was controversial because it was so unusual to cut rates when the economy was growing, and there was a lot riding on the meeting. But Williams's work was interrupted.

On Monday afternoon, Lorie Logan dispatched a message to Williams, Jay Powell, and Vice Chairman Richard Clarida. The repo market was seizing up, she reported, it wasn't stopping, and her team was simultaneously trying to understand the problem and come up with a plan to deal with it.

If the repo rates did not immediately subside from 5 percent back into a normal range between 2.25 and 2.5 percent, they could precipitate a cascading series of failures on Wall Street. All those hedge funds that used repo loans to pay their daily bills would be forced to find other ways to raise cash, and raise it quickly. This meant they would start selling off assets, like Treasury bills or mortgage-backed securities. When too many people do this at once, it creates a "deleveraging" event, meaning that everyone is liquidating their holdings at the same time, which causes prices to crash. The deleveraging event might even be, in the words of Jay Powell, "large and dynamic."

But this risk, as bad as it was, was only part of the problem. Williams and Logan worried about something even more fundamental. If the repo rates didn't fall, this would put pressure on other short-term rates, including the all-important Fed Funds that measured overnight loans. If the Fed Funds rate rose beyond the FOMC's target, the world's most powerful central bank would have lost control of the price of money.

The painful irony was that the Fed had used the repo market for many decades as its primary way to control short-term rates. The Fed traders in New York had a finely tuned system by which they injected or withdrew cash from the banking system, almost daily, by buying and selling repo contracts. These were the very "open market" operations referred to in the FOMC's name, the Federal Open Market Committee. The traders went out into the open markets to buy and sell repo loans as a way to manage the money supply.

This system was destroyed when Ben Bernanke's Fed decided to embark on years of quantitative easing and 0 percent interest rates. A side effect of QE was that the Fed swamped the delicate ecosystem of open market operations with so much cash. The Fed's own repo traders had bought and sold repos with precision, like a piano tuner who tightened or loosened strings to keep them at the precisely correct level of tension. The traders would buy only $6 billion or so of repo loans, or sell the same amount, in very targeted transactions that kept the money supply exactly where the Fed wanted it. Buying repo loans injected a little more cash while selling them removed a little cash. The important thing about all this cash was that it existed inside the reserve accounts of the big banks. Each reserve account was like a glass of water, filled right to the red line that represented the minimum level of required reserves. Banks didn't want to have any reserves above the level of that red line because they could be lending that money out for a profit. But they also didn't want the money to be below the red line because then they'd be violating the rules on keeping a minimum amount of reserves. This need to keep reserves right on the red line explains why there was a big market in overnight loans between banks. After the day's hectic activity, banks that ended up with too much money lent it out to banks that happened to have too little money. The Fed traders used their repo trades to gently fill more glasses with more water, reducing demand for overnight loans and therefore lowering interest rates. And they used reverse repo trades to gently remove money from the glasses, increasing demand for loans and causing rates to rise. This worked well in the long era of scarce bank reserves.

Quantitative easing didn't just overfill the glasses with excess reserves. It flooded the room in which the glasses were held. Then it replaced the glasses with silos, so that they could hold the trillions of dollars in new liquid reserves. This meant that doing little repo trades worth $6 billion was totally meaningless. It had no effect on the demand for overnight loans.

The Fed realized very early on that its open market operations would be an early casualty of the bailouts that happened in late 2007, as the mortgage market collapsed. William Dudley, who was the New York

Fed president, warned about this during an emergency FOMC conference call on December 6, 2007. "We cannot change the amount of reserves in the system if we want to keep the federal funds rate anchored at the target," he said.

Rather than hold back its bailouts, the Fed invented a new way to control short-term interest rates. Congress helped solve this problem by giving the Fed new powers that were buried in the emergency bailout act of October 2008, which authorized the $700 billion bailout known as the Troubled Asset Relief Program, or TARP. What went unnoticed was that the law also updated the Federal Reserve Act in a manner that paved the way for quantitative easing. It allowed the Fed for the first time to directly pay banks an interest rate on the cash they held in their Fed reserve accounts.* This might seem trivial, but it's what allowed the Fed to transform the financial system. Now the Fed didn't need repo operations to control short-term rates. There was no ceiling anymore on the level of excess bank reserves. Instead of controlling rates through repo trades, the Fed would control them by lifting or lowering the interest on excess reserves, or IOER, rate.

None of this mattered for many years because interest rates were at zero. Demand for overnight loans was basically zero because there were so many dollars in the system. The real test of how well this system worked would only come if the Fed tried to raise rates. When the Fed finally hiked rates at the end of 2015, it did so by raising the IOER rate. The whole thing was an experiment conducted in real time, and it carried big risks. Simon Potter, who ran the New York Fed trading desk before Lorie Logan, cowrote an academic study in early 2020 evaluating these risks. Potter tried to figure out what might happen if the Fed actually got serious about normalization and withdrew the excess bank

---

*The Fed was originally granted this authority back in 2006, but the original law didn't make the move effective until 2011. The 2008 law just moved up the date so the Fed could have more freedom to fight the financial crisis.

reserves. At some point, the reserves would hit a level where they were actually scarce again. At that moment, the interest rate banks charged for an overnight loan would probably not creep up in a steady and predictable way. It would likely jolt up as banks realized for the first time in a decade that reserves were scarce. Everything would be calm until it wasn't, and then interest rates would spike. The problem was that nobody knew exactly when this moment would hit. How low was too low?

The Fed seemed to have answered that question. The number where reserves turned out to be scarce was $1.39 trillion, which was the level hit on Monday morning.

Logan and her team worked until after seven in the evening on Monday to get an accurate picture of the repo markets. Around eight that night, Logan met with Williams in the lobby of the hotel in D.C. where the Fed officials stayed. She told him the situation was very bad. The repo panic was not abating. But even more worrisome, it looked like the Fed Funds rate was about to rise above the level set by the FOMC.

Williams was persuaded that something needed to be done. The situation seemed like a mini panic, a breakdown in the market that wasn't going to heal itself quickly. Williams believed that the traders on Wall Street were deeply uncertain about what was going on and the Fed needed to act fast to restore their confidence.

On Tuesday morning, Williams and Logan arrived early at the Eccles Building to hold an emergency meeting with Powell and Clarida. Logan presented the plan that her team had developed. If market conditions worsened, as the data seemed to predict, the Fed would be ready to act.

That morning, the price of a repo loan crossed 9.5 percent. This was the territory that caused financial meltdowns. That day, the Fed initiated an unprecedented intervention into repo markets, offering to pump $75 billion into the overnight markets. That was just the start of a long bailout, which would later come to include massive new rounds of quantitative easing. When the Fed announced these measures, it used a lot of technical terms and talked about the whole thing as if it were a plumbing job. But this obscured an important reality. The money that the Fed unleashed was not a neutral force. It benefited some people and disadvantaged others.

When the repo rate rose above 9 percent, it seemed like a scary but abstract number. This number, in fact, told a story. The number reflected a struggle that was going on between real people. On one side of the struggle were lenders like JPMorgan, who offered repo loans. On the other side of the struggle was someone who desperately needed a repo loan to stay in business. The intensity of this struggle was made clear as the repo-rate number went higher and higher. When the rate hit 9 percent, it meant that somebody out there was so terrified and desperate that they were willing to pay loan-shark rates of 8 percent to secure a totally collateralized overnight loan, which normally cost about 2 percent or less. But even more amazing than this, the person on the other side of the struggle was not willing to extend a super-safe overnight repo loan at the price of 8 percent. The lender wanted 9 percent.

This indicated that the lenders were very nervous about the people who wanted to borrow repo loans. The scarcity of bank reserves revealed this nervousness, but did not create it.

During the age of ZIRP, the repo market had transformed. Before the financial crisis, the market was mostly used by banks. But the banks didn't use repo loans as often now that they had so much cash. A new group of financial players stepped in and started using repos: hedge funds. The amount of overnight repo loans used by nonbank actors like hedge funds roughly doubled between 2008 and 2019, rising from about $1 trillion to $2 trillion. This figure, $2 trillion, understated just how important the repo market had become to hedge funds.

Hedge funds used repo loans as the cornerstone to build a much larger structure of debt. They got cash from a repo loan, then used that cash as the payment to make a larger bet in the marketplace. Wall Street called this technique leveraging up, meaning you borrowed a dollar to pay for a ten-dollar wager. The hedge funds used $2 trillion in overnight repo loans to build positions in the market that were much, much larger than the repo loans themselves.

Even the Federal Reserve was not entirely aware of what was going on. It was obvious that hedge funds were doing a lot more repo loans than they used to, but it wasn't clear why. What were they funding? And how risky were their activities? This remained a mystery because the hedge funds weren't regulated as tightly as banks. They were part of a shadow banking system that didn't face as much scrutiny from the FDIC and all the Dodd-Frank rules. The theory behind this was that hedge funds were sophisticated investors who could succeed or fail on their own merits.

Even months after the repo market collapsed in 2019, the Treasury Department wasn't entirely sure what the hedge funds had been up to. But, like forensic analysts digging through the debris of an explosion, they discovered some convincing clues.

The hedge funds had been piling into a very particular trade called a "basis risk" trade. The tactic was made possible by the very market tranquility that the Fed had manufactured over the years of quantitative easing and ZIRP. The basis trade worked well only in an environment of enforced tranquility, where traders knew that the Fed would step in and stop any violent market turmoil. When this condition was met, hedge funds felt justified in borrowing hundreds of billions of dollars to build a trade that was virtually risk-free as long as market volatility was dead.

The design was simple. A hedge-fund trader searched out a small wrinkle in financial markets that almost always occurred naturally. The wrinkle was the very minute difference in the price between a Treasury bill and a futures contract on that Treasury bill.* This difference in price between the Treasury bill you buy today and the price of a Treasury futures contract is called the basis. The hedge fund exploits the very tiny basis by purchasing a lot of the Treasury bills along with the futures contracts on the bills. The hedge fund then just holds on to the bills, and delivers them on the date they're due, collecting a profit that is the basis price difference.

This is where the repo market comes in. The profit margin on a basis trade was essentially guaranteed, but it's small. To make the trade pay off, a hedge fund needs to make the trade thousands of times over. They used the repo market to pull this off. The hedge fund takes the Treasury bill, uses it as collateral, and gets the cash needed to load up on Treasury futures contracts. The hedge funds were able to lever up their bets by a factor of fifty to one, meaning every dollar they had allowed them to borrow fifty more dollars to use for trading. Ultimately, the hedge funds built a mutually reinforced tripod of debt and risk between Treasury bills, repo loans, and Treasury futures. It was easy money, like collecting millions of loose pennies off the sidewalk. The hedge funds didn't have to report how much money they had put into a trade like this. But a subsequent Treasury Department investigation provided a good estimate. Between 2014 and 2019, the total value of "short" positions in the Treasury futures markets owned by hedge funds rose from about $200 billion to nearly $900 billion.† This position was key to making the basis trade work. The market for basis trades appears to have been dominated by a group of hedge funds called relative-value

---

*A futures contract is basically a promise to deliver a Treasury bill to someone on a certain date in the future at a certain price. The contracts are often dated in months, with a three-month futures contract promising delivery three months in the future. There are lots of good reasons to do something like this beyond mere speculation. Lots of futures contracts are used as insurance policies against certain future events.
†A short position is a bet that the price of something will fall.

funds. These included relatively obscure firms like LMR Partners and BlueCrest Capital Management.

The basis trade worked just fine as long as repo prices stayed low and stable. If the price of repo loans rose, it instantly demolished the profitability of the basis trade. The hedge funds found themselves obligated to make payments on their futures contracts but had to pay more money to keep the repo debt rolling. When repo rates spiked in mid-September, financial analysts on Wall Street started hearing alarming stories. Certain hedge funds were very, very desperate to raise cash and raise it quickly. Ralph Axel, an analyst with Bank of America, captured the moment in a report published months later. His message was chilling. He pointed out that the hedge funds' dependence on repo loans had doubled in a decade. If the repo market was closed off to hedge funds, then they would be forced to liquidate Treasury bills and mortgage securities at a level that was twice as large as the amount liquidated in 2008.

Always understated, Axel wrote, "The impact could be massive."

The financial world faced a forced liquidation event that could be twice as large as that in the horrific crash of 2008, and this was all happening during the apparently sunny weather of an economic boom, when markets were not just stable, but rising.

When the Fed entered the repo market on September 17, it bailed out any hedge funds that found themselves desperate for a repo loan. The going rate for such a loan was over 9 percent that day. The Fed offered such loans at 2.1 percent, using money it could create instantaneously.

The hedge funds could breathe. The repo market was once again available to them. It is difficult to quantify, financially, just how much money this was worth to the hedge funds. They saved a great deal of money on the repo loan itself. But they also saved a nearly incalculable amount by escaping the consequences of having entered basis risk trades that went bad. The Fed made sure that hedge funds did not need to liquidate their holdings.

The Fed had offered $75 billion in overnight repo loans the first day. The pace picked up over the following weeks. The program became open-ended and continued through the autumn, growing in size. By October 23, the Fed said that the minimum size of its overnight repos would be $120 billion. The central bank was offering a mix of overnight and longer-term repo loans. On October 29, it would boost its long-term repos from $35 billion to $45 billion a day, alongside the short-term overnight loans.

It appears that some hedge funds took the chance to unwind at least some of their basis trades while they had the chance. The volume of short positions on Treasury futures fell gradually through the fall and into early 2020, dropping from nearly $900 billion to less than $800 billion. But it was still roughly quadruple what it had been in 2014.

When the Fed announced its repo intervention, it didn't talk about hedge funds or basis trades or the fact that it was improvising a new system for controlling the overnight loan rates. As the repo bailout continued over weeks and months, Fed officials like Powell, Logan, and Williams talked about it as if it were a routine form of system maintenance.

The Fed focused narrowly on how the repo meltdown affected the Fed Funds rate. When that rate broke past its prescribed boundaries, it triggered something called the "standing directive" at the New York Fed. The standing directive was the order to keep short-term interest rates where the FOMC wanted them to be. That day in September the target rate was between 2 and 2.25 percent, which was breached. So the New York Fed initiated the repo intervention to get the rate back in line. The whole thing was reminiscent of a joke that circulated in Silicon Valley. The joke described a new artificial intelligence machine that was given unlimited power to fulfill a simple directive: Reduce the amount of spam email. The AI program analyzed the problem, realized that all spam emails were created by humans, and so launched a wave of nuclear warheads to wipe out humanity. No more spam. A simple directive, fulfilled by sweeping powers.

The repo bailout succeeded, and fulfilled the directive. The Fed Funds rate was pushed back into range. But the overnight repo loans were just the start of the operation. As the repo loans expanded during the following weeks, Powell was already discussing the next phase of the plan. The Fed was going to get back into the business of quantitative easing. During normalization, the Fed had drawn down bank reserves to $1.39 trillion, and discovered the bottom of the swimming pool. Even if the Fed offered cheap repo loans on a permanent basis, which it was considering, it needed to deal with the structural problem of scarce bank reserves.

On October 4, two weeks after the repo crisis, the FOMC held an emergency video conference call. The meeting began with a presentation from the Fed's staff, which showed that the repo intervention had worked, but the real problem hadn't gone away. Tax time rolled around quarterly, and banks might once again find themselves in a cash pinch. It was unclear what the markets might look like when that happened. To combat this uncertainty, the Fed needed to pump money back into the system. The most obvious way to do this was another round of quantitative easing. Every member of the FOMC agreed with the idea, according to minutes of the call.

As the Fed finalized its plans, Powell traveled to Denver to speak at an economics conference. He took the chance, during his speech, to announce what the Fed was about to do. "At some point, we will begin increasing our securities holdings to maintain an appropriate level of reserves. That time is now upon us," Powell said. "I want to emphasize that growth of our balance sheet for reserve management purposes should, in no way, be confused with the large-scale asset purchase programs that we deployed after the financial crisis."

Powell was saying that the Fed was going to do something that appeared to be quantitative easing but was not, in fact, quantitative easing. The key difference seemed to be the Fed's intent. The Fed wasn't pumping money into bank reserve accounts to stimulate the economy

this time. It was just doing it to keep reserve levels high, for maintenance. About a week later, the Fed announced it would buy about $60
billion worth of Treasury bonds per month. Between September 2019
and February 2020, the Fed created about 413 billion new dollars in
the banking system, judging by the increase of its balance sheet. This
was one of the largest financial interventions of any kind in many years.

The traders on Wall Street nicknamed the new program NQE,
short for "non-QE." But they had no illusions about what was happening. The Fed Put was being expanded and enmeshed more deeply into
markets. The deployment of overnight repo loans showed that the Fed
would not tolerate dangerous flare-ups in that market. The hedge funds
acted on this insight, borrowing more money and using it to buy shares
of stock. A Goldman Sachs index showed that debt-fueled hedge-fund
trades rose sharply after the repo bailout and the dawn of NQE. In
February 2020 alone, the leverage ratio of hedge funds (meaning their
debt compared to assets) rose by 5 percent, the biggest increase in years.

On January 13, 2020, the Dow Jones Industrial Average broke
above 29,000 points, marking a record high.

By early 2020, Thomas Hoenig had migrated away from the center of
American economic power and decision-making. There wasn't exactly
a booming market for Hoenig's political philosophy about the banking system or market structures. After he left the FDIC, Hoenig started
spending a lot more time around his house in Kansas City. He wrote a
series of academic lectures on the financial system, and wrote periodic
opinion pieces about banking and monetary policy. He got a job as a
senior fellow at the Mercatus Center, a libertarian-leaning think tank
based at George Mason University, in suburban Washington, D.C.

Hoenig's perch at Mercatus reflected the fractured public discussion about the Federal Reserve. Most people who criticized the Fed still
tended to be conservative. Many of the bank's prominent defenders and
former officials migrated to the liberal-leaning think tank the Brookings

Institution, which gave fellowships to Ben Bernanke, Janet Yellen, and other former Fed employees. Bernanke joked that his hallway at Brookings housed the new FOMC, meaning the "Former Open Market Committee." Brookings hosted events in downtown D.C. featuring Jay Powell and other luminaries. Hoenig's views, by contrast, rarely seemed to capture headlines.

On Monday, March 2, Hoenig traveled a few minutes from his house to a local shopping district known as Brookside, a row of quaint one-story retail outlets along the moderately busy thoroughfare of Sixty-Third Street. There was a dime store, an ice cream shop, and a drugstore that the locals still called McDaniel's, even though it had been bought out by the CVS chain many years prior. Hoenig went to a Starbucks that was a relatively recent addition to the neighborhood. He grabbed a table near a window and took off his coat. He was there to meet with a journalist, who was reporting on the Fed's repo intervention. Maybe Hoenig was in a hurry that day, maybe he was overly busy, or maybe something personal was stressing him out. But Hoenig didn't seem like his usual placid self. He seemed irritable. His irritation became evident as he started talking about the repo bailout. The galling thing about it wasn't just its size or scope, or what it said about the fragility of modern financial markets. It was also the fact that nobody seemed to know it had happened. The extraordinary had become routine. The distorted had become ordinary. The massive bailout had become the tool of daily maintenance.

"They're trapped!" he said about the Fed. What he meant was that the Fed was trapped by its own past actions. It was committed to a level of intervention and money creation that would have once seemed wildly improbable. This was what it took to keep basic markets functioning. Hoenig had been portrayed, during 2010, as an inflexible person, even an unsophisticated person, when he voted against quantitative easing and 0 percent rates. One of his chief warnings was that quantitative easing would be very difficult to undo once it started. Almost a decade later, the difficulty was apparent.

This state of affairs was obscured by the very distortions it created. In early 2020, the economy looked fine from the outside thanks to the dazzling effects of cheap debt, rising asset prices, and a reach for yield that propped up risky investments like corporate junk bonds. It was true that the unemployment rate was at the lowest level in decades, at an astoundingly small 3.5 percent. But the job boom was just only starting to nudge higher after many years of stagnating. The real prosperity was being enjoyed at the highest peaks of the economic system by the people who owned most of the assets. When hedge funds borrowed money and plowed it into the stock market, the daily reports on cable news seemed quite cheerful: "The Dow closed at a record high today . . ." Who could complain?

In retrospect, Tom Hoenig's trip to Starbucks seemed like an especially poignant moment. He didn't know it at the time, but this was the closing chapter on an epoch of American economic history. The daily headlines were about a growing viral epidemic. A novel coronavirus was quickly spreading around the world. One hundred and fifty-eight cases of coronavirus infection had been reported in the United States on March 4. This was scary, but the guests at Starbucks with Hoenig entered and left freely. Nobody wore a face mask. It was still taken for granted that people shook hands when they met. Things seemed normal. Nobody seemed aware of the fact that this was as good as things were going to be for a long, long time.

CHAPTER 14

INFECTION

(2020)

The first waves of volatility arrived on U.S. shores in January 2020, with the strange news coming from the industrial city of Wuhan, China. The first dispatches had a science fiction quality to them: A mysterious pneumonia-like disease prompted the Communist authorities to shut down train service and flights to and from a city of 11 million people. Cable news shows carried weird images of backhoes and cranes and construction sites where China's government was building new hospitals, apparently to accommodate the infected. The financial types on Wall Street tried to digest this news and figure out what it meant for the economy. Jim Bianco, an investor in Chicago, grew alarmed in early January. He was worried that the virus might shut down China's gargantuan manufacturing sector, which was the workhorse of the world. If Chinese factories were closed for months, it could interrupt the supply of medicine, iPads, toys, and television sets. It might even precipitate a recession. What seemed to concern Bianco even more was the general attitude on Wall Street, where the virus was treated like an afterthought. People seemed to believe that the virus would be contained quickly, like the SARS epidemic in 2003.

Then very bad news came out of Italy. The novel coronavirus was detected in the northern part of the country, and was spreading quickly. On February 24, the Italian government ordered people in the north to cease travel and remain at home. They called it a lockdown, and it was a shocking thing at the time. More people started to worry about the virus and wonder if the problem might spill far outside of China. On February 26, a U.S. health official turned this concern into a panic. Her name was Nancy Messonnier, and she worked at the U.S. Centers for Disease Control and Prevention. During a conference call with reporters, Messonnier said that the virus was spreading quickly, humans had no natural immunity to it, and there was no vaccine. The United States was probably going to have to do things like close schools and keep people at home. "I understand this whole situation may seem overwhelming and that disruption to everyday life may be severe," Messonnier said. "But these are things that people need to start thinking about now."

The traders on Wall Street did start thinking about them now. An investor named Scott Minerd joined the ranks of very worried people like Jim Bianco. Minerd was the chief investment officer of Guggenheim Investments, which managed about $246 billion in assets. Minerd had a lot of money on the line, and had to figure out how to position it in the face of a viral epidemic. People like Minerd and Bianco saw a similar picture when they examined the American economy after a decade of ZIRP and QE. Corporate debt levels were at a record high, giving companies very little room to maneuver in the face of a downturn. Assets across the board—from bonds to stocks to commercial real estate—were "priced to perfection," meaning that they were trading at the very upper limits that could be justified under the most optimistic scenarios. And the investment community had for years been pushing its money in one direction, toward risk, way out onto the thin ice of the yield curve.

This system was not well positioned for what appeared to be coming.

"Corporate America started out from a place of being highly leveraged and being very illiquid," Minerd said. The rise of cheap debt had increased fragility in the system. "At some point there was bound to be an exogenous shock to the economy—something that would be totally unexpected. And it was going to cause a massive unwinding in leverage."

On Thursday, February 27, the day after Messonnier sent her warning, the Dow Jones Industrial Average fell by nearly 1,200 points, or 4 percent. It was the worst day in the stock market since 2008.

The mood inside the New York Federal Reserve was surprisingly calm that day. The traders who worked for Lorie Logan held their usual meeting in the afternoon, where they compared notes and patched in their colleagues from Chicago on the video screen. No one seemed panicked.

The waves continued to gain strength until Sunday, March 8, when the real flood damage began. That afternoon, the government of Saudi Arabia announced it would increase oil production, even as oil prices were falling. This was cataclysmic for global oil markets, which were already glutted by excess oil from American frackers. Oil prices crashed. People in the financial world did not sleep well that night because they knew what was coming. Jim Bianco, in Chicago, realized that there were big differences between the 2003 SARS outbreak and the coronavirus outbreak of 2020. The new outbreak wasn't just worse. It was hitting at a moment when the markets were extraordinarily fragile. "This was a bubble in search of a pin. And we found a big pin," Bianco said.

On Monday morning, the stock market opened and promptly crashed so hard it triggered an automatic shutdown, halting trading for fifteen minutes. This was the first time the trigger had been activated since 1997. Over the next two weeks, the shutdown trigger would be activated three more times. The news about the stock market was all very bad, but it did not reflect the full nature of the financial crisis that started to gather strength on that Monday morning. The real crisis was in the market for U.S. Treasurys.

Ten-year Treasury bonds are the bedrock of modern finance. On the morning of Monday, March 9, the interest rates on these Treasury bonds convulsed in ways that were previously unthinkable.

The previous Friday, 10-year Treasury yields had been 0.76 percent. On Monday morning they plunged to 0.31 percent. Throughout the day they rose again to 0.6 percent. These numbers seem tiny to outsiders, but they were tiny in the way that when a street buckles during an earthquake, it only heaves upward by five feet above sea level, then ends the day collapsed ten feet below sea level. To the people walking on that street, these changes are acutely noticeable. The Treasury bill volatility felt the same way to financial traders. As the *Financial Times* later put it: "Such turmoil simply shouldn't be possible in the Treasury market, analysts say."

The turmoil largely escaped public notice for several reasons. The Treasury market wasn't as widely discussed as the stock markets. And the Treasury market seized up at the moment when American society shut down. That was the week when the NBA suspended its season, and the NCAA canceled its March Madness tournament. Most important, schools began to shut their doors, leaving frantic parents to figure out what to do with their kids. Home offices and remote classrooms were arranged on kitchen tables for the first time.

Inside the Federal Reserve, the Treasury market collapse was an urgent concern. It made the repo market seizure of September seem like a placid event. The Fed analysts could see what the turmoil signified. The financial world was panicking. Everyone was seeking to hold the safest, most easily tradeable thing imaginable: cash. People didn't even want to hold Treasurys, considered the safest investment on Earth. They wanted to liquidate everything, including Treasurys, to gather whatever piles of cash they could obtain. This happens when people believe the entire system is on the brink of collapse. This rush to get cash intensified each day. On Thursday the truly unthinkable happened. Some Treasury bills couldn't even find a price, meaning that no one was willing to buy them and trade their cash for them. The broader consequences of this liquidation were enormous and immediate.

The hedge funds that had loaded up on basis trade bets were imperiled. They would need to unload whatever assets they had to raise cash, at the very moment that everyone else was doing the same thing. The hedge funds seemed to have drawn down some of their basis trade bets since September, but the level of such bets was still historically high. And these weren't the only hedge-fund bets that were going bad. A class of hedge funds called "risk parity funds" had borrowed money to make bets on futures contracts for things like bonds, stocks, and commodities. They allocated their bets in a way that was supposed to reflect the relative risk of each asset. But the simultaneous—and once-unthinkable—downturn in stocks and Treasurys scrambled all the equations about relative risk. The risk-parity hedge funds found themselves in a squeeze, forced to find cash at the moment when the entire market was hoarding cash.

Powell responded to this crisis by authorizing the Fed to respond with nearly unprecedented force.

In September, when the repo market had collapsed, the Fed shocked markets by offering $75 billion in repo loans. On Thursday, March 12, the Fed announced that it would offer $500 billion in repo loans, and would offer $1 trillion in repo loans the following day. The Fed was offering $1.5 trillion in immediate assistance to Wall Street. It did virtually nothing to help. The Dow continued to plunge and closed the day down 2,300 points, or 10 percent.

On Friday, things were hectic at the Federal Reserve. The Eccles Building would soon close down, and the Fed staff and board of governors would be sent home to work remotely. But before that happened, Jay Powell agreed to hold one last emergency meeting. The American financial system had developed a certain muscle memory by this point. When the volatility got out of control, all attention turned to the Federal Reserve. The central bank would meet on Sunday afternoon to figure out how to respond.

The massive polished table at the center of the Fed's boardroom gets quite crowded during FOMC meetings. It's considered a status symbol to be seated at the table during meetings, rather than occupying a chair along the outside wall. As the Fed created new divisions and senior positions over the years, the crowd at the boardroom table grew larger until they were crowded close together with all their binders, papers, and cups of coffee. This made the meeting of Sunday, March 15, all the more striking. The table was virtually empty. Two large video monitors had been erected at either side of the table, and the faces of FOMC board members began to flicker onto the screens as the meeting began. The few staff members who still arrived at the Eccles Building sat at the big table, arranged several feet apart from one another. One participant said it was like sitting in a haunted house.

The New York Fed staff opened the meeting with an overview of economic conditions. Not surprisingly, this was a horror show. The Treasury markets, bond markets, oil markets, and stock markets were all in free fall. The staff focused on three markets that were particularly troubling. The first was corporate debt markets, which appeared to be grinding to a halt, although things hadn't yet gotten as bad as they were in 2008. There was growing stress in markets for commercial mortgage-backed securities, or CMBSs, the loan portfolios that the analyst John Flynn discovered were based on overoptimistic assumptions when he went through all those spreadsheets. The second market they discussed was the Treasury market, which had suffered an "acute decline" in trading. Finally, they discussed the markets for short-term corporate loans, or short-term commercial paper, as it is generally called. These loans were supposed to be traded almost as easily as cash, but these markets were also seizing up.

The FOMC members began to discuss what they ought to do about this. When faced with a viral pandemic, the Fed had very limited tools at its disposal. The Fed could not give money to hospitals, nor to people who were being laid off or told to stay at home. The Fed could not slow the virus's passage nor help produce the materials for face masks, which were in such direly short supply. When considering such problems, the Fed could look to its own past actions. One of the lessons the Fed took from the 2008 crisis was that it was better to move faster and bigger. "They moved too slowly in 2008," said Claudia Sahm, a former senior economist at the Fed who participated in a series of "lessons learned" studies inside the bank that examined the 2008 response. When the Fed did break through the zero bound, and employed tools like quantitative easing, this made it easier to do so again. Now the Fed had a suite of tools to use and had practice using them. And the theory was that the quicker these tools were employed, the better things would be. "The best opportunity that you have to short-circuit a recession, and make it less severe, is right at the start," Sahm said. This thinking appears to have become predominant inside the Fed's leadership team. That Sunday in March, Jay Powell and his team proposed a sweeping set of actions.

Powell's Fed would do virtually everything that Ben Bernanke's had done in 2008 and 2009, but this time did it in one weekend, rather than over several months. It slashed interest rates to near zero. It opened up their "swap lines" with foreign central banks, flooding them with dollars in exchange for their local currencies (this was important because so much global debt is denominated in dollars). It executed a new round of quantitative easing, worth a total of $700 billion, and bought the bonds at a faster rate than before. The Fed would buy $80 billion worth of bonds before the following Tuesday, meaning that it pushed as much money into the banking system in forty-eight hours as it had done in the span of a month during earlier rounds of QE. It gave forward guidance, promising to keep rates pinned near zero as long as necessary. And it launched all of this in one day.

The FOMC voted almost unanimously to pass the emergency actions. One regional bank president, Loretta Mester of the Cleveland

Fed, voted against the plan because she thought the interest rate should have been dropped only as low as 0.5 percent rather than 0.1 percent.

When the meeting adjourned, Powell hosted a conference call for journalists, announcing the emergency set of measures. His voice was tinny, as if he were calling from overseas, and the whole thing had a very disorganized feel to it. The scale of the Fed's actions was meant to soothe investors, but it appeared instead to terrify them. It was unnerving to hear Powell's voice on Sunday afternoon, an effect that was amplified by the fact that the FOMC had been scheduled to meet the following Tuesday. If the Fed couldn't wait forty-eight hours to do what it was doing, then things must be really dire. Once again, on a Sunday evening, financial traders experienced surges of adrenaline and started making frantic calls to rearrange their holdings in light of the bad news. They knew what would come when the trading week began.

The next morning, markets opened in free fall. The Dow fell by 13 percent. That was the Monday when the financial crisis, which had started gathering power a week earlier, fully engulfed the economy.

The week of March 16 was when people on Wall Street saw things happen that they didn't think were possible. Scott Minerd, the chief investment officer at Guggenheim, was amazed when he saw the market for Treasury bills essentially freeze. There had been a similar collapse in the mortgage bond market, back in 2008, which led to a global panic and collapse. But to see it happen in the $20 trillion market for ultrasafe Treasurys wasn't just scary. It was difficult to comprehend.

When somebody like Minerd looks at a debt market, they look at something called the "spread." The spread is the difference between a seller's price for something and what the buyer is willing to pay. If a person offers to sell a bond for $10, but buyers are willing to pay only $9.90, then the spread is 10 cents, or 1 percent. Typically, the spread on a Treasury bill is way less than 1 cent. That's because there are so many buyers and sellers, conducting so many trades, which makes finding a price relatively easy. A Treasury spread is typically something like 0.031 percent or 0.016 percent. During the March crisis, Minerd saw the spread on some Treasurys widen to as high as 4 percent. At some points, the screen that should have shown bids and offers on Treasurys just went blank, meaning that no agreed-upon price could be found.

This chaotic breakdown filtered out to every kind of debt. The spreads on corporate debt, which is riskier than Treasury debt, began to widen quickly. "At the height of the thing, the bid/offer spread was, in some cases, thirty percent" on corporate debt, Minerd said. "That is unthinkable."

In Chicago, the trader Jim Bianco was basically locked in his home with his family and his dogs. The city felt haunted. Weekday traffic slowed to a pace typical during the early morning hours on a Sunday. The financial markets felt similarly shaken and hollowed out.

Bianco was very concerned about the health of the big banks, which were the core of the financial system. The stock value of the big banks fell by 48 percent between the stock market's peak in February and March 23. Shares of JPMorgan Chase, the biggest of the big banks, were down by 43 percent during that time. "Really, what we're looking at is destruction in the banking industry that is maybe even bigger than '08," Bianco said. The banks hadn't failed, and they still had a lot of cash in their reserve accounts. But Bianco and others could see that their failure was on the horizon, and the horizon was not too far off.

On Monday, March 16, the eight biggest banks made a joint announcement that all of them would step forward to take out emergency loans from the Fed's "discount window." These banks had bogged down the discussions over living wills and stress tests for years, but they acted with rapidity now. In the past, banks avoided loans from the Fed's emergency lending discount window because taking the loans signaled weakness. By stepping forward all together, the banks shielded one another from the stigma of emergency borrowing. The banks said that they didn't need the money immediately, but had made the declaration to keep the option open if they needed it. Bianco estimated that if bank stocks declined by another 15 percent, then bank failures would begin.

The turmoil revealed the extraordinary weakness that record levels of debt had woven into the fabric of corporate America. Big companies weren't just desperate to get cash to keep their doors open and their lights on during a shutdown. They were desperate to get cash because they had to make regular payments on leveraged loans and corporate bonds that they'd taken out at a record pace over the previous decade, encouraged at every step by the Federal Reserve. Corporate bonds had the unforgiving structure that Powell would have learned about during his days at Dillon, Read and Carlyle. When a company borrowed $1 million in bonds or leveraged loans, it paid only the interest on the debt until the final day it was due, at which point it had to pay off the entire debt or refinance it in the market by selling it and rolling it over. When the economy shut down, customers stayed home and the cash stopped rolling in. Companies from Southwest Airlines to AT&T to Ford had to pay the full interest payments on their full debt loads, or face default.

The fragility of the corporate debt markets created an interlocking set of crises, each linked to the next like a chain, that threatened to take down the banking system. The first, immediate crisis arose from the indebted corporations that were scrambling to get cash. In their panic, these companies rapidly drew upon a source of emergency debt called a revolving credit facility, which allowed them to quickly borrow cash up to a certain limit. After markets crashed on March 16, Southwest Airlines drew down a $1 billion revolving credit facility. The hotel operator Hilton drew down $1.75 billion. General Motors, the following week, would draw down $16 billion. This helped explain why bank stocks fell by almost half in a matter of weeks. The revolving credit facilities threatened to bleed the banks dry even as they struggled to cope with the market volatility. What was even more troubling to analysts like Jim Bianco was that the lines of credit were still probably insufficient to save many troubled corporations, meaning that the companies would draw cash out of the banks and then take it over the cliff with them when they declared bankruptcy anyway.

The second link in the chain of failures would happen when companies started to miss debt payments and default on the loans. This would force debt-rating agencies, like Standard & Poor's and Moody's, to downgrade companies like Ford, moving many into the realm of junk debt. A wave of such downgrades looked inevitable, and it carried a grave consequence for the big banks. The downgrades would be like a torpedo in the side of the CLO industry. The banks had been compiling leveraged loans into packages of CLOs and selling them to pension funds, but the banks had also been buying CLOs for themselves. In 2019 alone, the value of CLOs held by big banks jumped by 12 percent to $99.5 billion. JPMorgan had boosted its own holdings by 57 percent that year. The vast majority of these CLO investments were held by three big banks: JPMorgan, Wells Fargo, and Citigroup, who together owned about 81 percent of all CLO bank holdings. The approaching tide of credit downgrades posed a serious risk to the value of the CLOs. Most CLOs contained a contract clause that allowed them to hold only so much junk debt. If more of the leveraged loans inside the CLOs were downgraded, then this would breach the standards of the contracts, and the CLOs would have to start selling off their junk debt and replace it, or write down the value of the whole CLO.

The prospect of trying to sell junk debt was sobering. Investors were already dumping assets in a stampede of sales. One financial trader, who granted an interview during this period on the condition of anonymity, sounded shaken after his day at work. He was one of those jaded, even cynical Wall Street types, who prided himself on being unsentimental about turmoil in the marketplace. But in mid-March, he had a real tinge of fear in his voice. He said that big investors were selling off assets with a level of desperation that was terrifying. He likened it to watching people sell an apartment building for $100. While it was thrilling to buy an apartment building for $100, it was also unsettling because of what it signified. A mass liquidation was under way and it heralded even worse things ahead.

Few chairmen of the Federal Reserve were in a better position to understand what was going on than Powell. His long career could be considered an extended training course in the modern financial system and its shortcomings. He had personally helped build and sell big structures of leveraged loans and corporate bonds. He had overseen the division of the Treasury Department that auctioned off government debt. And he had warned for years about the systemic fragility that the Fed was encouraging. In retrospect, one of Powell's warnings took on particular significance. In 2013, he had predicted how hard it would be for the Fed to contain the damage when asset prices corrected. "In any case, we ought to have a low level of confidence that we can regulate or manage our way around the kind of large, dynamic market event that becomes increasingly likely, thanks to our policy," he had said.

The emergency actions Powell initiated on March 15 were a show of overwhelming force, by any standard. They were more far-reaching, larger, and faster-paced than any previous intervention ever taken by the central bank. But by Friday evening, March 20, a week of financial carnage proved that the Fed's actions weren't enough to stem the panic.

By this point, Powell was already designing the next phase of the Fed's bailout, which would push the central bank into areas it had never been to before. The bank would, for the first time, directly purchase corporate bonds, CLOs, and even corporate junk debt. This would expand the Fed Put to entirely new realms of the economic system, changing the debt markets from that point forward. This phase of the plan was not debated in formal FOMC meetings, which were transcribed for history. It was hashed out during a series of frantic phone calls between Jay Powell, John Williams at the New York Fed, and Fed officials like Governor Lael Brainard.

But Powell wasn't just talking to people inside the central bank.

Many of his calls were routed to the U.S. Department of the Treasury. If the Fed was going to expand its reach where it needed to, it needed approval from the Treasury Department. This happened to be a lucky break. The department was run by one of Powell's strongest allies in Washington: Steven Mnuchin.

CHAPTER 15

WINNERS AND LOSERS

(2020)

Steven Mnuchin was quick to point out that he had personally recommended Jay Powell as the next Fed chairman, when President Trump was reviewing candidates. Such a recommendation went a long way in the Trump administration. A good word from someone like Mnuchin could be decisive in Trump's decision making; Mnuchin was one of the few cabinet secretaries who served throughout Trump's full administration. While Trump had been impressed by Janet Yellen, Mnuchin had a stronger bond with Jay Powell. Both men had a long background in the world of private equity and leveraged loans. They spoke the same vocabulary of banking and deal-making, and had a shared sensibility about the world. After Powell got the job, Mnuchin and Powell had lunch at least once a week.

Mnuchin, like Powell, also had a granular understanding of markets and trading. He got his professional start at Goldman Sachs, where his father had been an influential partner. After nine years at the firm, Mnuchin also made partner. He left Goldman in 2002 with company stock worth about $46 million. Mnuchin then joined a private equity fund called ESL Investments, then started his own hedge fund called Dune Capital. Mnuchin made a killing after the housing market crash of 2008 when he organized a group of investors, including Michael Dell (founder of the computer company) and George Soros. They bought a failed bank in California called IndyMac, which had been a major provider of failed home loans. They renamed the company OneWest and went on a home foreclosure spree, eventually selling the bank for $3.4 billion in 2015. Mnuchin knew how to manage sensitive situations and how to deal with problematic investors and clients. He also had a preternatural ability to blend into the background of the Trump administration while also retaining influence. Mnuchin could do this, in part, because he excelled at doing what Trump hated doing most, which was getting involved in details.

When the coronavirus pandemic crushed the American economy, it was Mnuchin, not Donald Trump, who took the lead role in negotiating with Congress on behalf of the White House. This was a delicate job, since the House was controlled by Democrats and the Senate controlled by Republicans. Mnuchin talked frequently with Nancy Pelosi, the Democratic Speaker of the House, building a bridge between the White House and the opposition party. Congress had become a graveyard of ideas, ambition, and public purpose during the administration of Donald Trump. After passing the tax cut and a criminal justice reform law, Congress had done little else. Senate Majority Leader Mitch McConnell focused most of his energy on appointing federal judges, which required only a bare majority of Republican votes. Nobody had big hopes for Congress when it came time to address the pandemic. Trump encouraged Congress to pass some kind of relief bill, without offering much in the way of guidance or support. Trump spent hours of his day performing manic monologues in front of the television cameras. By March 18, Congress had passed two relief bills totaling roughly $230 billion, which were wholly inadequate for the problem. A familiar rhythm developed in which promising signs of action would dissipate as soon as any plans for action moved to the poisonous atmosphere of the Senate, where McConnell helped suffocate them.

This left America to depend upon, yet again, the Federal Reserve. But the Fed could not act alone if it was going to do the things that Powell was considering. During this period of March, Mnuchin and Powell talked on the phone roughly twenty times a day. There was a legal reason that Powell needed to talk with the Treasury secretary. Congress had limited the Fed's emergency powers after the crash of 2008, when the Fed extended loans that were arranged quickly and with little oversight. When Congress passed the Dodd-Frank reform law of 2010, it included new restrictions on the Fed that required the bank to get approval from the U.S. Department of the Treasury for emergency actions that were not spelled out in the Fed's charter. When Congress created the Fed in 1913, lawmakers were cautious in defining the scope of the central bank's powers. They were just as careful in setting strict limits on what the bank could *not* do as they were in defining what it could do. The Fed was denied the power to lend directly to corporations, or to take on risky debt like leveraged loans. This was designed in part so the Fed could not pick winners and losers in the economy by directly subsidizing some industries over others. The Fed arguably went outside this stricture in 2008, when it arranged loans for failing investment firms like Bear Stearns. But Dodd-Frank gave the Treasury secretary clear oversight over such actions.

This is why Powell had a copy of Dodd-Frank on his desk when he started working from home in March. Over the weekend of March 20, he finalized the details on a complex rescue package that would include several interlocking bailouts, each targeting different parts of the financial system. This would be the largest, most far-reaching, and most consequential intervention in the history of the Federal Reserve. It would change the central bank's role in the American economy for at least decades to come, and dramatically increase the Fed's financial footprint. The package was arranged during phone calls between Powell and

Mnuchin, Fed governors, and senior Fed staff members. Unlike formal FOMC meetings, these conversations were private and not transcribed for the public to review. The full FOMC did not vote on the program once it was finalized. Because the program was an emergency lending effort, it only required the approval of a handful of members on the board of governors.

One participant in these discussions described the process as being the opposite of creative. The Fed wasn't trying to do anything innovative or novel. It was just figuring out which corners of the financial world were engulfed in flames, and then pointing the Fed's flood of new money in that direction. The Fed decided to resurrect a certain legal tool that it pioneered during the 2008 financial crisis, called a special-purpose vehicle, or SPV. An SPV was basically a shell company that allowed the Fed to get around the limits placed on its lending authority, using the U.S. Department of the Treasury as a partner. Many of the phone calls in March were between the Fed's lawyers in Washington and the Fed's financial team in New York, which would create the new SPVs. Each SPV was basically a company, formed jointly between the Fed and the Treasury Department. The company was registered in the state of Delaware, at a cost of about ten dollars. The Treasury Department would invest taxpayer cash in each SPV, and then the Fed would use that cash as seed money to start making loans, lending as much as ten dollars for every dollar invested by the Treasury. This taxpayer money is what allowed the Fed to go outside its usual limits and start buying risky debt and extending loans to new parts of the economy. If there were any losses, the losses would be paid for first by the taxpayers, which helped the Fed make the legal argument that it was not, in fact, making risky loans. Powell would cite this fact as a justification for the programs. The Fed might be taking on more risk and expanding its mission, but the Treasury Department had oversight of the whole thing, which meant that there was some level of democratic oversight.

The Fed created three important SPVs by the end of that weekend.

The first two SPVs would allow the Fed to buy corporate debt. The motivation behind this was obvious. The Fed saw what was coming in the chain of failures as corporations defaulted on their loans, damaging the banks and hollowing out the value of CLOs. To prevent this calamity, the Fed expanded the Fed Put into an entirely new area of finance. People who traded stocks now assumed that the Fed would step in with a rescue package if the stock market ever crashed. Now people who traded corporate bonds and leveraged loans would have the same assurance. This had consequences that reverberated far beyond the corporate debt-trading desks. The interest rates on corporate debt were supposed to measure the underlying risk of that debt. Risky companies had to pay very high interest rates, while safe companies paid low rates. Now that the Fed had stepped in and become a major buyer of corporate debt, providing a floor for the market, it changed the very nature of interest rates on the debt. Those rates didn't just reflect the risk of the company, but also reflected the Fed's appetite to buy the bond. Critically, once the Fed bought corporate bonds, it could never undo the action. The eager eyes on Wall Street would always remember what they had seen. Every time the Fed intervened, its future intervention was assumed.

Perhaps the most ground-breaking SPV was the third one, which would buy debt of midsize businesses that were too small to get leveraged loans or corporate bonds. This program was wildly experimental. The Fed lawyers who constructed it only had the broad outlines in place when the program was announced. They planned to fill in the details later. The guiding principle of the program was that it would move the Fed's reach beyond the confines of Wall Street. Instead of using the primary dealers to implement this plan, the Fed would use regional banks as its conduit. The banks would give loans to small business, and the Fed would buy 95 percent of the loan, letting the regional bank hold the remainder. The Fed called this program the Main Street Lending Program.

The final piece of the rescue plan was not a new SPV, but a massive influx of money in the form of a large-scale, near-permanent quantitative easing program. The parameters of this new round of QE would be left intentionally vague. The Fed would create as much money as it decided was necessary, for as long as it was needed. The scale was unprecedented. In one week, the Fed bought $625 billion in bonds, more than it purchased during the entire program that Tom Hoenig voted against.

By Sunday evening, March 22, the plan was largely pulled together. But there was one small problem. The plan called for the Treasury Department to invest about $454 billion into the new SPVs, which would enable the Fed to loan about $4 trillion in new debt. But Congress had not yet passed a relief bill that would authorize the use of $454 billion of taxpayer money.

Powell and his team decided they would not wait on Congress. They would announce the new SPVs on Monday morning, March 23, before the markets opened.

The Fed's announcement on that morning was radical, and it was enough to stop the panic. In roughly ninety days, the Fed would create $3 trillion. That was as much money as the Fed would have printed in roughly three hundred years at its normal pace, before the 2008 financial crisis.

There was virtually no public opposition to the Fed's actions, and Powell expanded the Fed's efforts. Within less than three weeks of its first rescue package, the Fed announced new actions that built on what it had already done. Once again, the plan was not voted upon by the full FOMC, and there are no transcripts available to determine the thinking behind the new initiatives, parts of which were approved by a unanimous, closed-door vote on April 8.*

The Fed announced on April 9 that it wouldn't only buy corporate

---

*The vote was taken by Powell, his vice chairman Richard Clarida, and the governors Randal Quarles, Lael Brainard, and Michelle Bowman.

bonds—it would also buy even riskier bonds, which were rated as junk debt. The junk bond purchases would not be unlimited. The Fed would only buy debt that had been rated as investment-grade before the pandemic. These bonds were called fallen angels on Wall Street, and they included debt from companies like Ford Motor Co. By purchasing the debt of fallen angels, the Fed was also helping out the much larger pools of even riskier corporate junk, such as Rexnord's, that already existed. When the debt of fallen angels crashed down the ratings scale, it would displace these other loans and make them far less attractive to purchase. The Fed had stopped this potential cascade.

Also that day, the Fed updated a separate new program (called TALF, for "term asset-backed-securities loan facility") so that it could directly purchase, for the first time, big chunks of CLO debt, which was composed of leveraged loans. This was a significant extension of the Fed's safety net, and it played a large role in quelling the anxiety around the hundreds of billions of dollars' worth of CLOs that faced loan write-downs and breaches of their standard caps. It also helped the big banks that owned billions in CLO debt.

All of this barely penetrated the public conversation, or the cable news landscape. The reasons were predictable: Everything was cloaked in language that was obtuse and incomprehensible. As the Fed put it: The SMCCF* was amended and expanded, while the TALF added a new asset class to support the flow of credit to households and businesses. Not thrilling stuff. And even less compelling on a day when 35,000 new coronavirus cases were reported (compared to 201 on the same day of the preceding month) and states were closing down restaurants and stores.

But to people who actually traded bonds, and who packaged and sold them, the news was shocking. It was one of those things that

*The Secondary Market Corporate Credit Facility, as the Fed called one of its corporate bond buying programs.

divided history: There was the way things worked before the SPVs were created, and the way things worked afterward.

"Fundamentally we have now socialized credit risk. And we have forever changed the nature of how our economy functions," said Scott Minerd, the Fed advisor and senior trader at Guggenheim Investments. "The Fed has made it clear that prudent investing will not be tolerated."

Just the announcement of the Fed's program was enough to soothe bond dealers and CLO operators. The Fed bought only a tiny fraction of available corporate bonds, not nearly enough to prop up the entire market, but it had telegraphed that it would be there if the trouble resumed, and its pocketbook was bottomless. This was evidence of the program's success, in the eyes of its creators. Steven Mnuchin, at the Treasury, was particularly pleased.

"The day we jointly announced that transaction—and the commitment to it—that unlocked the entire corporate bond market," Mnuchin later said.

These actions, as dramatic as they were, directly benefited only a small group of people: those who owned assets or those who made a living trading them. But the financial crisis the Fed was fighting was a different thing than the much broader crisis of the coronavirus pandemic. The virus was inflicting incalculable damage across American society, in areas the Fed could not address. The hospital system was overwhelmed. Emergency room nurses wore improvised protective gear made out of garbage bags. The virus spread more quickly because many workers who got sick did not have paid sick leave, so they stayed on the job and infected others. State governors had to compete with one another to obtain necessary supplies, such as viral testing kits. Governor Larry Hogan of Maryland smuggled a planeload of test kits from South Korea, which were kept under armed guard when they arrived. Restaurants, theaters, stores, and schools closed down, in order to slow the infection. But while they were closed, the federal government failed entirely to implement any kind of unified response to the virus. This failure left businesses and schools with a terrible choice in late spring: They could either reopen, with the pandemic worse than before, or remain shut. During this period, roughly 22 million American jobs disappeared, creating the worst jobs crisis since the Great Depression. The central bank could not address these things, and for many years central bank leaders had complained that their counterparts in Congress did not do enough to address the many deep problems that afflicted the economy. Jay Powell had echoed these thoughts, and had launched key parts of the March rescue package without waiting for Congress.

But just days after the Fed's groundbreaking SPVs were announced, Congress would step into the breach. It would pass one of the largest, most expensive bills in modern history, called the CARES Act. This was the chance for Mnuchin, Trump, Pelosi, and McConnell to show that they could solve big problems, and that the U.S. government could lend a hand when it was needed.

The CARES Act authorized $2 trillion in spending to counteract the pandemic, including $454 billion in taxpayer money to fund the Fed's SPVs. The part of the CARES Act that got the most attention was the roughly $292 billion chunk of the spending that went directly to people. There was good reason for this spending to get the attention that it did. The impact was immediate and beneficial for the millions of people who received it. And the government had never truly done something like this before, sending direct payments to people regardless of their previous level of tax payments, or even of their current level of need. These direct benefits were coupled with more benefits for those who had been directly affected by the lockdowns. Unemployment insurance benefits, administered by the states, were boosted by $600 a week through July. That benefit was partially extended that summer, although at a lower level.

The spending that went straight into people's bank accounts was the most visible part of the CARES Act. But it was a relatively small part of the overall relief spending approved by Congress, which included the CARES Act and three smaller bills. Over half of all that money was aimed at businesses, according to an analysis by *The Washington Post* based on data from the Committee for a Responsible Federal Budget. A vanishingly small share of the $4 trillion was allocated to address the public health crisis created by the pandemic, or to slow the virus's spread.

The largest chunk of the money, totaling $670 billion, funded an emergency loan program called the Paycheck Protection Program, or PPP. The idea was that the businesses would get a PPP loan, keep their employees, and then the loan would be forgiven when the businesses reopened and everyone went back to work. This money could have potentially helped a huge and diverse population of business owners who had suffered terribly during the long and punishing lockdowns. And it did help millions of businesses. But more than half of all the PPP money went to just 5 percent of the companies that received the loans. Even that figure understated the narrowness of the impact. Fully 25 percent of all the PPP went to 1 percent of the companies. These were the big law firms and national food chains, which got the maximum PPP amount of $10 million. Those beneficiaries included the Boston Market restaurant chain and the high-powered law firm of Boies Schiller Flexner. An analysis by the Federal Reserve and others found that the PPP program saved about 2.3 million jobs at a cost of $286,000 per job, after President Trump claimed it would save or support 50 million jobs.

About $651 billion of the CARES Act was in the form of tax breaks for businesses, which were often complicated to obtain. This meant that the tax benefits went largely to the big companies that could hire the best tax lawyers. The Cheesecake Factory restaurant chain, for example, claimed a tax break of $50 million, even as it furloughed 41,000 people. About $250 billion of the tax breaks were given to any business in any industry, without regard to how much they might have been hurt by the pandemic. People who owned businesses were given tax breaks worth $135 billion, meaning that about 43,000 people who earned more than

$1 million a year each got a benefit worth $1.6 million. By and large, these billions of dollars were quietly absorbed into corporate treasuries and personal bank accounts around the country. The wildly unequal distribution of the money was not made public until months later, after *The Washington Post* won an open-records lawsuit that made the information public.

The unequal distribution of federal aid, from both Congress and the Federal Reserve, exposed the underlying structure of America's economic system in 2020. As the dollars flowed through the nation's financial plumbing, they illuminated which parts of that system worked quite well, and which did not. The system that the Fed used to deliver money to the primary dealers, for example, worked with the speed, smoothness, and efficiency of a hypermodern and well-maintained network. The money for everyone else migrated through a neglected, leaky network that failed to deliver the relief that was advertised. One reason the PPP loans failed to make their way to small businesses in need was that the loans were processed through the Small Business Administration, which was supposed to work with participating banks. The SBA was a sleepy agency that had never administered an emergency program of this scale. Not surprisingly, the companies that fared the best in this system were the companies that could best navigate a complex and overwhelmed bureaucracy.

Inside the Trump administration, the intervention was seen as a success. Steven Mnuchin, for one, wanted to get the emergency money out the door quickly, even if some of it went to companies or people that might not need it. He didn't want the ideally perfect program to be the enemy of the realistically good one. Mnuchin knew that some of the money was misdirected—he publicly chastised the Los Angeles Lakers for taking a $4.6 million loan, calling it "outrageous." But Mnuchin believed the rapid response, combining the fiscal spending with the monetary stimulus, was the only thing that staved off a worse disaster.

"Never in the history of the Fed has there been coordinated action with the Treasury and the Fed, the way there was in March and April of that year. Nothing in the financial crisis comes even close to this," Mnuchin recalled later. "I think that if we had collectively not done what we did—certain actions we did together and certain actions [the Fed] did independently—I think we would have had a Great Depression."

There was a growing sensitivity inside the Federal Reserve about the central bank's public image. Jay Powell led an effort to portray the bank as a vehicle to help the middle class. In 2019, before the pandemic, Powell had gone on a "listening tour," to hear the concerns and ideas of working people, and to discuss how the bank might help them. There was a strategic reason for this. Senior leaders at the Fed knew that it was unpopular to help the very rich while everyone else languished. The Fed's bailouts in 2008 and 2009 played a formative role in animating both the Tea Party movement on the right and the Occupy Wall Street movement on the left. The conservative backlash was particularly intense and led to strident calls for the Fed to be audited, more tightly regulated, or even disbanded altogether. This was recognized by those who participated in the Fed's internal "lessons learned" sessions, including the former senior economist Claudia Sahm. "The Fed always gets slammed. Because it's easy. No one understands what the heck they are. They seem like they care about Wall Street. So they will get hit," Sahm said. After the Fed announced its new programs in late March, Sahm and others were worried about the backlash. "I mean, the 'End the Fed' movement in four years, I don't even want to think about what it looks like," she said.

It was difficult to argue that buying junk bonds and CLOs would help a Starbucks barista who was out of a job. But the Fed did have one program that it could point to when it made the case that it was working hard to help people outside Wall Street. This was the Main Street Lending Program. The program was kind of like the checks sent to people under the CARES Act. It got a lot of attention. It was new, and even shocking to the people who followed the history of the Fed. It would push the Fed into the terrain of giving credit directly to companies that could tap the bond market, all across America. The Fed was breaking barriers and expanding its reach, and was doing it all to help small businesses.

The Main Street program allowed the Fed to argue that it wasn't just bailing out asset owners and hedge funds and Wall Street banks. In April, the conservative and influential economist Glenn Hubbard told *The Wall Street Journal* that the success of the Main Street program was important. It would show that the Fed could use its creative energies to help people outside of Wall Street.

"I'm really worried it's not going to work," Hubbard told the newspaper.

It did not work. The Main Street program was unwieldy, complicated, and difficult to use. It relied on local and regional banks to first make loans to small businesses, which the Fed would then buy. But the Fed also insisted that the local banks keep 5 percent of the loan value, meaning the banks had to absorb some risk. The banks were also deterred by the expense and work entailed with making loans to so many companies that might be in dire straits, with little chance of survival. The Main Street program had been built to purchase as much as $600 billion in loans. It had purchased a little more than $17 billion in loans by December, the month that it was shut down.

This didn't mean that the Fed's bailout programs were ineffective. It's just that they were effective only for certain people. The real bailout, the successful bailout, was shockingly strong and swift. This was the bailout for people who owned assets. The owners of stock were made entirely whole within about nine months of the pandemic crash. So were the owners of corporate debt. Starting in March, when the Fed intervened, the stock market began one of the largest, fastest booms in its history, with the Dow Jones Industrial Average exploding in value.

The market hit its low point in mid-March, when the Treasury market collapsed. But between that day and the middle of June—in just three months—the market's value surged by 35 percent. In the three months after that, it rose by another 7 percent. By then, stocks were trading at the same value they had when restaurants, movie theaters, hotels, and cruise ships were operating at full capacity. The average monthly returns on leveraged loans were restored as early as April. By August, so many new investment-grade bonds were issued that the previous record, set in 2017, was broken.

As always, asset price inflation was portrayed in the media as a boom. And this time the boom was so intense that it was almost surreal. Millions of people were out of work, millions more were in constant danger of being evicted, restaurants were shuttered, and hundreds of thousands of people were dying. But the debt and equity markets were on fire.

During the summer of 2020, the stock market was personified by an overcaffeinated man in his mid-forties named David Portnoy, who sat alone in a big empty room and shouted into a computer camera that livestreamed his thoughts. Portnoy was one of those Internet-famous people who knew exactly how to capture attention and maintain it. In 2003 he had launched a free newspaper in Boston called *Barstool Sports*, which evolved over the years into a well-trafficked website. *Barstool Sports* was richly baited to draw interest and produce outrage. One series of articles assigned letter grades to female teachers who got arrested for molesting students. (One teacher was graded harshly with a C for not sharing explicit photos of herself.) All of it kept people talking about Portnoy, and in return he kept giving people things to talk about. In the spring and early summer of 2020, Portnoy started to talk about the stock market, launching a show called "Davey Day Trader Global." He sat in front of his webcam and talked about stocks the way radio hosts talked about baseball stats. Because stock prices were rising, then rising again, gambling in the stock market gained an addictive edge. Portnoy took callers as he broadcast his show, including a man who apparently went by the name "Balls," and who told Portnoy to buy stock in the fast-food chain Shake Shack.

"Balls said: 'Go long.' I'm going long! Another half a mill on Shake Shack," Portnoy shouted during one video. Portnoy bragged about his profits and advertised the thrill of it all.

Viewers who wanted to join the fun could do so by creating an account on the stock trading platform called Robinhood, which had been founded in 2013. Robinhood charged no fees for trading stock, enticing people to open up 10 million accounts on its platform by the end of 2019. These were average people who put their stock trades on credit cards, or paid for them with home equity loans. This made Robinhood's platform look like something that democratized high finance, moving the riches of stock trading from Wall Street to the family living room. But Robinhood's business model was dominated by the same big players that already operated at the peak of financial power. The people who traded on Robinhood were not the company's real customers. Its real customers were big hedge funds and trading firms like Citadel Securities. Robinhood might have organized all the trading through its app, but the trades were actually executed by companies like Citadel. These firms paid Robinhood millions of dollars for the privilege because it allowed them to see what people were buying, then make trades based on that information as they filled the order. This was called paying for order flow. Robinhood earned about $19,000 from trading firms for each dollar that a normal retail investor had in their account. Robinhood's cash from order flow more than tripled from the start of 2020 to the same period in 2021. It is unclear how much money Citadel earned from the arrangement, because it is privately held.

Market swings were hard to predict, but Citadel had a good view into how things worked at the Federal Reserve. In 2015, the company hired Ben Bernanke to be a senior advisor. Bernanke said that he typically worked for Citadel only a few days a year, sharing his views on the economy or occasionally showing up for client events to be interviewed. He declined to say how much he earned for such events, but Citadel was shown to pay well. The company paid Janet Yellen between $710,000 and $760,000 to give speeches in 2019 and 2020, according to financial disclosure forms.

Firms like Citadel benefited when trading activity became feverish, as it did in the summer of 2020, helped along by media personalities like Portnoy. During one video, Portnoy seemed genuinely angry that some people cautioned against dumping money into the stock market.

"Where are the haters now?" he bellowed. "Now I have both hands on the steering wheel. And I'm taking this thing to the fucking *moon*. We're going to drive right over all the haters. And people are mad. Why are you mad? Get on board. BUY! Everyone makes money. Everyone makes money. Buy. Buy. Buy. We make money. Why the haters? Why are you shorting the market? Because you're wrong and outdated? Because I've proven you to be a fool in two months? Turn these machines on."

They did turn the machines on. Robinhood added 3 million new accounts in 2020.

The insanity of all this seemed distant from the world of Jay Powell. He continued giving speeches and engaging in listening tours, which were virtual now. He testified before Congress, and projected the image of a steadfast leader. Jay Powell was, by and large, hailed as a hero.

The crisis response of 2020 marked a high point in Powell's career. He had quietly served in the background at very powerful institutions like the Treasury Department, the Carlyle Group, and the Fed. But now he was the central actor of the world's most powerful central bank. There was no political downside, ever, to acting aggressively at the Fed in times of distress. The balance sheet of the Fed, which had been a source of worry when it was $4.5 trillion, would grow to $7.4 trillion with no sign of stopping. The controversial programs that Ben Bernanke had employed to go below zero were now background operations, employed as standard practice. The real attention was on the new experimental actions, and what might come next. Virtually no one believed that the Fed was finished.

Powell's predecessors—and virtually everyone else in a position of power in the world of banking, monetary policy, or governance— praised him for what he did. They also acknowledged that it would take years, if not decades, to unwind the actions the Fed had taken in a matter of months. But that problem would be left for tomorrow.

Ben Bernanke began an interview, in April 2020, with an unsolicited comment: "Jay Powell has done an excellent job in a difficult situation," he said. Janet Yellen went further when asked about the Fed's recent actions. "I think they're heroic, and I'm really supportive. I'm really impressed by what they did."

In supporting Powell's actions, Yellen provided an expansive view of the Fed's power, and its role in America. The Fed wasn't just supposed to maintain a stable money supply and be the lender of last resort to banks in times of trouble. That view was outdated, she suggested, in part because the financial system had become so dominated by hedge funds, private equity firms, or other entities that were sometimes referred to as the "shadow" banking system. The Fed was there to back them all up, in times of crisis. "This is why the Fed was invented and this is what they're doing now," Yellen said. She portrayed the coronavirus pandemic as something like a bank panic that went beyond the banks and affected the entire American economy. The Fed was now the lender of last resort for everyone. "When [the coronavirus] came along and people realized how very serious it was going to be, there was just a huge, broad-based flight from risky assets of every type. And that's like a modern-day bank run. Again, you know, fortunately the banks, the core banking system, is in good shape. Again this was centered in the shadow banking system. People are terrified of losses and they're running from lending and want to be in the safety of cash. The role of the central bank is to take risks, to avoid harm to the economy, when no one else is willing to do so," Yellen said.

The bailout of 2020—the largest expenditure of American public resources since World War II—solidified and entrenched an economic regime that had been quietly and steadily constructed, largely by the Federal Reserve, during the previous decade. The resources from this bailout went largely to the entities that were strengthened by the policies of ZIRP and QE. It went to large corporations that used borrowed money to buy out their competitors; it went to the very richest of Americans who owned the vast majority of assets; it went to the riskiest of financial speculators on Wall Street, who used borrowed money to build fragile positions in global markets; and it went to the very largest U.S. banks, whose bigness and inability to fail was now an article of faith.

And all of this happened at a moment when Americans were more distracted, more beleaguered, and more financially distressed than at any moment in modern history. It was difficult to even comprehend the impact of what had happened. But the impact would make itself visible in the months, years, and likely decades to come.

CHAPTER 16

THE LONG CRASH

(2020–2021)

After he was laid off from Rexnord, John Feltner was determined to keep his life on track. He and Nina had been planning for a long time to save up enough money to buy the house they rented near Silver Spoon Drive. The couple didn't seem willing to let go of that goal. In the first few months after he lost his factory job, Feltner bounced around between temporary gigs. He got a job doing maintenance work at a grocery store. He later got a contracting job, also in maintenance. He had suspected that he wouldn't be able to find a steady job that paid as much as his unionized position at Rexnord. He was right. But he kept pressing and he did eventually find a full-time position in the maintenance department of a big hospital. It paid less than Rexnord, but it was dependable. Nina had work in the human resources department of a company that provided at-home mental health care. It took some time, but they did save up the money, and they did buy their house. Also, thanks to luck, they worked in health care, one of the few industries that weren't shut down or interrupted by the coronavirus pandemic.

By the end of 2020, Feltner's workday started in the late afternoon.

He started getting ready a little after 2:00 in the afternoon, when he pulled out of his driveway and began his long commute. The quickest way to get to work took about forty minutes. The first part of the route went along Interstate 70, toward Indianapolis, past a monotonous background of farmland that was wide open and empty during the long winter months. From there, the route went north on the big highway loop around the edge of the city, to Community North Hospital, a large medical complex that looked like a self-contained office park. Feltner's shift ran from 3:30 in the afternoon to about 11:30 at night, when the complex was mostly quiet. The first COVID-19 case in Indiana was diagnosed at Community North, on March 6. By November the state had about 200,000 cases and 5,000 deaths. Another 5,000 people would die in the state in the following couple of months. The whole thing made life surreal for people like Feltner. The hospital eventually set up a temporary tent facility in a parking lot to conduct drive-through testing for the virus, creating the feel of emergency barracks. Feltner wore a face mask during his entire shift. His social life slammed to a halt, and Nina set up a home office in an upstairs bedroom. The couple's daughter lived at home, although her health care job took her out of the house. The Feltners stopped seeing their friends, and heard through the rumor mill when their neighbors got sick. Feltner stayed very busy at work, which was a blessing in its way. People in the restaurant and hotel businesses would be out of work for months. Feltner belonged to the group of workers deemed "essential," meaning that he didn't have the option to work from home, at a safe distance from others.

America's essential workers in 2020 put in very long hours and crisscrossed a largely abandoned landscape, delivering food, working at grocery store checkout counters, using their cars, staffing hospitals, and keeping factories and warehouses humming around the clock. They often did this at great personal risk, getting sick from COVID-19 at a far higher rate than workers who stayed at home. Feltner and Nina were among the fortunate; they never caught coronavirus, or at least didn't have any symptoms if they did. Neither did their daughter, even though her job took her on home visits to people who did have the virus. The federal bailouts did have a significant impact on these essential workers. Evictions were held at bay, and the emergency payments helped them meet bills. But the majority of the government's largesse bypassed places like the Feltners' neighborhood. The economic recovery of 2020 was a gated recovery, with the money flowing to selected, exclusive zip codes. The people who did well did very well, but the rest did not. The Fed surveyed businesses with fewer than five hundred employees and found that 90 percent of them were still suffering from a downturn in sales by the end of the year. About 30 percent of those companies said they would probably go out of business if they didn't get more federal aid.

For Feltner, the bailouts were a marginal issue, something that didn't matter very much in his daily life. The onetime payments mailed out to everyone didn't do anything to arrest the much longer downward slide that defined the decades of Feltner's working life. Before the financial crisis, when he worked at the auto parts maker Navistar, Feltner earned about $80,000 a year or more when overtime pay was included. At Rexnord, he earned about $60,000. At the hospital, he earned about $46,000. And at each job his benefits had been scaled back and his health care costs had risen. He wasn't alone in this regard. The middle class had experienced a very long and deep slide in its earning power, bargaining power, and wages. Virtually nothing had changed this trajectory during the decade between 2010 and 2020. The economy had grown, but the growth was captured by a smaller and smaller share of the population. Feltner and his neighbors weren't just excluded from the lion's share of the 2020 bailout. They had been excluded from the benefits of ZIRP and QE and the asset price inflation that those policies created. The entire bottom half of the U.S. population owned about 2 percent of all the nation's assets. The top 1 percent of the population owned 31 percent. This helped explain why the households in the very middle of America's income scale—meaning the middle 20 percent—saw their median net worth rise by only 4 percent between 1989 and 2016. During the same period, the net worth of people in the top 20 percent more than doubled. The wealth of the top 1 percent nearly tripled. Millions of people in the middle class were falling behind. To compensate for this fact they took on loads of cheap debt, which helped them feel like they were at least remaining in place. Consumer debt hit $14 trillion in late 2019, a record level even after adjusting for inflation. The only good news seemed to be that interest rates on the debt were lower. Households were spending about 10 percent of their disposable income in servicing debt in 2019, which was down from 13 percent right before the Global Financial Crisis.

Feltner was an optimistic guy, by nature. He talked about the local boom in construction that seemed to be under way in 2020, and the fact that skilled trade workers were in such high demand. His daughter found work as a home health care aide, and his two sons also had full-time jobs, doing maintenance work on vehicles for a local school district. Things were pretty good at the end of the day. One of Feltner's sons welcomed a new baby during the pandemic, which helped keep everyone's mind off the gloomier realities of what was going on. But Feltner also felt a nagging fear about his kids' futures. All of them had started working when they were young, and they knew how to work hard and be dependable. But it wasn't clear anymore that hard work was a pathway to a dependable living or a stable life. Feltner didn't know if his kids could expect to earn even as much as he had earned. "It scares the hell out of me. It really does," he said. "It's almost like we've become the commodities ourselves, you know what I'm saying?" Feltner said.

The value of workers had been diminished, but the value of other commodities was on the rise. The Fed was making sure of it.

Jay Powell had become a figure like the Wizard of Oz by December 2020. To most people, Powell was a disembodied face that flickered on a large screen, delivering proclamations from on high. The Fed's press conferences were now held by video conference after each FOMC meeting. The choreographed events began with an image of Powell, standing in front of a large blue curtain and reading scripted comments. When he was finished, Powell took questions from reporters who suddenly appeared on screen, each of them a small face framed within squares arranged in a large grid across the screen. The reporters were sitting in various home offices and apartments, and they spoke into awkwardly angled cameras.

On December 16, Powell made a big announcement. Some of the most important emergency measures the Fed had deployed during the spring would now be made semipermanent. While the Main Street Lending Program was sputtering to a quiet end, other parts of the bailout would endure. The Fed would keep interest rates at zero, and would now conduct $120 billion in quantitative easing every month for the foreseeable future. That was about a decade's worth of money creation, at historic rates, conducted every thirty days. It would continue, Powell said, until "substantial further progress has been made" toward healing the economy. When that might occur was anyone's guess.

Powell said the Fed would continue to intervene as long as price inflation didn't rise above 2 percent for an extended period of time, an eventuality that he said was unlikely in the near future. The price of certain items had spiked because of supply disruptions, but weak growth and weak demand were smothering prices overall. Asset price inflation, however, was accelerating without restraint.

The stock market was doing so well in December that it didn't even make sense to the people who were making money off it. A Web-based food delivery company called DoorDash went public that month, and its stock nearly doubled immediately. The online rental company Airbnb went public and its shares more than doubled. This might sound great for those companies, but when share prices jump so quickly it means that the firm's original owners have lost out on a lot of money because they've priced their shares too low. A video game company called

Roblox suspended its initial public offering in December "as it tried to make sense of the market," according to *The Wall Street Journal*. The value of stock market shares was as high as any time since the dot-com boom, when compared to actual company revenue. If that didn't make sense to people, then things weren't going to make sense for a long time. The market broke records and then broke them again in the months to come.

The market for corporate debt was just as strong. By the end of 2020, companies issued more than $1.9 trillion in new corporate debt, beating the previous record that was set in 2017. Business for leveraged loans and CLOs was booming. American companies would carry this debt for many years to come because of the way it was structured. Companies had to either roll the debt by selling it again, or pay it in full when the loan expired. The corporate debt binge brought a new and troubling term into corporate America's lexicon, something called the "zombie company." A zombie company was a firm that carried so much debt that its profits weren't enough to cover its loan costs. The only thing that kept zombie companies out of bankruptcy was the ability to roll their debt perpetually. During 2020, nearly two hundred major publicly traded companies entered the ranks of the zombie army, according to an analysis by Bloomberg News. These weren't just marginal or risky firms, but included well-known firms like Boeing, ExxonMobil, Macy's, and Delta Airlines. When Bloomberg analyzed three thousand large, publicly traded firms, it found that about 20 percent of them were zombies. These companies posed a risk beyond their own financial stability. Their existence suppressed economic productivity because they consumed investments and resources that might have gone to new firms or entrepreneurs.

Powell's political standing in Washington had never been higher. His fortunes seemed to rise even higher in November, when President Trump lost his bid for reelection to the Democrat Joe Biden, the former vice president. Word soon leaked out that Biden's pick for Treasury secretary was Powell's former boss and colleague Janet Yellen. Experts in D.C. expected that the Fed and the White House would now have one of the most cooperative relationships in recent memory. On the way out of office, Trump's administration had a final spat with the Fed. Mnuchin, who had worked so closely with Powell, announced that the Treasury would no longer support the special-purpose vehicles the Treasury and the Fed had created together (like the program that bought corporate junk debt). The vehicles would be closed down at the end of the year. The Federal Reserve opposed this move, and released a statement saying as much. But Mnuchin said that his reasoning was simple. The CARES Act specifically said that the Fed's emergency SPVs should close at the end of 2020. There seemed to be little reason to extend the programs now that markets for stocks and corporate bonds were booming. "I had every intention of following what I saw as the clear interpretation of the law," Mnuchin later said.

The Fed pressed Mnuchin to keep the facilities open in case markets reversed, but he felt that doing so would come with a cost. "The downside was that some future Treasury Secretary is going to have to go back to Congress at some point in the next hundred years and ask for these [kinds of emergency programs]. And I think the fact that I was a good steward of this, and gave back the capital as the law was written, will be a good precedent for future Treasury secretaries."

When Mnuchin announced that the programs would close, it did not disrupt the booming market for corporate debt or stocks. Investors had seen that the Fed would intervene on their behalf, and that was apparently enough to keep them optimistic.

On January 6, 2021, thousands of violent extremists laid siege to the United States Capitol. Inside the building, members of Congress were conducting the once-formal process of counting the electoral votes that were submitted by the states. Biden had won the election handily, but President Trump did not concede. Trump alleged that a wide-ranging and ever-shifting criminal conspiracy had stolen the election from him. Trump's followers smashed windows, broke open doors, sprayed police officers with bear repellent, and pushed their way into the House and Senate chambers, forcibly shutting down the transfer of power. For about six long hours, the U.S. political system hung in a suspended state. The transfer of power resumed that night, after police managed to regain control of the building and the rioters had been allowed to walk back to their hotels. It was the most effective attack on American democracy since the Civil War, and it marked an entirely new level of volatility in American society.

The following day, the Dow Jones Industrial Average jumped 1.4 percent, closing at a record high.

That month, millions of traders on the retail platform Robinhood helped drive up shares in a video-game rental company called Game-Stop. The company's rising share value was puzzling when compared against its underlying economic health—the storefront business was suffering massive losses of customer traffic during the coronavirus lock-downs, and was arguably being made technologically obsolete by Inter-net streaming. Its stock was jumping by double digits.

During a news conference in late January, Jay Powell was asked re-peatedly about the possibility that the Fed was fueling an asset bubble. Inside the FOMC meetings, the Fed's own experts talked repeatedly about the ways that quantitative easing boosted all asset prices, along with the stock market. Powell said that the Fed was monitoring asset prices, but wasn't overly concerned. When he was pressed on the topic, he seemed almost exasperated.

"I think that the connection between low interest rates and, and asset values is probably something that's not as tight as people think because a lot of—a lot of different factors are driving asset prices at any given time," he said.

————————

Tom Hoenig spent the long winter of 2020–2021 as so many people did, in isolation. Instead of visiting his grandchildren, he saw them through FaceTime chats. Once the weather got cold in Kansas City, Tom and Cynthia spent a lot of time around the house and rarely saw their friends. They figured out the little tricks of survival in the new world, like determining that the best time to do grocery shopping was on Wednesday afternoon, at about 3:00, when no one else seemed to be at the store. They wore double-layered face masks as they walked through the grocery aisles, which were now marked "One Way," and they stood a respectful distance from the cashier at the checkout counter, who wore a plastic face visor.

One thing that kept Tom Hoenig going was the feeling that he could do useful work. In the mornings, he woke up early and read the news on his iPad. He kept up with the Fed's actions through the coverage in the *Financial Times*, *The Wall Street Journal*, and *The Washington Post*, among other publications. He spent a lot of time in his home office, writing essays and opinion pieces that offered his best perspective on what the Fed and the bank regulators ought to be doing. He published some of these essays in *Discourse*, the online publication of the Mercatus Center think tank, where he was a senior fellow. In May 2020, Hoenig published an essay urging people to think about what the Fed's actions during the crisis might mean over the long term. Emergency spending was vital to fighting the pandemic, he wrote. "These policies, while necessary in the short term, place an ever larger mortgage against the nation's future income; and extending them beyond the crisis period could have significant negative unintended consequences."

Hoenig had made a similar argument in 2010. He was saying that the United States needed to think about what it was going to do when the immediate crisis was over. Would the country use democratically elected institutions to confront its problems, or would it rely on its central bank once again? When Hoenig went on his long spree of dissenting votes in 2010, the Fed's balance sheet had been $2.3 trillion. That was a radically high amount by historical standards, and was more than twice the size of the balance sheet before the 2008 financial crisis. In May 2020, the Fed's balance sheet was $7 trillion, and continuing to grow under the near-permanent flow of quantitative easing.

Hoenig's warnings in 2020 were different in one important way from his warnings a decade earlier. Now he could point to the historical record. In his essay, Hoenig compared the period of economic growth between 2010 and 2018 with the period a decade earlier, between 1992 and 2000. These periods were comparable because they were both long periods of economic stability after a recession, he argued. In the 1990s, labor productivity in the United States increased at an annual average rate of 2.3 percent. During the decade of ZIRP, it rose by only 1.1 percent. Real median weekly earnings for wage and salary employees rose by 0.7 percent on average annually during the 1990s, but rose by only 0.26 percent during the 2010s. Average real GDP growth, a measure of the overall economy, rose an average of 3.8 percent annually during the 1990s, but by only 2.3 percent during the recent decade. The only part of the economy that seemed to benefit under ZIRP was the market for assets. The stock market more than doubled in value during the 2010s. Even after the crash of 2020, the markets continued their stellar growth and returns.

Hoenig wasn't optimistic about what American life might look like after another decade of weak growth, wage stagnation, and booming asset values that primarily benefitted the rich. This was something he talked about a lot, both publicly and privately. In his mind, economics and the banking system were tightly intertwined with American society. One thing affected the other. When the financial system benefited only a handful of people, average people started to lose faith in society as a whole. When they saw the biggest banks get bailed out while middle-class wages faltered, it made people feel like the system was rigged. Hoenig argued in public speeches that this was a good reason to pursue bank reform. Over coffee at a bakery in downtown Washington, in 2019, Hoenig said that the misallocation of resources under ZIRP very likely contributed to the undercurrents tearing apart American society. "Do you think that we would have had the political, shall we say turmoil, revolution, we had in 2016, had we not had this great divide created? Had we not had the effects of the zero interest rates that benefited some far more than others?" Hoenig asked. "I don't know. It's a counterfactual. But it's a question I would like to pose."

In 2021, as he sat at home in Kansas City, Hoenig seemed interested in talking about one issue above all. It was the need for long-term thinking. He recalled a piece of advice he'd once gotten from a Swiss central banker that always stuck with him. "We are responsible for the long run, so the short run can take care of itself," the central banker had said. The Fed was supposed to be an ideal institution for long-term thinking because it was insulated from voters and elections. But Hoenig didn't believe that long-term thinking dominated the decisions of 2010 or beyond. "The short run was the focal point," he said. This wasn't just a problem that afflicted central bankers. It seemed to increasingly dominate the thinking of corporations, government institutions, and the concerns of average citizens. "Everyone had a short-term need that makes the long term impossible to look to," Hoenig said.

This mattered a lot, because long-term thinking would be indispensable to confronting America's economic problems in 2021. The financial crash that happened in the spring of 2020 was smothered so rapidly, by so much new money from the Fed, that most people didn't know it had happened. But the consequences of the crash were dire.

On the morning of March 11, 2021, as Hoenig was reading *The Wall Street Journal*, he came across a particularly alarming story. Like so much of the important news about America's money and debt, this article carried a seemingly benign headline: "Wave of New Debt to Test Treasury Market." The story explained the deep vulnerability roiling beneath the surface of a financial system that seemed to be growing smoothly. This vulnerability was not new, and it had to do with the very delicate balance on the financial seesaw of risk. The safe side of the seesaw held reliable assets, like Treasury bonds. The other side of the seesaw held risky assets, like stocks and corporate debt. The Fed was pumping $80 billion* a month onto the safe side of the seesaw by purchasing Treasury bonds, which in turn depressed the interest rates, or yield, on those bills. As had been happening for a decade, this forced investors to push their money to the risky side, seeking yield. Something worrisome started to happen in March. Treasury interest rates had started to climb, regardless of the Fed's intervention. There were lots of reasons for the yields to rise—investors expected the economy to grow, which pushed up rates, for example—but the *Journal* article highlighted another, potentially more dangerous reason: the sheer amount of debt the U.S. government was issuing. President Trump and the Republicans in Congress had passed a tax cut in 2017 that forced the government to borrow $1 trillion every year to keep the government running, even when the economy was at its peak in 2019. When the pandemic hit, Congress approved more than $2 trillion in spending in the CARES Act alone, all of it financed by deficit spending. In March, President Biden signed a new $1.9 trillion rescue package. This was heralded as the first major rescue bill in decades that steered the majority of its spending to poor and working-class people. All of this meant that the U.S. Treasury would be selling about $2.8 trillion in Treasurys during 2021. The *Journal* article documented the troubling fact that there might not be enough demand for all that debt to keep Treasury interest rates down at the low levels where the Fed had been pushing them. Demand was worryingly soft during a couple of Treasurys auctions that month. Analysts believed there might be a "buyer's strike" for some Treasurys, which would require the government to pay higher interest rates to entice buyers. If Treasury rates rose, all that investment cash on Wall Street would

---

*The Fed was spending $120 billion a month in quantitative easing, with $80 billion going toward Treasury bonds and $40 billion going toward mortgage-backed securities.

be enticed to move toward the safe end of the seesaw, finding shelter in the higher, safer yields that had been denied for so long. This would drain cash out of the markets for leveraged loans, stocks, CLOs, and all the risky structures that Wall Street had been busily building for many years. Powell and his team would then face a familiar choice. They could let the risky structures fall, or intervene once again with more quantitative easing and emergency programs. Powell faced a similar choice when money rushed out of risky assets in late 2018, and he chose the path of creating more money to soothe markets. This encouraged more speculation and asset inflation. Hoenig believed that the Fed would almost certainly once again choose the path of money creation if debt prices rose and markets teetered. "You see the complications we're building for ourselves going forward," Hoenig said.

Hoenig kept churning out his essays and his white papers. He was seventy-four years old, and at the end of his career his ideas didn't seem much more popular than they were before. His papers were not read widely. He was rarely invited to speak on cable news shows. But Hoenig's arguments were as relevant in 2021 as they were a decade earlier. This didn't reflect the consistency of his views so much as the intractability of America's long-term problems.

In many important ways, the financial crash of 2008 had never ended. It was a long crash that crippled the economy for years. The problems that caused it went almost entirely unsolved. And this financial crash was compounded by a long crash in the strength of America's democratic institutions. When America relied on the Federal Reserve to address its economic problems, it relied on a deeply flawed tool. All the Fed's money only widened the distance between America's winners and losers and laid the foundation for more instability. This fragile financial system was wrecked by the pandemic and in response the Fed created yet more new money, amplifying the earlier distortions.

The long crash of 2008 had evolved into the long crash of 2020. The bills had yet to be paid.

NOTES

Some of the information in this book comes from knowledge I derived after spending more than ten years writing about the U.S. economy. Some background facts, such as general descriptions of the Global Financial Crisis in 2008, for example, come from my personal reporting over the years. These notes do not list every article I wrote to substantiate that reporting.

CHAPTER 1: GOING BELOW ZERO

3 *Thomas Hoenig woke up early on November 3*: Thomas Hoenig, interviews by author, 2016–2021; transcript of the meeting of the Federal Open Market Committee, November 2–3, 2010.

4 *For a year now, Hoenig had been voting no*: Transcripts of the meetings of the Federal Open Market Committee, January, March, April, May, June, August, September, October, and November 2010; Hoenig, interviews with author, 2016–2021; Ben Bernanke, interview with author, 2020; Sewell Chan, "Fed's Contrarian Has a Wary Eye on the Past," *New York Times*, December 13, 2010; Ben Bernanke, *The Courage to Act: A Memoir of a Crisis and Its Aftermath* (New York: Norton, 2015).

6 *Between 1913 and 2008, the Fed gradually increased the money supply*: Figures of money supply, or "M1 Money Stock," taken from Economic Research Federal Reserve Bank of St. Louis database, https://fred.stlou isfed.org/series/M1NS.

6 *Only about twenty-four special banks*: List of Primary Dealers, Federal Reserve Bank of New York, accessed June 10, 2021.

6 *The amount of excess money in the banking system swelled*: Figures of excess reserves, or "Excess Reserves of Depository Institutions," taken from

Economic Research Federal Reserve Bank of St. Louis database, https://
fred.stlouisfed.org/series/EXCSRESNS.

9 *The politics of money used to be a charged political issue*: Roger Lowenstein, *America's Bank: The Epic Struggle to Create the Federal Reserve*, 23 (New York: Penguin Press, 2016).

9 *The things that bothered Hoenig*: Hoenig, interviews with author, 2016–2020.

11 *When the Fed's regional bank presidents came to town*: Hoenig, interviews with author, 2016–2021; all descriptions of Hotel Fairmont are taken from author's notes, video, and photographs taken at the hotel in 2020, and from the hotel's marketing photos at https://www.fairmont.com/washington/.

11 *There was a deep feeling of collegiality among the bank presidents*: Impressions and understanding of regional bank president and FOMC culture taken from author interviews with Janet Yellen, Richard Fisher, Jeffrey Lacker, Jerome Powell, Ben Bernanke, Thomas Hoenig, Betsy Duke, and Sarah Bloom Raskin, 2020–2021; select transcripts of the meetings of the Federal Open Market Committee, 1991–2015.

13 *The previous day had been Election Day across America*: Peter Baker, "In Republican Victories, Tide Turns Starkly," *New York Times*, November 2, 2010; Kate Zernike, "Tea Party Comes to Power on an Unclear Mandate," *New York Times*, November 2, 2010.

15 *A columnist at* The Wall Street Journal *wrote a regular column*: Sudeep Reddy, "The Lone Dissenter: Kansas City's Hoenig Stands Firm," *Wall Street Journal*, March 16, 2010; Sudeep Reddy, "The Lone Dissenter: Kansas City's Hoenig Goes Four for Four," *Wall Street Journal*, June 23, 2010; Sudeep Reddy, "The Lone Dissenter: Thomas Hoenig Hits Seven," *Wall Street Journal*, November 3, 2010; Sudeep Reddy, "The Lone Dissenter: Kansas City's Hoenig Goes Out with a Record," *Wall Street Journal*, December 14, 2010.

15 *They asked if he was* sure: Hoenig, interviews with author, 2016–2021.

15 *When the cars arrived*: Hoenig, interviews with author, 2016–2021; all descriptions of the driving route between the Hotel Fairmont and the Eccles Building are taken from author's notes, video, and photographs, 2020.

16 *Even the basic politics of the Federal Reserve are confusing*: Observations of Federal Reserve politics taken from interviews with current and former Federal Reserve officials and economists; Christopher Leonard, "How

Jay Powell's Coronavirus Response Is Changing the Fed Forever," *Time*, June 11, 2020.

18 *The historical record shows that this narrative is entirely wrong*: Transcripts of the meetings of the Federal Open Market Committee, January, March, April, May, June, August, September, October, and November 2010; Mary Anastasia O'Grady, "The Fed's Monetary Dissident," *Wall Street Journal*, May 15, 2010; Thomas Hoenig lecture, Anderson Chandler Lecture Series, University of Kansas School of Business, October 26, 2010, https://kansaspublicradio.org/kpr-news/thomas-hoenig; Thomas Hoenig speech, "Hard Choices," Town Hall Meeting, Lincoln, Nebraska, August 13, 2010.

19 *When Hoenig talked about allocative effects*: Hoenig, interviews with author, 2016–2021.

21 *Hoenig's ride continued south toward the Fed headquarters*: Descriptions of the driving route between the Hotel Fairmont and the Eccles Building are taken from author's notes, video, and photographs, 2020.

22 *When Ben Bernanke published a memoir*: Ben Bernanke, interview with author, 2020. Bernanke, *The Courage to Act*.

23 *Bernanke published papers on this concept*: Laurence M. Ball, "Ben Bernanke and the Zero Bound," *National Bureau of Economic Research Working Paper 17836* (February 2012).

24 *Members of the FOMC were worried about this*: Transcripts of the meetings of the Federal Open Market Committee, January, March, April, May, June, August, September, October, and November 2010.

24 *He explained his heightened worries*: Transcript of the meeting of the Federal Open Market Committee, August 10, 2010, 119–20.

25 *In August, Bernanke began a public campaign*: Sewell Chan, "Fed Ready to Dig Deeper to Aid Growth, Chief Says," *New York Times*, August 27, 2010; "The Economic Outlook and Monetary Policy," remarks by Ben S. Bernanke, chairman, Board of Governors of the Federal Reserve System, at the Federal Reserve Bank of Kansas City Economic Symposium, Jackson Hole, Wyoming, August 27, 2010.

25 *The basic mechanics and goals of quantitative easing*: This description of quantitative easing is based on the author's interviews with current and former Federal Reserve officials, financial traders, financial analysts, and senior members of the New York Federal Reserve Bank who designed and implemented the program, 2016–2020; Brett W. Fawley and Christopher J. Neely, "Four Stories of Quantitative Easing," Federal Reserve

Bank of St. Louis, *Review*, January/February 2013; Stephen Williamson, "Quantitative Easing: Does This Tool Work?," St. Louis Federal Reserve Bank, *The Regional Economist*, Third Quarter 2017; *Quantitative Easing Explained*, Economic Information Newsletter, Research Library of the Federal Reserve Bank of St. Louis, April 2011; *QE and Ultra-Low Interest Rates: Distributional Effects and Risks*, McKinsey Global Institute discussion paper, November 2013.

27   *During the FOMC meeting in September*: Transcript of the meeting of the Federal Open Market Committee, September 21, 2010, 105–107.

29   *These comments irritated Ben Bernanke*: Bernanke, *The Courage to Act* (New York: Norton, 2017), 485–92.

29   *When the Fed gathered to vote on the quantitative easing plan in November*: Transcript of the meeting of the Federal Open Market Committee, November 2–3, 2010.

29   *"Good morning everybody," Bernanke said*: Ibid.

CHAPTER 2: SERIOUS NUMBERS

35   *When Thomas Hoenig was nine years old*: Thomas Hoenig, interviews with author, 2020; Kathleen Kelley, interview with author, 2020; Arlene M. Hoenig obituary, January 2011; Scott Lanman, "Thomas Hoenig Is Fed Up," *Bloomberg Businessweek*, September 23, 2010; Sewell Chan, "Fed's Contrarian Has a Wary Eye on the Past," *New York Times*, December 13, 2010.

36   *Tom decided to go to college*: Hoenig, interviews with author, 2020; Kathleen Kelley, interview with author, 2020.

38   *Hoenig and McKeon worked together in a small bunker*: Jon McKeon, interview with author, 2020. Images of Vietnam-era fire-control bases and FADAC computers taken from online diaries and blogs of Vietnam veterans and military historians.

39   *As fire control specialists, Hoenig and McKeon sat on a committee*: Hoenig and McKeon, interviews with author, 2020.

40   *When he got back home to Fort Madison*: Hoenig, interviews with author, 2020.

41   *It helped that Hoenig had a new life to move toward*: Cynthia Hoenig, interview with author, 2020.

42   *When Tom Hoenig studied economics at Iowa State*: Hoenig, interviews with author, 2020; Thomas M. Hoenig, "Anticipating State Revenue for Iowa Through Regression on Personal Income," Iowa State University

Capstones, Theses and Dissertations, 1972; Thomas M. Hoenig, "Commercial Banking: Competition and the Personal Loan Market," Iowa State University Capstones, Theses and Dissertations, 1974.

44 *There is nothing in the U.S. Constitution that demands . . . a central bank*: Roger Lowenstein, *America's Bank: The Epic Struggle to Create the Federal Reserve* (New York: Penguin Press, 2016); William Greider, *Secrets of the Temple: How the Federal Reserve Runs the Country* (New York: Simon & Schuster, 1987).

48 *The tension was also encoded into the Fed's structure*: Peter Conti-Brown, *The Power and Independence of the Federal Reserve* (Princeton, N.J.: Princeton University Press, 2016).

49 *Hoenig's job involved a lot of arguments*: Hoenig, interviews with author, 2020–2021.

CHAPTER 3: THE GREAT INFLATION(S)

53 *Hoenig was thirty-three years old when the banking*: Thomas Hoenig, interviews with author, 2016–2021.

54 *An asset is anything a person can buy*: Financial traders, speaking on background, 2016–2021; John Kenneth Galbraith, *The Great Crash, 1929* (New York: Mariner Books, 1997), 1–23.

55 *Tom Hoenig watched*: Hoenig, interviews with author, 2020.

56 *Volcker recognized that when he was fighting*: Paul Volker, *Keeping At It: The Quest for Sound Money and Good Government* (New York: Public Affairs, 2018), 220–40; William Greider, *Secrets of the Temple*, 75–123; Tim Barker, "Other People's Blood," *n+1*, Spring 2019; Bill Medley, "Volcker's Announcement of Anti-Inflation Measures October 1979," *Federal Reserve History*, November 22, 2013.

57 *The reporters pressed Volcker*: Transcript of press conference with Paul A. Volcker, chairman, Board of Governors of the Federal Reserve System, held in boardroom, Federal Reserve Building, Washington, D.C., October 6, 1979.

57 *The price of farmland fell by 27 percent*: Alex J. Pollock, "A Bubble to Remember—and Anticipate?," American Enterprise Institute for Public Policy Research, November 2012.

58 *Hoenig's team spent most of the early 1980s doing one thing*: John Yorke and Hoenig, interviews with author, 2020.

58 *A true bank panic broke out in 1982*: "History of the Eighties: Lessons

for the Future. Vol. 1. An Examination of the Banking Crises of the 1980s and Early 1990s," report by Federal Deposit Insurance Corporation, 1997, 14–15; Yorke and Hoenig, interviews with author, 2020.

60   *Perhaps the most detailed account of how the Federal Reserve*: Allan H. Meltzer, *A History of the Federal Reserve, Volume 2, Book 2, 1970–1986* (Chicago: University of Chicago Press, 2014), 843–1007.

60   *It was monetary policy, set by the Fed, that primarily created the problem*: Ibid., 864.

61   *But the problem was more fundamental*: Edward Nelson, "The Great Inflation of the Seventies: What Really Happened?," Federal Reserve Bank of St. Louis Research Division, Working Paper 2004-001, January 2004.

62   *This lesson of the banking crisis stuck with Tom Hoenig*: Hoenig, interviews with author, 2016–2021.

63   *Penn Square was run by a guy named Bill*: Phillip L. Zweig, *Belly Up: The Collapse of the Penn Square Bank* (New York: Crown, 1985); Robert A. Bennett, "Penn Square's Failed Concept," *New York Times*, August 16, 1982; Yorke and Hoenig, interviews with author, 2020.

65   *But the really important thing about the failure*: Sebastian Mallaby, *The Man Who Knew: The Life and Times of Alan Greenspan* (New York: Penguin Press, 2016), 297–301; Renee Haltom, "Failure of Continental Illinois," *Federal Reserve History*, November 22, 2013.

67   *Paul Volcker's career as chairman did not end pleasantly*: Volker, *Keeping At It*; Hoenig, interviews with author, 2020; Associated Press, "President of Federal Reserve Bank of Kansas City to Retire," March 18, 1991.

CHAPTER 4: FEDSPEAK

71   *On October 1, 1991, Tom Hoenig walked*: Hoenig, interviews with author, 2016–2021; transcript of the meeting of the Federal Open Market Committee, October 1, 1991; descriptions of FOMC boardroom and headquarters building taken from archival news photos and video.

72   *Hoenig joined the FOMC at a very strange inflection point*: Stephen K. McNees, "The 1990–91 Recession in Historical Perspective," *New England Economic Review*, January/February 1992; Jennifer M. Gardner, "The 1990–91 Recession: How Bad Was the Labor Market?," *Monthly Labor Review*, June 1994; Carl E. Walsh, "What Caused the 1990–91 Recession?" *Economic Review, Federal Reserve Bank of San Francisco*, 1993,

Number 2; Natalia Kolesnikova and Yang Liu, "Jobless Recoveries: Causes and Consequences," *The Regional Economist*, 2011; Mallaby, *The Man Who Knew*, 391–445.

73 *This was the puzzle faced by Greenspan*: Transcript of the meeting of the Federal Open Market Committee, October 1, 1991.

73 *In 1993, a young Princeton economist*: Ben S. Bernanke, "Credit in the Macroeconomy," *Federal Reserve Bank of New York Quarterly Review*, Spring 1992–93.

74 *Even Greenspan was perplexed*: James Sterngold, "Fed Chief Says Economy Is Resisting Remedies," *New York Times*, October 15, 1992.

74 *If the economy had broken with past patterns*: Hoenig, interviews with author; Mallaby, *The Man Who Knew*, 391–445; select transcripts of meetings of the Federal Open Market Committee, 1991–94.

76 *A typical hearing occurred on June 10*: Testimony of Chairman Alan Greenspan: An update on economic conditions in the United States Before the Joint Economic Committee, U.S. Congress, June 10, 1998; images of event taken from archived C-SPAN coverage, https://www.c-span.org/video/?107135-1/monetary-policy-economic-outlook.

79 *The largest burst of fiscal action*: David M. Kennedy, *Freedom from Fear: The American People in Depression and War, 1929–1945* (New York: Oxford University Press, 1999).

80 *The Federal Reserve presented elected politicians*: Nicholas Lemann, *Transaction Man: The Rise of the Deal and the Decline of the American Dream* (New York: Farrar, Straus and Giroux, 2019), 57–64.

81 *In 1989, interest rates had been close to 10 percent*: Figures of interest rates, or "Effective Federal Funds Rate," taken from Economic Research Federal Reserve Bank of St. Louis database, https://fred.stlouisfed.org/series/FEDFUNDS; Hoenig, interviews with author, 2016–2020; vote tallies taken from select transcripts of meetings of the Federal Open Market Committee, 1991–2006.

81 *Behind the cloud of Fedspeak, there were . . . disputes*: Mallaby, *The Man Who Knew*; select transcripts of meetings of the Federal Open Market Committee, 1991–2000; Hoenig, interviews with author, 2016–2020; transcript of the meeting of the Federal Open Market Committee, July 5–6, 1995.

83 *Greenspan had a solid rationale*: Mallaby, *The Man Who Knew*, 432; Hoenig, interviews with author, 2016–2020; select transcripts of meetings of the Federal Open Market Committee, 1991–2000.

84 *This is why Hoenig was worried*: Transcript of the meeting of the Federal Open Market Committee, November 17, 1998.

86 *In 1999, shares of stock*: Floyd Norris, "The Year in the Markets, 1999: Extraordinary Winners and More Losers," *New York Times*, January 3, 2000; Chris Gaither and Dawn C. Chmielewski, "Fears of Dot-Com Crash, Version 2.0," *Los Angeles Times*, July 16, 2006; David Kleinbard, "The $1.7 Trillion Dot.com Lesson," CNNMoney, November 9, 2000; Alex Berenson, "Market Paying Price for Valuing New-Economy Hope Over Profits," *New York Times*, December 21, 2000; Elizabeth Douglass, "Qualcomm Stock May Need Reality Check," *Los Angeles Times*, November 18, 1999.

86 *The FOMC increased rates sharply*: Gretchen Morgenson, "The Markets: Market Place; Shift in Stance by Federal Reserve Deals Blow to Wall Street," *New York Times*, December 21, 2000; "Effective Federal Funds Rate," taken from Economic Research Federal Reserve Bank of St. Louis database, https://fred.stlouisfed.org/series/FEDFUNDS.

87 *The cleanup job in 2000*: Transcripts of meetings of the Federal Open Market Committee, May 15 and December 11, 2001; Mallaby, *The Man Who Knew*, 569–614; Hoenig, interviews with author, 2016–2020.

CHAPTER 5: THE OVERMIGHTY CITIZEN

91 *It started in 2001*: "World Markets Shatter; Terrorist Attack Near Wall Street Spreads Consequences Around World," CNNMoney, September 11, 2001; transcript of the meeting of the Federal Open Market Committee, March 20, 2001.

92 *Over the next few years*: Mallaby, *The Man Who Knew*, 569–671; Paul Krugman, "Running Out of Bubbles," *New York Times*, May 27, 2005; Hoenig, interviews with author, 2020.

93 *In 2006, Alan Greenspan retired*: Bernanke and Hoenig, interviews with author, 2020; Bernanke, *The Courage to Act*; transcript of the meeting of the Federal Open Market Committee, June 28–29, 2006.

94 *By 2006, Hoenig had a coherent view*: Hoenig, interviews with author, 2016–2020.

96 *In late October, Hoenig was invited*: Hoenig, interviews with author, 2020; meeting agenda, 2006 Western States Director Education Foundation Symposium, October 29–31, 2006; images of Tucson Starr Pass hotel taken from the resort's website; transcript of Thomas Hoenig's

speech, "This Time It's Different (Or Is It?)," retrieved from Kansas City
Federal Reserve Bank.

99 *A few months later . . . Bernanke was invited*: Transcript of testimony from
Chairman Ben S. Bernanke, "The Economic Outlook," before the Joint
Economic Committee, U.S. Congress, March 28, 2007.

99 *The problems were not contained*: Alan S. Blinder, *After the Music Stopped:
The Financial Crisis, the Response, and the Work Ahead* (New York: Pen-
guin Press, 2013); Andrew Ross Sorkin, *Too Big to Fail: The Inside Story of
How Wall Street and Washington Fought to Save the Financial System—and
Themselves* (New York: Viking, 2009); Sheryl Gay Stolberg, "Obama and
Republicans Clash over Stimulus Bill, One Year Later," *New York Times*,
February 17, 2010; Renae Merle, "A Guide to the Financial Crisis—10
Years Later," *Washington Post*, September 10, 2018.

101 *These fiscal programs were dwarfed*: Adam Tooze, *Crashed: How a Decade of Financial Crises Changed the World* (New York: Viking, 2018),
153–219; Bernanke, *The Courage to Act*.

101 *It is easiest to grasp the scale of the Fed's*: Figures of money supply, or "M1
Money Stock," taken from Economic Research Federal Reserve Bank
of St. Louis database, https://fred.stlouisfed.org/series/M1NS; Hoenig's
voting tally taken from transcripts of FOMC meetings, 2008–2009.

102 *When the crash of 2008 ended*: "UCLA Anderson Forecast: National
Recovery Linked to Global Solutions," States News Service, March 25,
2009; transcript, House Committee Hearing on Economic Budget
Challenges, January 27, 2009; Sheryl Gay Stolberg, "Obama and Re-
publicans Clash Over Stimulus Bill, One Year Later," *New York Times*,
February 17, 2010.

103 *All of this put even more pressure on central banks*: Paul Tucker, *Unelected
Power: The Quest for Legitimacy in Central Banking and the Regulatory
State* (Princeton, N.J.: Princeton University Press, 2018).

104 *In nearly twenty years as an FOMC member*: Daniel L. Thornton and
David C. Wheelock, "Making Sense of Dissents: A History of FOMC
Dissents," *Federal Reserve Bank of St. Louis Review*, Third Quarter 2014;
Sudeep Reddy, "The Lone Dissenter: Kansas City's Hoenig Goes Out
with a Record," *Wall Street Journal*, December 14, 2010; transcripts
of FOMC meetings when Thomas Hoenig dissented: July 1995, May
2001, December 2001, and October 2007.

104 *Hoenig could sense the uneasiness in the room*: Hoenig, interviews with
author, 2020.

CHAPTER 6: THE MONEY BOMB

107   *After he had cast his vote*: Thomas and Cynthia Hoenig, interviews with author, 2020.

108   *The Fed's policies were an obsession*: Carola Binder, "Federal Reserve Communication and the Media," *Journal of Media Economics*, October 2017; Carola Binder, interview with author, 2020.

109   *On the night that Hoenig cast his dissent*: "Americans Spending More Time Following the News," Pew Research Center, September 12, 2010; "Political Polarization & Media Habits," Pew Research Center, October 21, 2014. Glenn Beck monologue, "Devaluing the Dollar," 2010, uploaded to YouTube: https://www.youtube.com/watch?v=-QmPJAIbTwI; survey of Drudge Report and Huffington Post coverage taken from the Internet Archive at archive.org.

111   *The Fed was, in fact, trying to devalue*: Transcript of meeting of the Federal Open Market Committee, November 2–3, 2010.

112   *Ben Bernanke helped entrench*: Video and transcript of Ben Bernanke's appearance on *60 Minutes*. Bernanke's 2009 appearance: https://www.youtube.com/watch?v=QWJC__mz1Pc; Bernanke's 2010 appearance: https://www.youtube.com/watch?v=CMeB9sqWZqc; Bernanke, *The Courage to Act*.

113   *Beginning on November 4, 2010, the American financial system*: Notes from author's tour of New York Federal Reserve Bank trading floor, February 2020; author interviews with six current and former senior officials at the New York Federal Reserve Bank, 2020–2021, speaking on background. Three of these officials directly implemented the quantitative easing program.

117   *To understand the effects of ZIRP*: Author interviews with financial traders, on background, 2016–2020. The author is particularly indebted to one trader who prefers to remain anonymous, and who has a keen grasp of how markets work. Among many, many sources documenting the search for yield is *QE and Ultra-Low Interest Rates: Distributional Effects and Risks*, McKinsey Global Institute discussion paper, November 2013. Céline Choulet, "QE and Bank Balance Sheets: The American Experience," *Conjoncture*, July-August 2015.

120   *In early 2011, Hoenig retired*: Frank Morris, "Fed Dissenter Thomas Hoenig Retires," *All Things Considered*, September 28, 2011; transcript

of Thomas Hoenig speech, "Monetary Policy and the Role of Dissent," delivered at the Central Exchange, January 5, 2011.

120 *Between November 2010 and June 2011*: Figures of money supply, or "M1 Money Stock," taken from Economic Research Federal Reserve Bank of St. Louis database, https://fred.stlouisfed.org/series/M1NS; figures of excess reserves, or "Excess Reserves of Depository Institutions," taken from Economic Research Federal Reserve Bank of St. Louis database, https://fred.stlouisfed.org/series/EXCSRESNS.

121 *Bernanke's strongest opposition*: Jerome H. Powell and Betsy Duke, interviews with author, 2020; Bernanke, *The Courage to Act*, 531–63; selected transcripts of meetings of the Federal Open Market Committee, 2012–2014.

CHAPTER 7: QUANTITATIVE QUAGMIRE

125 *When Jerome Powell joined the Fed board*: Jerome H. Powell and Elizabeth "Betsy" Ashburn Duke, interviews with author, 2020; former Fed official, background interviews with author, 2020; Bernanke, *The Courage to Act*, 502–533; transcripts of meetings of the Federal Open Market Committee, January, March, April, June, July, and September 2012.

126 *The Fed had already employed two*: "Large-Scale Asset Purchases" timeline, Federal Reserve Bank of New York, accessed 2020; "Review of Monetary Policy Strategy, Tools, and Communications; Timelines of Policy Actions and Communications: Balance Sheet Policies," Federal Reserve Board, accessed 2020; Nick Timiraos, "Fed Releases Transcripts of 2012 Policy Meetings," *Wall Street Journal*, January 5, 2018.

127 *Powell began to work closely*: Duke, interviews with author, 2020; Jon Hilsenrath, "How Bernanke Pulled the Fed His Way," *Wall Street Journal*, September 28, 2012; transcripts of meetings of the Federal Open Market Committee, January, March, April, June, July, and September 2012; Bernanke, *The Courage to Act*, 502–533.

128 *When Bernanke lobbied the Fed governors*: Duke, interviews with author, 2020; two former FOMC members, interviewed on background by author, 2020; Richard Fisher, interviews with author, 2020; Jon Hilsenrath, "How Bernanke Pulled the Fed His Way," *Wall Street Journal*, September 28, 2012.

129 *In his very first meeting at the FOMC, Powell*: Duke, interviews with

author, 2020; two former FOMC members, interviewed on background by author, 2020; transcript of the meeting of the Federal Open Market Committee, June 19–20, 2012; Christopher Leonard, "How Jay Powell's Coronavirus Response Is Changing the Fed Forever," *Time*, June 11, 2020.

130 *One of Bernanke's secret weapons*: Duke and Yellen, interviews with author, 2020; transcripts of meetings of the Federal Open Market Committee, January, March, April, June, July, and September 2012.

131 *Fisher said that he had*: Transcript of meeting of the Federal Open Market Committee, July 31–August 1, 2012; Fisher, interviews with author, 2020; Peter Conti-Brown, *The Power and the Independence of the Federal Reserve* (Princeton, N.J.: Princeton University Press, 2017), 91.

132 *During the July meeting*: Powell and Duke, interviews with author, 2020; transcript of the meeting of the Federal Open Market Committee, July 31–August 1, 2012.

132 *The weather was beautiful*: Archived television and photographic coverage of Jackson Hole symposium; Jon Hilsenrath, "Fed Sets Stage for Stimulus," *Wall Street Journal*, August 31, 2012; Martin Feldstein, August 2012 interview with FoxBusiness, uploaded to YouTube, https://video.foxbusiness.com/v/1816772227001#sp=show-clips.

133 *Bernanke's speech that year*: "Monetary Policy Since the Onset of the Crisis," transcript of remarks by Ben S. Bernanke, chairman, Board of Governors of the Federal Reserve System, at the Federal Reserve Bank of Kansas City Economic Symposium, Jackson Hole, Wyoming, August 31, 2012; Jon Hilsenrath, "Fed Sets Stage for Stimulus," *Wall Street Journal*, August 31, 2012; Bernanke, *The Courage to Act*, 531–33.

134 *In Europe, the financial crisis of 2008*: Tooze, *Crashed*, 396–421, 91–117; Jackie Calmes, "Next on the Agenda for Washington: Fight over Debt," *New York Times*, April 9, 2011; Binyamin Appelbaum, "Debt Ceiling Has Some Give, Until Roof Falls In," *New York Times*, May 4, 2011; Jackie Calmes, "Demystifying the Fiscal Impasse That Is Vexing Washington," *New York Times*, November 15, 2012.

136 *On September 12*: Duke, Bernanke, Fisher, and Powell, interviews with author, 2020; two former FOMC officials, background interviews with author, 2020; transcript of the Meeting of the Federal Open Market Committee, September 12–13, 2012.

137 *The presentation was written by Seth Carpenter*: Seth Carpenter, interview with author, 2020; Seth B. Carpenter and Michelle Ezer, "Material for

Briefing on Potential Effects of a Large-Scale Asset-Purchase Program,"
September 12, 2012; figures on interest rates, or "Effective Federal
Funds Rate," taken from Economic Research Federal Reserve Bank of St.
Louis database, https://fred.stlouisfed.org/series/FEDFUNDS; Figures
on 30-year home loan rates, or "30-Year Fixed Rate Mortgage Average
in the United States," taken from Economic Research Federal Reserve
Bank of St. Louis database, https://fred.stlouisfed.org/series/MORT
GAGE30US; figures on value of Fed bonds in the New York trading
account taken from "System Open Market Account Portfolio," https://
www.newyorkfed.org/data-and-statistics/data-visualization/system
-open-market-account-portfolio; figures on price inflation taken from
"Median PCE Inflation," Federal Reserve Bank of Cleveland, https://
www.clevelandfed.org/our-research/indicators-and-data/median-pce
-inflation.aspx; all data accessed in 2020.

139 *These forecasting errors were not an isolated incident*: Brian Fabo, Martina
Jancokova, Elisabeth Kempf, and Lubos Pastor, "Fifty Shades of QE:
Conflicts of Interest in Economic Research," National Bureau of Eco-
nomic Research Working Paper No. 27849, September 28, 2020.

140 *These arguments were tame*: Transcript of the meeting of the Federal
Open Market Committee, September 12–13, 2012.

141 *When the Fed announced that its QE*: Duke, Fisher, Powell, and Bernanke,
interviews with author, 2020; FOMC, "Monetary Policy Alternatives,"
Tealbook presentation to FOMC members, September 6, 2012; "Options for an Additional LSAP Program," staff report from Federal Reserve
Board of Governors and Federal Reserve Bank of New York, August 28,
2012; Bernanke, *The Courage to Act*, 502–563; transcript of the meeting
of the Federal Open Market Committee, March 19–20, 2013.

144 *After the June meeting*: Transcript of Chairman Bernanke's press conference, June 19, 2013; archived news footage of press conference; Bernanke, *The Courage to Act*, 498.

145 *What happened next was . . . a kind of market shock*: Duke, Bernanke,
and Powell, interviews with author, 2020; two former FOMC officials,
background interviews with author, 2020; financial trader speaking on
background to author, 2016–2021; Nick Summers, "Market's 'Taper'
Tantrum Extends to Fourth Day," Bloomberg News, June 24, 2013;
Anusha Chari, Karlye Dilts Stedman, and Christian Lundblad, "Taper
Tantrums: QE, Its Aftermath and Emerging Market Capital Flows," National Bureau of Economic Research Working Paper 23474, June 2017.

147   *Even within hours of the press conference*: Duke, interviews with author, 2020; FOMC "Monetary Policy Alternatives," Tealbook presentation to FOMC members, September 6, 2012; "Options for an Additional LSAP Program," staff report from Federal Reserve Board of Governors and Federal Reserve Bank of New York, August 28, 2012.

148   *One of the Fed's own economists*: Transcript of meeting of the Federal Open Market Committee, September 12–13, 2012, 16; transcript of meeting of the Federal Open Market Committee, March 19–20, 2013, 22–24; transcript of meeting of the Federal Open Market Committee, January 29–30, 2013.

CHAPTER 8: THE FIXER

151   *When Jay Powell was a senior*: Powell, interview with author, 2020; "Notable Alumni," Georgetown Preparatory School; descriptions of Georgetown Prep taken from notes by author, 2020, and campus map from the school's website; Patricia H. Powell obituary, 2010; Jerome Powell (senior) obituary, 2007; "Elissa Leonard to Wed Jerome H. Powell," *New York Times*, September 15, 1985.

152   *As an adult, Jay Powell knew*: Josh Boak and Christopher Rugaber, "As Fed Chief, Powell Would Bring a Knack for Forging Consensus," Associated Press, November 5, 2017; Gary Siegel, "Market Sees Powell Nomination as Continuation of Policy," Bondbuyer.com, November 2, 2017; "Jerome Powell, Trump's Multi-Millionaire Pick for Fed Chief," Agence France Presse, November 2, 2017; "Jay Powell: From Warren Buffett to Fed Chair," AFR Online, November 3, 2017; "Jerome Powell's Nomination as Fed Chair Means 'More of the Same,' and Markets Love It," *Washington Post*, November 2, 2017; "Trump's Fed Chair Choice Largely Down to Powell or Taylor," *Washington Post*, October 26, 2017; Neil Irwin, "Experts Rate the Odds on Trump's Choice to Lead the Fed," *New York Times*, September 23, 2017; Zachary A. Goldfarb, "Obama Makes Bipartisan Fed Picks," *Washington Post*, December 28, 2011; "GEF Adds to Investment Team," Business Wire, July 8, 2008.

153   *When journalists describe Dillon, Read*: "Banker Joins Dillon Read," *New York Times*, February 17, 1995; Anthony Bianco, "The Wonder Woman of Muni Bonds," *Bloomberg Businessweek*, February 23, 1987; Catherine Austin Fitts, "Dillon Read & Co. Inc. and the Aristocracy of Prison Profits," 2006, http://www.jamlab.us/downloads/Documents/DillonRead_1.112506as.pdf.

153 *It might seem odd that a lawyer*: Catherine Austin Fitts, interview with author, 2020.

155 *There are two basic kinds of corporate debt*: Greg Nini, Vicki Bryan, and Austin Fitts, interviews with author, 2020; testimony of Dr. Greg Nini, Assistant Professor, Drexel University, before the U.S. House Committee on Financial Services Subcommittee, June 4, 2019.

156 *In 1988, the company's chairman*: Austin Fitts, interview with author, 2020; David E. Rosenbaum, "The Treasury's 'Mr. Diffident,'" *New York Times*, November 19, 1989.

157 *The problem started inside the large bureaucracy*: Kurt Eichenwald, "Salomon Is Punished by Treasury, Which Partly Relents Hours Later," *New York Times*, August 19, 1991; Stephen Labaton, "Salomon Inquiry Widened," *New York Times*, September 4, 1991; Robert A. Rosenblatt, "Salomon Cornered Market," *Los Angeles Times*, September 5, 1991; Diana B. Henriques, "Treasury's Troubled Auctions," *New York Times*, September 15, 1991; "Former Salomon Chief Fined in Bond Scandal," *Chicago Tribune*, December 4, 1992; Keith Bradsher, "Former Salomon Trader to Pay $1.1 Million Fine," *New York Times*, July 15, 1994; Mike Dorning, "Former Salomon Chief Fined in Bond Scandal," *Chicago Tribune*, December 4, 1992; Keith Bradsher, "Former Salomon Trader to Pay $1.1 Million Fine," *New York Times*, July 15, 1994.

158 *Powell's boss*: Steve Bell, interview with author, 2020.

161 *Leveraging the connections and influence of Washington*: Senior Carlyle Group executive, background interview with author, 2020; transcript of David Rubenstein interview with CNBC's *Power Lunch*, July 18, 2018; Thomas Heath, "Now in Their Own Orbits, Carlyle's Stars Keep Rising," *Washington Post*, July 24, 2007; "The Carlyle Group Alumni," *Washington Post*, July 24, 2007; Dan Freed, "Carlyle Tightens Its Focus on Consumer Products," *Corporate Financing Week*, March 21, 2004; Christa Fanelli, "Carlyle Picks Up Trio of Heavy Hitters," *Private Equity Week*, May 7, 2001; Irene Cherkassky, "Adventures in Venture Capitalism," *Beverage World*, September 15, 2000; Dan Briody, *The Iron Triangle: Inside the Secret World of the Carlyle Group* (Hoboken, N.J.: John Wiley & Sons, 2003).

163 *Our offices were so boring*: Christopher Ullman, interview with author, 2020.

163 *Rexnord's headquarters were located*: Images of Rexnord headquarters retrieved from Google Maps and Google Street View, 2020.

164 *Tom Jansen started working*: Tom Jansen, interviews with author, 2020; "REG—Invensys PLC Strategy Review," February 19, 2002; Thomas Content, "Rexnord Corp. Again Up for Sale," *Milwaukee Journal Sentinel*,

February 23, 2002; "Carlyle to Buy Rexnord," *Washington Post*, September 30, 2002; "The Carlyle Group Completes Rexnord Acquisition," Business Wire, November 25, 2002; Nicola Hobday, "Carlyle Buys Invensys Power Unit for $880M," *Daily Deal*, September 30, 2002; Thomas Content, "Rexnord Is Acquired by Carlyle Group," *Milwaukee Journal Sentinel*, November 27, 2002; "Rexnord Corp. Reports Fourth Quarter and Full Year Results," *Business Wire*, June 15, 2005; Paul Sharke, "Big Hold from Small Screws," *Mechanical Engineering*, November 1, 2001.

165   *The debt put pressure on Rexnord*: Jansen, interview with author, 2020; Rick Romell, "Rexnord to Close Plant in West Milwaukee for Week; Union Agrees to Shutdown to Help Save Money, Jobs," *Milwaukee Journal Sentinel*, July 27, 2006.

166   *After Powell joined Rexnord's board*: Jansen, interview with author, 2020; one current and one former senior employee at the Carlyle Group interviewed on background by author, 2020; images of Doral Country Club taken from hotel's website.

168   *In early 2005, Rexnord still carried*: Rexnord financial figures taken from Rexnord Form 10-K filings with U.S. Securities and Exchange Commission, 2003–2009; select Moody's Debt Ratings reports on Rexnord.

168   *First, Rexnord toyed with the idea of going public*: Jansen, interview with author, 2020; "Apollo Management to Buy Rexnord in $1.83 Billion Deal," *Wall Street Journal*, May 25, 2006; "Carlyle Flips Parts Maker to Apollo for $1.8 Billion," *New York Times*, May 25, 2006; "Rexnord to Be Acquired from Carlyle by Apollo Management for $1.8 Billion," *Machinery and Equipment MRO*, June 1, 2006.

169   *The payoff to Jay Powell and his team was immense*: Former senior Carlyle Group employee, interview on background with author, 2020; "Jerome Powell, Trump's Multi-Millionaire Pick for Fed Chief," Agence France Presse, November 2, 2017; financial figures on Rexnord sale taken from sources in note above; Rexnord Form 10-K filings, 2003–2012; select Moody's debt ratings reports on Rexnord.

170   *One person who helped underwrite*: Rexnord Incremental Assumption and Debt Agreement, August 21, 2013.

CHAPTER 9: THE RISK MACHINE

171   *Some of the most profitable products*: Robert Hetu, interviews with author, 2020; various Rexnord debt-financing and debt-rating documents

including: Rexnord Incremental Assumption and Debt Agreement, August 21, 2013; RBS Global, Inc., and Rexnord LLC Form 8-K, filed with U.S. Securities and Exchange Commission, April 17, 2012; Rexnord Corp., Form 8-K filing, November 2, 2016; Rexnord Form 10-K filings with SEC, 2010–2020; Moody's Investors Service Credit Opinion on Rexnord Corp., December 10, 2003; Moody's Investors Service Credit Opinion on Rexnord Corp., August 5, 2016; Moody's Investors Service Credit Opinion on Rexnord Corp., August 18, 2020.

171 *Hetu's office overlooked*: Hetu, interviews with author, 2020; descriptions of Credit Suisse office taken from Google Maps and Street View and Hetu's descriptions of office interior.

174 *This name, CLO, might sound familiar*: Hetu and Greg Nini, interviews with author, 2020; the author is deeply indebted to Alexander Holt, an independent researcher who developed a detailed portfolio on the history, structure, and financing of CLOs during the winter of 2020, also providing hours of invaluable discussion on the topic; Sally Bakewell, "CLOs: Corporate Loans Sliced, Diced and Worrisome," *Bloomberg Businessweek*, March 29, 2019; Tom Metcalf, Tom Maloney, Sally Bakewell, and Christopher Cannon, "Wall Street's Billionaire Machine, Where Almost Everyone Gets Rich," Bloomberg News, December 20, 2018; Lisa Lee, "Battered CLO Investors Are About to Get a Look at Their Losses," Bloomberg News, April 20, 2020; Sunny Oh, "Here's Why the Fed and Global Regulators Are Ringing the Alarm over Leveraged Loans and CLOs," *MarketWatch*, March 12, 2019; Kelsey Butler, "Shadow Bank Lending Vehicles on Pace for Worst Quarter on Record," Bloomberg News, March 25, 2020; Jane Baird, "CDO Market Seen Shrinking by Half in Long Term," Reuters, October 1, 2007.

174 *Credit Suisse was a leading producer of CLOs*: Hetu, interviews with author, 2020; Glen Fest, "Banks' Warehouse Loans Play Big Role in CLO Resurgence," *American Banker*, August 11, 2014; Matthew Toole, "Records Broken in Global Capital Markets During Q3," *Refinitiv Deals Intelligence*, November 2, 2020; "CLO Asset Manager Handbook," *Fitch Ratings*, April 2017.

175 *Popp looks like a trustworthy guy*: John Popp, "Beyond the Core: Preparing Portfolios for a Post-Treasury-Rally World," Credit Suisse Asset Management report, May 2012; descriptions of Popp's appearance taken from his portrait included in report and other Credit Suisse marketing material.

175 *The key innovation of CLOs*: Nini, Hetu, and Holt, interviews with author, 2003; ibid., sources in Note 3.

177 *Credit Suisse helped Rexnord roll its debt*: Hetu, interviews with author; notes on Rexnord debt offerings, ibid., Note 1.

177 *It was around this time*: Vicky Bryan, interview with author, 2020.

178 *All that money*: CLO Yearbook 2018, Credit Flux, accessed 2020 at: https://www.creditflux.com/CLOYearbook2018; Sally Bakewell, "CLOs: Corporate Loans Sliced, Diced and Worrisome," *Bloomberg Businessweek*, March 29, 2019.

178 *Hetu described this situation*: Hetu, interviews with author, 2020.

180 *The Cov-lite loan, once an exotic debt instrument*: Jim Edwards, "The Risky 'Leveraged Loan' Market Just Sunk to a Whole New Low," *BusinessInsider*, February 17, 2019; Sean Collins, "A Quick Look at the Future for Business Development Companies," Deloitte *Perspectives*, March 20, 2019.

182 *It would be easy, years later, to point fingers*: Transcript of the meeting of the Federal Open Market Committee, September 12–13, 2012.

CHAPTER 10: THE ZIRP REGIME

185 *When Jay Powell sat on Rexnord's board*: Tom Jansen, interview with author, 2020; Tom Daykin, "Rexnord Moving into City; Executives Will Work at Global Water Center," *Milwaukee Journal Sentinel*, April 1, 2014; description of Rexnord's headquarters taken from Google Maps and Street View, 2020.

185 *These factories were seen as assets*: Jansen, interview with author, 2020; Debt ratings analyst, background interview with author, 2020; Rexnord Corp., 10-K filings with U.S. Securities and Exchange Commission, 2013–2020; Moody's Investors Service Credit Opinion on Rexnord Corp., August 18, 2020; "Rexnord Announces President & Chief Executive Officer's Appointment," Business Wire news release, September 14, 2009; Rexnord Corp. 14A Proxy filings with SEC, 2012–2020.

186 *When Todd Adams talked publicly*: Todd Adams, Rexnord marketing video, "A Message from CEO Todd Adams," accessed at company's website, https://rexnordcorporation.com/en-US/Rexnord-Business-System; compensation figures taken from Rexnord 10-K and 14A Proxy filings.

188 *When John Feltner got the chance to interview*: John Feltner, interviews with author, 2020–2021; Rick Barrett, "Rexnord Workers Stuck in

Middle," *Milwaukee Journal Sentinel*, December 9, 2016; Robert King, "Rexnord Worker Feels Pain of Coming Closure; Indiana Plant Shifts Positions to Mexico," *Milwaukee Journal Sentinel*, March 1, 2017; Farah Stockman, "Becoming a Steelworker Liberated Her. Then Her Job Moved to Mexico," *New York Times*, October 14, 2017.

190 *From the view of Rexnord's headquarters office*: Debt figures taken from Rexnord Corp. 10-K filings with U.S. Securities and Exchange Commission, 2013–2020; ownership stakes taken from Rexnord 14A filing, 2014; Rick Barrett, "Rexnord Stock Gains 11% in Debut; Shares Close at $20 a Day After IPO Priced at $18," *Milwaukee Journal Sentinel*, March 30, 2012.

192 *Stock buybacks were made legal in 1982*: William Lazonick, "Profits Without Prosperity," *Harvard Business Review*, September 2014; Liyu Zeng and Priscilla Luk, "Examining Share Repurchasing and the S&P Buyback Indices in the U.S. Market," *S&P Dow Jones Indices*, March 2020; Sirio Aramonte, "Mind the Buybacks, Beware of the Leverage," *BIS Quarterly Review*, September 2020.

193 *The most boring-seeming companies in America*: Antoine Gara and Nathan Vardi, "Inside the $2.5 Trillion Debt Binge That Has Taken S&P 500 Titans Including Boeing and AT&T from Blue Chips to Junk," *Forbes*, July 2020.

193 *Rexnord was considering a stock buyback in 2015*: Rexnord 10-K and 14A Proxy filings, 2013–2020.

194 *Feltner was a longtime union guy*: Feltner, interviews with author, 2020–2021; James Briggs, "Manufacturer Rexnord Plans to Move 300 High-Paying Jobs to Mexico," *Indianapolis Star*, October 14, 2016; King, "Rexnord Worker Feels Pain of Coming Closure"; Robert King, "Laid Off from Rexnord, Once-Bitter Worker Settles into a 'New Norm,'" *Indianapolis Star*, February 9, 2018. All Rexnord debt figures taken from Rexnord Corp. 10-K filings with SEC, 2015–2020; Moody's Investors Service Credit Opinions on Rexnord Corp., 2015–2020.

195 *In May 2016, Rexnord made*: Brooke Sutherland, "Toilet Maker May Suit Buyer Flush with Cash; With Industrials Desperate for Deals, a Rexnord Sale Makes Sense," Bloomberg News, May 25.

196 *Looking back, Rexnord employees would say*: Feltner, interviews with author, 2020–2021; Stockman, "Becoming a Steelworker Liberated Her"; Briggs, "Manufacturer Rexnord Plans to Move 300 High-Paying Jobs to Mexico"; King, "Rexnord Worker Feels Pain of Coming Closure";

King, "Laid Off from Rexnord, Once-Bitter Worker Settles into a 'New Norm.'"

197 *They convened at the Mount Olive Ministries church*: "Carrier and Rexnord Workers Pray to Save Their Jobs in Indianapolis," WRATV Indianapolis, uploaded to YouTube, https://www.youtube.com/watch?v=7bk1QNTXqpA.

198 *Todd Adams never managed to find a buyer*: All Rexnord debt, income, and compensation figures come from Rexnord Corp. 10-K and 14A Proxy filings with SEC.

199 *John Feltner did his "Play-Doh" routine*: Feltner, interviews with author, 2020–2021.

199 *Jay Powell had earned his personal fortune*: Figures on corporate debt, or "Nonfinancial Corporate Business; Debt Securities and Loans; Liability, Level," taken from Economic Research Federal Reserve Bank of St. Louis database, https://fred.stlouisfed.org/series/BCNSDODNS.

200 *Hoenig also had other things on his mind*: Hoenig, interview with author, 2020.

CHAPTER 11: THE HOENIG RULE

201 *After Thomas Hoenig left*: Thomas Hoenig, interviews with author, 2016–2021. The author is deeply indebted to Kelly Kullman, a 2020 student reporter at the Watchdog Writers Group, a nonprofit journalism institute at the University of Missouri School of Journalism. Kullman spent months researching Tom Hoenig's tenure at the Federal Deposit Insurance Corporation, along with the history of that institution going back to the Great Depression. Kullman's reporting and insights were invaluable in writing this chapter.

202 *Everybody knew where Tom Hoenig stood*: Transcript of Thomas Hoenig speech, "Back to Basics: A Better Alternative to Basel Capital Rules," delivered to the American Banker Regulatory Symposium, September 14, 2012; transcript of Hoenig speech, "Financial Stability Through Properly Aligned Incentives," delivered to the Exchequer Club, September 19, 2012; Barbara A. Rehm, "For Megabanks, It's Time to Shape Up or Break Up," *American Banker*, July 26, 2012.

203 *But very early on, the warning signs*: Transcript, U.S. Senate Committee on Banking, Housing and Urban Affairs Hearing on Pending Nominations, November 17, 2011.

204   *Hoenig was called before a Senate hearing*: Hoenig, interviews with au-
       thor, 2020; transcript, U.S. Senate Hearing on Limiting Federal Support
       for Financial Institutions, Panel 2—Committee Hearing, May 9, 2012;
       Allan Sloan, "Taking Stock Five Years After the Meltdown," *Washington
       Post*, June 17, 2012.

205   *With this support, Hoenig kept pushing*: Transcript of Thomas Hoe-
       nig speech, "Financial Stability Through Properly Aligned Incentives,"
       delivered to the Exchequer Club, September 19, 2012; Scott Lanman,
       "Thomas Hoenig Is Fed Up," *Bloomberg Businessweek*, September 23, 2010.

206   *Hoenig made the rounds on Capitol Hill*: Hoenig, interviews with author,
       2020; Ryan Tracy, "FDIC's Hoenig Keeps Wall Street on Edge," Dow
       Jones Newswires, September 25, 2014.

207   *The very complexity of Dodd-Frank*: Haley Sweetland Edwards, "He Who
       Makes the Rules," *Washington Monthly*, March/April 2013; Gina Chon,
       "FDIC Is Last Defense Against Dodd-Frank Rollbacks," Reuters News,
       September 22, 2017.

208   *In 2013, the big banks submitted their living wills*: Thomas Hoenig, in-
       terviews with author, 2020; Alan Zibel, "FDIC to Offer Guidance to
       Banks, Online Lenders," Dow Jones Newswires, September 26, 2013;
       Ronald Orol, "Hoenig: Banks Get One Year to Fix Wills or Face Dives-
       titures," *The Deal*, September 23, 2014; Barney Jopson, "Regulators Re-
       ject 'Living Wills' of 5 Big US Banks," *Financial Times*, April 13, 2016;
       Ronald Orol, "FDIC's Hoenig Urges More Public Disclosure of Big
       Bank 'Living Wills,'" *The Deal*, March 2, 2015; Ronald Orol, "Repub-
       licans Take Issue with Big Bank Living Wills," *The Deal*, July 16, 2014;
       Gina Chon and Tom Braithwaite, "Living Wills Raise Liquidity Fears,"
       Financial Times, November 3, 2014.

208   *One group of people who seemed to have zero*: Rob Blackwell and Donna
       Borak, "Gruenberg Confronts Doubts That FDIC Will End TBTF,"
       American Banker, May 11, 2012.

209   *There was a reason that the banks*: Hoenig, interviews with author, 2016–
       2020; FDIC's Global Capital Index, fourth quarter, 2013; Simon John-
       son, "The Fed in Denial," *Project Syndicate*, July 22, 2014; "FDIC Vice
       Chairman Hoenig Issues Statement on Global Capital Index," Targeted
       News Service, April 13, 2017.

211   *Between 2007 and 2017, the Fed's balance sheet*: Figures on Fed's balance
       sheet, or "Total Assets," taken from Economic Research Federal Reserve
       Bank of St. Louis database, https://fred.stlouisfed.org/series/WALCL;

QE and Ultra-Low Interest Rates: Distributional Effects and Risks, McKinsey Global Institute discussion paper, November 2013.

212   *The search for yield . . . corporate debt and stocks*: "Who Owns U.S. CLO Securities?" *FEDS Notes*, July 19, 2019; Paul J. Davies, "Tense Time for Buyers of Riskier Corporate Loans," *Wall Street Journal*, January 6, 2020; Olen Honeyman, Hanna Zhang, Tejaswini Tungare, and Ramki Muthukrishnan, "When the Cycle Turns: The Continued Attack of the EBITDA Add-Back," S&P Global Ratings, September 19, 2019; Frank Partnoy, "The Looming Bank Collapse," *The Atlantic*, July/August 2020.

213   *The search for yield . . . oil industry*: Bethany McLean, "The Next Financial Crisis Lurks Underground," *New York Times*, September 1, 2018; Bradley Olson, Rebecca Elliott, and Christopher M. Matthews, "Fracking's Secret Problem—Oil Wells Aren't Producing as Much as Forecast," *Wall Street Journal*, January 2, 2019; Rebecca Elliott and Christopher M. Matthews, "As Shale Wells Age, Gap Between Forecasts and Performance Grows," *Wall Street Journal*, December 29, 2019; Ryan Dezember, "Energy Industry Faces Reckoning After Oil Prices Crash," *Wall Street Journal*, March 10, 2020; Sam Goldfarb and Matt Wirz, "Borrowing Binge Reaches Riskiest Companies," *Wall Street Journal*, February 15, 2021; Lukas Ross, Alan Zibel, Dan Wagner, and Chris Kuveke, "Big Oil's $100 Billion Bender," joint report by Bailout Watch, Friends of the Earth, and Public Citizen, September 1, 2020; Ares Capital 10-K filing with Securities and Exchange Commission, December 31, 2017.

214   *The search for yield . . . into commercial real estate*: John Flynn, interview with author, 2020; Heather Vogell, "Whistleblower: Wall Street Has Engaged in Widespread Manipulation of Mortgage Funds," *ProPublica*, May 15, 2020; Cezary Podkul, "Commercial Properties' Ability to Repay Mortgages Was Overstated, Study Finds," *Wall Street Journal*, August 11, 2020; David Dayen, "Look at That, Fraud in Mortgage Markets!," *American Prospect*, May 19, 2020.

216   *The search for yield . . . government debt of developing nations*: David J. Lynch, "Turkey's Woes Could Be Just the Start as Record Global Debt Bills Come Due," *Washington Post*, September 3, 2018; David J. Lynch, "Turkey Went on a Building Spree as Its Economy Boomed. Now the Frenzy Is Crashing to a Halt," *Washington Post*, September 25, 2018; Matt Phillips and Karl Russell, "The Next Financial Calamity Is Coming. Here's What to Watch," *New York Times*, September 12, 2018; Peter S. Goodman, "For Erdogan, the Bill for Turkey's Debt-Fueled

Growth Comes Due," *New York Times*, June 24, 2019; Anusha Chari, Karlye Dilts Stedman, and Christian Lundblad, "Taper Tantrums: QE, Its Aftermath and Emerging Market Capital Flows," National Bureau of Economic Research, Working Paper 23474, June 2017; *QE and Ultra-Low Interest Rates: Distributional Effects and Risks*, McKinsey Global Institute discussion paper, November 2013.

217 *Finally, the world's central banks . . . yield upside down*: Financial trader, background interviews with author, 2016–2020; Daniel Kruger, "Negative Yields Mount Along with Europe's Problems," *Wall Street Journal*, February 18, 2019; Jeff Sommer, "In the Bizarro World of Negative Interest Rates, Saving Will Cost You," *New York Times*, March 5, 2016; Brian Blackstone, "Negative Rates, Designed as a Short-Term Jolt, Have Become an Addiction," *Wall Street Journal*, May 20, 2019.

218 *This was happening as Tom Hoenig*: Thomas Hoeing, interview with author at FDIC headquarters, 2016.

CHAPTER 12: TOTALLY NORMAL

221 *During most of Jay Powell's career*: Jay Powell, interview with author, 2020; transcript of the meeting of the Federal Open Market Committee, January 28–29, 2014; Christopher Leonard, "How Jay Powell's Coronavirus Response Is Changing the Fed Forever," *Time*, June 11, 2020.

223 *During Yellen's first year on the job*: Janet Yellen, interview with author, 2020; transcripts of the meetings of the Federal Open Market Committee, January, March, April, June, July, September, October, and December 2014; Federal Reserve Board, "Timelines of Policy Actions and Communications: Policy Normalization Principles and Plans," February 22, 2019; Jon Hilsenrath, "Fed Sets Stage for Rate Hikes in 2015," *Wall Street Journal*, December 17, 2014; "Policy Normalization Principles and Plans," Federal Reserve press release, September 17, 2014; Neil Irwin, "Quantitative Easing Is Ending. Here's What It Did, in Charts," *New York Times*, October 29, 2014; Michael S. Derby and Jon Hilsenrath, "Fed's Dudley: Still Likely on Track for 2015 Rate Rise," *Wall Street Journal*, September 28, 2015.

224 *Experts grappled with this puzzle*: Brookings Institution event accessed 2020 at https://www.brookings.edu/events/whats-not-up-with -inflation/.

224 *Jay Powell, in 2014, was determined*: Transcript of meeting of the Federal Open Market Committee, June 17–18, 2014.

225 *Roughly seven months after delivering*: Richard Fisher, interview with author, 2020; former FOMC member, background interview with author, 2020; transcript of Jerome H. Powell speech, "'Audit the Fed' and Other Proposals," delivered at Catholic University of America, Columbus School of Law, February 9, 2015.

226 *In closed-door meetings*: Transcript of meeting of the Federal Open Market Committee, September 16–17, 2015.

227 *In December 2015, the Fed raised rates*: Transcript of meeting of the Federal Open Market Committee, December 15–16, 2015; Jon Hilsenrath and Ben Leubsdorf, "Fed Raises Rates After Seven Years Near Zero, Expects 'Gradual' Tightening Path," *Wall Street Journal*, December 16, 2015; Nick Timiraos, "Fed Raised Interest Rates in 2015 Despite Concerns over Growth," *Wall Street Journal*, January 8, 2021.

227 *The Fed was normalizing slowly*: Figures of excess reserves, or "Excess Reserves of Depository Institutions," taken from Economic Research Federal Reserve Bank of St. Louis database, https://fred.stlouisfed.org/series/ EXCSRESNS; figures on Fed's balance sheet, or "Total Assets," taken from Economic Research Federal Reserve Bank of St. Louis database, https://fred.stlouisfed.org/series/WALCL.

228 *Trump's animosity toward most government*: Trump's debate comments on "bubble" accessed in 2020 via YouTube at https://www.youtube.com/ watch?v=4xn9jLy_TB4.

228 *Jay Powell was hardly considered a front runner*: Steven Mnuchin, interview with author, 2020; "Jerome Powell's Nomination as Fed Chair Means 'More of the Same,' and Markets Love It," *Washington Post*, November 2, 2017; "Trump's Fed Chair Choice Largely Down to Powell or Taylor," *Washington Post*, October 26, 2017; "US Federal Reserve Calls Historic End to Quantitative Easing," *Financial Times*, September 20, 2017.

230 *It was unclear, at first, what Trump's victory*: Thomas Hoenig, interviews with author, 2020–2021; Ryan Tracy, "FDIC's Thomas Hoenig Said to Be Interested in Job in Trump Administration," *Wall Street Journal*, November 14, 2016; Robert Schmidt and Jesse Hamilton, "Ten Years After the Crisis, Banks Win Big in Trump's Washington," *Bloomberg Businessweek*, February 9, 2018.

230 *In April 2018, Hoenig left the FDIC*: Jesse Hamilton, "Wall Street's Least Favorite Regulator Is Calling It Quits," Bloomberg News, April 27, 2018.

231 *Becoming Fed chairman presented Jay Powell*: "Timelines of Policy Actions

and Communications: Policy Normalization Principles and Plans," Federal Reserve Board, February 22, 2019; "US Federal Reserve Calls Historic End to Quantitative Easing," *Financial Times*, September 20, 2017; Jeff Cox, "Janet Yellen Calls Stock Market, Real Estate 'High' in Last Interview Before Exit as Fed Chief," CNBC.com, February 4, 2018; Ben Casselman and Jim Tankersley, "More Jobs, Faster Growth and Now, the Threat of a Trade War," *New York Times*, April 6, 2018; figures of interest rates, or "Effective Federal Funds Rate," taken from Economic Research Federal Reserve Bank of St. Louis database, https://fred.stlouisfed.org/series/FEDFUNDS.

231 *On Monday, February 5, 2018*: Akane Otani, "Dow Drops More Than 1,100 Points in Stock-Market Route," *Wall Street Journal*, February 5, 2018; Corrie Driebusch, Riva Gold, and Daniel Kruger, "Dow Drops More Than 650 Points on Worries About Inflation," *Wall Street Journal*, February 2, 2018; Ben Leubsdorf, "U.S. Gained 200,000 Jobs in January as Wages Picked Up," *Wall Street Journal*, February 2, 2018; Nick Timiraos, "Market Turmoil Greets New Federal Reserve Chairman," *Wall Street Journal*, February 5, 2018; Gunjan Banerji and Alexander Osipovich, "Market Rout Shatters Lull in Volatility," *Wall Street Journal*, February 5, 2018; Matt Phillips, "Dow Jones and S.&P. Slide Again, Dropping by More Than 4%," *New York Times*, February 5, 2018; James Mackintosh, "What Should We Make of the Stock-Price Drop?," *Wall Street Journal*, February 5, 2018; Akane Otani, Riva Gold, and Michael Wursthorn, "U.S. Stocks End Worst Week in Years," *Wall Street Journal*, March 23, 2018.

231 *The market turbulence was not a sideshow*: Mohamed A. El-Erian, *The Only Game in Town: Central Banks, Instability, and Avoiding the Next Collapse* (New York: Random House, 2016).

232 *Powell's leadership on this front was steady*: Ibid., Note 13. Nick Timiraos, "President Trump Bashes the Fed. This Is How the Fed Chief Responds," *Wall Street Journal*, November 30, 2018; Christopher Condon, "Key Trump Quotes on Powell as Fed Remains in the Firing Line," Bloomberg News, December 17, 2019.

233 *As Powell built support*: Jim Tankersley and Neil Irwin, "Fed Raises Interest Rates and Signals 2 More Increases Are Coming," *New York Times*, June 13, 2018; Nick Timiraos, "Fed Raises Interest Rates, Signals One More Increase This Year," *Wall Street Journal*, September 26, 2018; Matt Phillips, "The Hot Topic in Markets Right Now: 'Quantitative Tightening,'" *New York Times*, January 30, 2019; Amrith Ramkumar and Nick Timiraos,

"Fed Chairman's Remarks Spark Market Rally," *Wall Street Journal*, November 28, 2018; Nick Timiraos, "Fed Weighs Wait-and-See Approach on Future Rate Increases," *Wall Street Journal*, December 6, 2018.

234 *The direct relationship between the Fed's actions*: Jack Ewing, "Europe's Central Bank Ends One of the Biggest Money-Printing Programs Ever," *New York Times*, December 13, 2018; Federal Reserve Board of Governors, Financial Stability Report, November 2018; Corrie Driebusch, Akane Otani, and Jessica Menton, "Jittery Investors Deepen Stock Fall," *Wall Street Journal*, October 11, 2018.

235 *December was the pivotal month*: Jay Powell, interview with author, 2020; transcript of Chairman Powell's press conference, December 19, 2018; Matt Phillips, "Investors Have Nowhere to Hide as Stocks, Bonds and Commodities All Tumble," *New York Times*, December 15, 2018; Matt Phillips, "The Hot Topic in Markets Right Now: 'Quantitative Tightening,'" *New York Times*, January 30, 2019.

236 *On Christmas Eve, a normally quiet*: Janna Herron, "Dow, Stocks End Sharply Lower on Christmas Eve After Weekend of Washington, D.C., Turmoil," *USA Today*, December 24, 2018.

236 *On January 25, 2019, a story was leaked*: Nick Timiraos, "Fed Officials Weigh Earlier-Than-Expected End to Bond Portfolio Runoff," *Wall Street Journal*, January 25, 2019; Nick Timiraos, "Fed Signals Hold on Interest Rate Increases," *Wall Street Journal*, January 30, 2018.

236 *After the FOMC meeting that month*: Jim Bianco and Scott Minerd, interviews with author, 2020; financial trader speaking on background, interviews with author, 2019–2020; Akane Otani, "Bond Rally Suggests the Stock Market Honeymoon Is on Borrowed Time," *Wall Street Journal*, February 3, 2019; Nick Timiraos, "Fed Keeps Interest Rates Unchanged; Signals No More Increases Likely This Year," *Wall Street Journal*, March 20, 2019.

237 *Deflation was a central problem*: Financial trader speaking on background, interviews with author, 2019–2020; Akane Otani and Georgi Kantchev, "Stocks, Bond Yields Fall Amid Anxiety over World Economy," *Wall Street Journal*, March 22, 2019; Akane Otani and Joe Wallace, "Stock Market Rally Trips on Global Growth Fears," *Wall Street Journal*, March 24, 2019; Jon Hilsenrath, "The World Braces for Slower Growth," *Wall Street Journal*, January 21, 2019; Nick Timiraos, Tom Fairless, and Brian Blackstone, "Slow Growth Prods Central Banks," *Wall Street Journal*, March 7, 2019; Greg Ip, "For a Change, It's the World That Is Pulling

Down the U.S. Economy," *Wall Street Journal*, October 2, 2019; Greg Ip, "Powell's Critics Miss the Mark," *Wall Street Journal*, March 27, 2019; Nick Timiraos, "Fed Keeps Interest Rates Unchanged; Signals No More Increases Likely This Year," *Wall Street Journal*, March 20, 2019.

238   *In July, Powell led . . . something extraordinary*: Heather Long, "With the Economy on the Line, the Fed Prepares to Take Its Biggest Gamble Yet," *Washington Post*, July 29, 2019; Nick Timiraos, "Fed Chief Wedged Between a Slowing Economy and an Angry President," *Wall Street Journal*, August 18, 2019; Greg Ip, "The Era of Fed Power Is Over. Prepare for a More Perilous Road Ahead," *Wall Street Journal*, January 15, 2020; Corrie Driebusch, Britton O'Daly, and Paul J. Davies, "Dow Sheds 800 in Biggest Drop of Year," *Wall Street Journal*, August 14, 2019; Josh Mitchell and Jon Hilsenrath, "Warning Signs Point to a Global Slowdown," *Wall Street Journal*, August 14, 2019; Damian Paletta, Thomas Heath, and Taylor Telford, "Stocks Losses Deepen as a Key Recession Warning Surfaces," *Washington Post*, August 14, 2019; Sarah Chaney, "Modest August Job Growth Shows Economy Expanding, but Slowly," *Wall Street Journal*, September 6, 2019; Paul Vigna, "U.S. Stocks Drop on Worries About Growth," *Wall Street Journal*, October 2, 2019.

238   *If Powell felt like he had control*: Senior trading officials at the New York Federal Reserve, background interviews with author, 2020.

CHAPTER 13: THE INVISIBLE BAILOUT

A note on sources:

It is common practice for the public relations office at the Federal Reserve Bank of New York to arrange background interviews for reporters with senior officials at the bank. The interviews are provided if reporters agree not to directly quote the officials. On February 14, 2020, the public relations office arranged a background interview for the author with two senior officials at the New York Federal Reserve Bank of New York's Markets Group, who were directly involved in the events described in this chapter.

On February 27, 2020, the public relations team arranged an interview by the author with the New York Fed's president, John Williams, and Lorie Logan, executive vice president of the bank's Markets Group. The interview was focused entirely on the events described in this chapter. At the time, the author was reporting a story about the New York Fed's 2019 intervention in the repo markets for *Time* magazine, a story that later evolved into one about the Fed's COVID-19 bailout. For this interview, it was agreed that the author could use quotes from the interview, but only after letting the public relations team check the quotes for accuracy. The interviews were digitally recorded, and quotes in this book are taken from a direct transcript of the interview.

The author also conducted independent background interviews with three former senior officials at the Federal Reserve Bank of New York who were directly involved in operating the bank's trading operations. These interviews provided background context and knowledge for this chapter and are not always directly cited in the notes below.

The author is particularly indebted to Alexander Holt, who spent weeks helping to research the nature, origins, and impact of the Fed's repo intervention. Among many other accomplishments, Holt discovered the academic paper, cited below, "Monetary Policy Implementation with an Ample Supply of Reserves," and helped translate it into plain English while sketching graphs on a legal pad. His insights and explanations were indispensable.

241 *At 9:05 on the morning of Friday, September*: Lorie Logan, interview with author, 2020; two senior New York Fed Markets Group officials, background interviews with author, 2020; descriptions of Markets Group trading floors and offices taken from notes during author's tour of the Markets Group, February 27, 2020.

243 *The Fed itself was directly responsible*: Gara Afonso, Kyungmin Kim, Antoine Martin, Ed Nosal, Simon Potter, and Sam Schulhofer-Wohl, "Monetary Policy Implementation with an Ample Supply of Reserves," Federal Reserve Bank of Atlanta Working Paper Series 2020-2 (January 2020); Bank for International Settlements Study Group chaired by Lorie Logan and Ulrich Bindseil, "Large Central Bank Balance Sheets and Market Functioning," Bank for International Settlements Markets Committee report, October 2019; Todd Keister and James J. McAndrews, "Why Are Banks Holding So Many Excess Reserves?," New York Federal Reserve Bank of New York *Current Issues in Economics and Finance*, December 2009; Scott A. Wolla, "A New Frontier: Monetary Policy with Ample Reserves," Federal Reserve Bank of St. Louis *Page One Economics*, May 2019.

244 *On the following Monday*: Federal Reserve officials, background interviews with author, 2020; Sriya Anbil, Alyssa Anderson, and Zeynep Senyuz, "What Happened in Money Markets in September 2019?," *FEDS Notes*, February 27, 2020; Nick Timiraos, " 'Why Were They Surprised?'

Repo Market Turmoil Tests New York Fed Chief," *Wall Street Journal*, September 29, 2019; Alex Harris, " 'This Is Crazy!': Wall Street Scurries to Protect Itself in Repo Surge," Bloomberg News, September 17, 2019; Emily Barrett and Jesse Hamilton, "Why the U.S. Repo Market Blew Up and How to Fix It," Bloomberg News, January 6, 2020.

245 *On Monday morning, September 16*: Logan John Williams, interview with author, 2020; Federal Reserve officials, background interviews with author, 2020; other sources, ibid., Note 3.

247 *This system was destroyed when Ben Bernanke's Fed*: Fed officials, background interviews with author, 2020; ibid., Note 2; "Policy Tools: Interest on Required Reserve Balances and Excess Balances," Federal Reserve Board of Governors website, updated January 2021.

250 *Williams was persuaded*: Williams and Logan, interview with author, 2020; Federal Reserve press release, September 18, 2019.

251 *Hedge funds used repo loans as the cornerstone*: Stephen Spratt, "How a Little Known Trade Upended the U.S. Treasury Market," Bloomberg News, March 17, 2020; Daniel Barth and Jay Kahn, "Basis Trades and Treasury Market Illiquidity," Office of Financial Research Brief Series, July 16, 2020; Jeanna Smialek and Deborah B. Solomon, "A Hedge Fund Bailout Highlights How Regulators Ignored Big Risks," *New York Times*, July 23, 2020; Nishant Kumar, "LMR Raises Capital After Hedge Fund Drops 12.5%," Bloomberg News, March 19, 2020; Gregory Zuckerman, Julia-Ambra Verlaine, and Paul J. Davies, "Traders Caught in Market Downdraft Are Forced to Unwind Leveraged Strategies," *Wall Street Journal*, March 12, 2020; "Hedging Repo Exposure in the Treasury Basis with One-Month SOFR Futures," CME Group, March 7, 2019.

254 *The basis trade worked just fine*: Ralph Axel, interviews with author, 2020; "Liquid Insight: Fed's Purchase Program May Have Costs," Bank of America Merrill Lynch analyst report, November 13, 2019.

255 *When the Fed announced its repo*: Federal Reserve press release, September 18, 2019; Federal Reserve officials, background interviews with author, 2020.

256 *On October 4, two weeks after*: Minutes of the Federal Open Market Committee, October 29–30, 2019.

256 *As the Fed finalized its plans*: Rich Miller and Steve Matthews, "Powell Sees Fed Resuming Balance-Sheet Growth, But It's Not QE," Bloomberg News, October 8, 2019; Rich Miller and Christopher Condon, "Fed to Start Buying $60 Billion of Treasury Bills a Month from October 15,"

Bloomberg News, October 11, 2019; Federal Reserve Statement Regarding Monetary Policy Implementation, October 11, 2019.

257　*By early 2020, Thomas Hoenig had migrated*: Thomas Hoenig, interview with author, March 2, 2020; Thomas Hoenig, "Emergency COVID-19 Stimulus Programs Are a Short-Term Solution," Mercatus Center white paper, May 20, 2020.

CHAPTER 14: INFECTION

261　*The first waves of volatility*: Sui-Lee Wee and Vivian Wang, "China Grapples with Mystery Pneumonia-Like Illness," *New York Times*, January 6, 2020; Fanfan Wang, "China Reports First Death from New Coronavirus," *Wall Street Journal*, January 11, 2020; Michael Levenson, "Scale of China's Wuhan Shutdown Is Believed to Be Without Precedent," *New York Times*, January 22, 2020; Jason Horowitz, "Italy Locks Down Much of the Country's North over the Coronavirus," *New York Times*, March 7, 2020; transcript of the CDC Telebriefing Update on COVID-19, February 26, 2020.

262　*The traders on Wall Street did start thinking*: Jim Bianco and Scott Minerd, interviews with author, 2020.

263　*On Thursday, February 27*: Catherine Thorbecke, "Dow Jones Plunges Most Since 2008 on Coronavirus Fears," ABC News, February 27, 2020.

263　*The mood inside the New York Federal Reserve*: Author notes and interviews inside New York Federal Reserve, February 27, 2020.

263　*The waves continued to gain strength*: Bianco, interviews with author, 2020; Clifford Krauss and Stanley Reed, "Oil Prices Dive as Saudi Arabia Takes Aim at Russian Production," *New York Times*, March 8, 2020.

263　*On Monday morning, the stock market*: Liz Hoffman, "Diary of a Crazy Week in the Markets," *Wall Street Journal*, March 14, 2020.

264　*Ten-year Treasury bills are the bedrock*: Bianco and Miner, interviews with author, 2020; financial trader, background interviews with author, 2020; Colby Smith and Robin Wigglesworth, "US Treasuries: The Lessons from March's Market Meltdown," *Financial Times*, July 29, 2020.

264　*Inside the Federal Reserve*: Jay Powell, interview with author, 2020; senior Federal Reserve official, speaking on background, 2020.

265　*The hedge funds that had loaded up*: Stephen Spratt, "How a Little Known Trade Upended the U.S. Treasury Market," Bloomberg News, March 17, 2020; Daniel Barth and Jay Kahn, "Basis Trades and Treasury

Market Illiquidity," Office of Financial Research Brief Series, July 16, 2020; Jeanna Smialek and Deborah B. Solomon, "A Hedge Fund Bailout Highlights How Regulators Ignored Big Risks," *New York Times*, July 23, 2020; Nishant Kumar, "LMR Raises Capital After Hedge Fund Drops 12.5%," Bloomberg News, March 19, 2020; Gregory Zuckerman, Julia-Ambra Verlaine, and Paul J. Davies, "Traders Caught in Market Downdraft Are Forced to Unwind Leveraged Strategies," *Wall Street Journal*, March 12, 2020.

265 *In September, when the repo market*: Federal Reserve Statement Regarding Treasury Reserve Management Purchases and Repurchase Operations, March 12, 2020; Alex Harris, "Fed Pledges More Than $500 Billion to Keep Funding Markets Calm," Bloomberg News, March 11, 2020; Pippa Stevens, Maggie Fitzgerald, and Fred Imbert, "Stock Market Live Thursday: Dow Tanks 2,300 in Worst Day Since Black Monday," CNBC.com, March 12, 2020.

266 *The massive polished table at the center*: Senior Federal Reserve official present at the meeting described, background interview with author, 2020; Claudia Sahm, interview with author, 2020; minutes of the meeting of the Federal Open Market Committee, March 15, 2020; Federal Reserve press release, March 15, 2020.

268 *The week of March 16 was when*: Minerd and Bianco, interviews with author, 2020; financial trader, background interview with author, 2020.

269 *On Monday, March 16*: David Benoit, "JPMorgan's Jamie Dimon and His Brush with Death: 'You Don't Have Time for an Ambulance,'" *Wall Street Journal*, December 24, 2020.

270 *The fragility of the corporate debt*: Greg Nini, interview with author, 2020; financial trader, background interview with author, 2020; Lisa Lee, "Battered CLO Investors Are About to Get a Look at Their Losses," Bloomberg News, April 20, 2020; Amelia Lucas, "General Motors Will Draw Down $16 Billion in Credit, Suspends 2020 Outlook," CNBC.com, March 24, 2020; "Big Firms Draw Down Billion Dollar Credit Lines," Pymnts.com, March 17, 2020; "Europe's Leveraged Loan Issuers Draw on Revolving Credits to Preserve Liquidity," S&P Global *Market Intelligence*, March 24, 2020.

272 *By this point, Powell was already*: Powell, interview with author, 2020; senior Federal Reserve official, background interview with author, 2020; Christopher Leonard, "How Jay Powell's Coronavirus Response Is Changing the Fed Forever," *Time*, June 11, 2020.

CHAPTER 15: WINNERS AND LOSERS

275   *Steven Mnuchin was quick to point out*: Steven Mnuchin, interview with author, 2020; Sheelah Kolhatkar, "The High-Finance Mogul in Charge of Our Economic Recovery," *The New Yorker*, July 13, 2020; Christopher Leonard, "How Jay Powell's Coronavirus Response Is Changing the Fed Forever," *Time*, June 11, 2020.

278   *One participant in these discussions*: Senior Federal Reserve official, background interview with author, 2020.

278   *The Fed created three important SPVs*: Powell, and a senior Fed official speaking on background, interviews with author, 2020; Federal Reserve press release, March 23, 2020; Nick Timiraos, "Fed Unveils Major Expansion of Market Intervention," *Wall Street Journal*, March 23, 2020.

280   *The Fed's announcement on that morning*: Figures on Fed's balance sheet, or "Total Assets," taken from Economic Research Federal Reserve Bank of St. Louis database, https://fred.stlouisfed.org/series/WALCL.

280   *The Fed announced on April 9*: Federal Reserve press release, "Federal Reserve Takes Additional Actions to Provide up to $2.3 Trillion in Loans to Support the Economy," April 9, 2020; Federal Reserve Board Vote Tally, https://www.federalreserve.gov/aboutthefed/boardvotes2020.htm, accessed 2021; Nick Timiraos, "Fed Expands Corporate-Debt Backstops, Unveils New Programs to Aid States, Cities and Small Businesses," *Wall Street Journal*, April 9, 2020; Olivia Raimonde and Molly Smith, "Ford Becomes Largest Fallen Angel After S&P Downgrade to Junk," Bloomberg News, March 25, 2020.

281   *But to people who actually traded*: Minerd and Mnuchin, interviews with author, 2020; financial trader, background interview with author, 2020.

282   *These actions, as dramatic as they were*: Steve Thompson, "Hogan's First Batch of Coronavirus Tests from South Korea Were Flawed, Never Used," *Washington Post*, November 20, 2020; Jeanna Smialek, Ben Casselman, and Gillian Friedman, "Workers Face Permanent Job Losses as the Virus Persists," *New York Times*, October 3, 2020.

283   *The CARES Act authorized $2 trillion*: Emily Cochrane and Sheryl Gay Stolberg, "$2 Trillion Coronavirus Stimulus Bill Is Signed into Law," *New York Times*, March 27, 2020.

283   *The spending that went directly to people*: Steven Mnuchin, interview with author, 2021; Peter Whoriskey, Douglas MacMillan, and Jonathan O'Connell, "'Doomed to Fail': Why a $4 Trillion Bailout Couldn't

Revive the American Economy," *Washington Post*, October 5, 2020; Jonathan O'Connell, Andrew Van Dam, Aaron Gregg, and Alyssa Fowers, "More Than Half of Emergency Small-Business Funds Went to Larger Businesses, New Data Shows," *New York Times*, December 1, 2020; Stacy Cowley and Ella Koeze, "1 Percent of P.P.P. Borrowers Got Over One-Quarter of the Loan Money," *New York Times*, December 2, 2020; Sydney Lake, "These 16 Va. Companies Received $10M PPP Loans," *Virginia Business*, December 2, 2020; Fred Imbert, "Treasury Secretary Mnuchin Says It Was 'Outrageous' for the LA Lakers to Take a Small Business Loan," CNBC.com, April 28, 2020.

286 *There was a growing sensitivity inside the Federal Reserve*: Claudia Sahm, interview with author 2020; Heather Long, "'It Doesn't Feel Like a Boom Yet': Many Americans Urge the Federal Reserve to Boost the Economy," *Washington Post*, October 29, 2019.

287 *The Main Street program allowed*: Nick Timiraos, "Fed Had a Loan Plan for Midsize Firms Hurt by Covid. It Found Few Takers," *Wall Street Journal*, January 4, 2021; Nick Timiraos and Jon Hilsenrath, "The Federal Reserve Is Changing What It Means to Be a Central Bank," *Wall Street Journal*, April 27, 2020; Jeanna Smialek and Peter Eavis, "With $2.3 Trillion Injection, Fed's Plan Far Exceeds Its 2008 Rescue," *New York Times*, April 9, 2020; Jeanna Smialek, "The Fed's $4 Trillion Lifeline Never Materialized. Here's Why," *New York Times*, October 21, 2020.

287 *This didn't mean that the Fed's bailout*: Peter Brennan, "Fed Keeps Corporate Bond Market Purring After COVID-19 Drove Record Issuance," S&P Global *Market Intelligence*, December 9, 2020; Marina Lukatsky, "US Leveraged Loans Gain 1.35% in December 2020, 3.12% in 2020 After Q4 Rebound," S&P Global *Market Intelligence*, January 4, 2021; Joy Wiltermuth, "U.S. Corporations Make Final Borrowing Push in a Record Breaking 2020," *MarketWatch*, November 10, 2020; value of Dow Jones average taken from Yahoo!Finance database, https://finance.yahoo.com/quote/%5EDJI?p=%5EDJI.

288 *During the summer of 2020*: "WELL WELL WELL WHAT DID I TELL YOU by Davey Day Trader Global," video uploaded to YouTube, https://www.youtube.com/watch?v=od6fxCD4KsM; "Davey Day Trader—March 23rd, 2020," video uploaded to YouTube, https://www.youtube.com/watch?v=MLIk_oHPCQQ; material from Bar Stool Sports retrieved from Internet Archive.

289 *Viewers who wanted to join the fun*: Nathaniel Popper, "Robinhood Has

Lured Young Traders, Sometimes with Devastating Results," *New York Times*, July 8, 2020; Sheelah Kolhatkar, "Robinhood's Big Gamble," *The New Yorker*, May 10, 2020.

289 *Market swings were hard to predict*: Ben Bernanke, email statement to author, 2021; Rob Copeland, "Former Fed Chief Ben Bernanke to Advise Hedge Fund Citadel," *Wall Street Journal*, April 16, 2015; Andrew Ross Sorkin and Alexandra Stevenson, "Ben Bernanke Will Work with Citadel, a Hedge Fund, as an Adviser," *New York Times*, April 16, 2015; Josh Zumbrun, "How Citadel and the Fed Crossed Paths Before the Hedge Fund Hired Ben Bernanke," *Wall Street Journal*, April 16, 2015; Tom Maloney, "Citadel Securities Gets the Spotlight," Bloomberg News, April 6, 2021; Edward Ongweso Jr., "Robinhood's Customers Are Hedge Funds Like Citadel. Its Users Are the Product," Vice.com, January 28, 2021; Douglas MacMillan and Yeganeh Torbati, "Robinhood and Citadel's Relationship Comes into Focus as Washington Vows to Examine Stock-Market Moves," *Washington Post*, January 29, 2021.

290 *The insanity of all this seemed distant*: Powell, Bernanke, and Janet Yellen, interviews with author, 2021; figures on Fed's balance sheet, or "Total Assets," taken from Economic Research Federal Reserve Bank of St. Louis database, https://fred.stlouisfed.org/series/WALCL.

CHAPTER 16: THE LONG CRASH

293 *After he was laid off*: John Feltner, interview with author, 2021; descriptions of Feltner's commute taken from Google Maps and Street View; Community Health Network news release, "COVID-19 Tent Testing Information 1," 2021; Eric Pointer, "1 Year Since Indiana's First Documented COVID-19 Case: Hoosiers Reflect on How Their Lives Were Impacted," Fox59 News, March 4, 2021.

294 *America's essential workers in 2020*: Michael S. Derby, "Business at Most Small Firms Below Pre-Pandemic Levels, Fed Survey Finds," *Wall Street Journal*, February 3, 2021; Justin Baer and Eric Morath, "On the Wrong Side of the Split Recovery: 'I Just Have to Keep Myself Going,'" *Wall Street Journal*, October 18, 2020.

295 *For Feltner, the bailouts*: Feltner, interviews with author, 2020–2021; AnnaMaria Andriotis, Ken Brown, and Shane Shifflett, "Families Go Deep in Debt to Stay in the Middle Class," *Wall Street Journal*, August 1, 2019.

296 *Jay Powell had become a figure*: Video of Jay Powell news conference,

December 16, 2020, uploaded to Federal Reserve Board of Governors website, https://www.federalreserve.gov/videos.htm.

297   *The stock market was doing so well*: Financial traders, background interviews with author, 2021; Eliot Brown and Maureen Farrell, "Sizzling Tech IPO Market Leaves Investors Befuddled," *Wall Street Journal*, December 13, 2020.

298   *The market for corporate debt*: Steven Mnuchin, interview with author, 2021; Joe Rennison, "US Corporate Bond Issuance Hits $1.919tn in 2020, Beating Full-Year Record," *Financial Times*, September 2, 2020; Ruchir Sharma, "The Rescues Ruining Capitalism," *Wall Street Journal*, July 24, 2020; Lisa Lee and Tom Contiliano, "America's 'Zombie' Companies Have Racked Up $1.4 Trillion of Debt," Bloomberg News, November 17, 2020; Jim Reid, John Tierney, Luke Templeman, and Sahil Mahtani, "The Persistence of Zombie Firms in a Low Yield World," Deutsche Bank analyst report, March 1, 2018; Dion Rabouin, "'Zombie' Companies May Soon Represent 20% of U.S. Firms," Axios, June 15, 2020; Jeff Stein and Rachel Siegel, "Treasury's Mnuchin Defends Ending Lending Programs, Fires Back at Federal Reserve," *Washington Post*, November 20, 2020.

299   *On January 6, 2021, thousands of violent*: Nicholas Fandos and Emily Cochrane, "After Pro-Trump Mob Storms Capitol, Congress Confirms Biden's Win," *New York Times*, January 6, 2021; "Stock Market News for January 7, 2021," Zacks Equity Research, via Yahoo!Finance, January 7, 2021.

300   *That month, millions of traders*: Matt Phillips, Taylor Lorenz, Tara Siegel Bernard, and Gillian Friedman, "The Hopes That Rose and Fell with GameStop," *New York Times*, February 7, 2021; video of Federal Reserve press conference, January 27, 2021, uploaded to Federal Reserve Board of Governors website: https://www.federalreserve.gov/videos.htm.

301   *Tom Hoenig spent the long winter*: Thomas Hoenig, interviews with author, 2016–2021; Thomas Hoenig, "Emergency COVID-19 Stimulus Programs Are a Short-Term Solution," Mercatus Center white paper, May 20, 2020; Sam Goldfarb, "Flood of New Debt Tests Bond Market," *Wall Street Journal*, March 10, 2021.

A PLAIN-ENGLISH GLOSSARY OF
IMPORTANT TERMS IN THIS BOOK

BALANCE SHEET: A balance sheet is a ledger that is divided into two parts: One part shows what a bank or a company *owns*, while the other part shows what it *owes*. In the case of a bank, the balance sheet shows the bank's assets (what it owns) and its liabilities (what it owes). The Federal Reserve's balance sheet also shows how much the Fed is intervening in the economy. When the balance sheet is big, it means the Fed is intervening a lot and creating a lot of money. When the balance sheet is small (by historical terms at least), it means the Fed is scaling back its money creation. The reason is simple: The Fed creates money by purchasing assets with dollars it creates out of thin air, and then storing those assets on its balance sheet. To use the Wall Street jargon, the Fed's balance sheet was about $900 billion before the crash of '08. Then it rose to $4.5 trillion in the age of ZIRP. The balance sheet hit $8 trillion after the bailouts of 2020 and continues to increase.

CDO: Basically a bundle of home loans. Best known for being at the center of the 2008 market crash, a collateralized debt obligation is a financial product sold on Wall Street. A CDO is built when a group of loans are bundled together. Investors can buy a portion of the CDO, and then collect the payments that are made on the underlying loans. If the loans default, investors can lose their money. CDOs usually refer to the home loans that were bundled together during the housing bubble of the 2000s.

CLO: A collateralized loan obligation, or CLO, is basically a bundle of leveraged loans. A CLO is built when a group of leveraged loans are bundled together, in a similar fashion to its Wall Street cousin. Investors can buy a portion of the CLO, and then collect the payments that are made on the underlying loans. If the loans default, investors can lose their money. CLOs fared much better during the crash of 2008, which made them an attractive investment during the 2010s.

COMPRESS THE YIELD CURVE: This is what the Fed did through quantitative easing, and it refers to the yield curve on U.S. Treasury bills (which basically affect the yield curve of everything else). In normal times, the yield curve rises on Fed Treasurys as they go out into the future, meaning the rates are higher on Treasurys out into the future. A Treasury due in ten years pays a higher rate, or yield, than a Treasury due in three months. The Fed "compressed" the difference between yields on long-term and short-term Treasurys. The Fed did this in order to pressure people to lend money. Long-term Treasurys were like a big fat savings account for Wall Street. By compressing the yield, the Fed reduced the incentive to save. It squeezed all that money from the future into the present, like toothpaste out of a tube.

CORPORATE BOND: This is a commonly used form of debt that is sold on Wall Street. Companies borrow money by issuing the corporate bond while agreeing to pay a certain interest rate. The bond is then sold on Wall Street to investors. Corporate bonds are rigidly structured, meaning they are largely standardized, which makes them easier to buy and sell. The financial structure of a corporate bond is not like a home loan or credit card loan in one important way: Companies don't pay down the debt along the way. Instead, they only pay the interest on the bond, and then pay off the full amount at the very end when the whole note is due. In practice, companies don't fully pay off their corporate bonds. They pay the interest, and then they "roll" the debt, meaning they sell a new corporate bond and use the money to pay off the existing bond. Companies can roll their debt forever, but it exposes them to interest-rate risk. If rates jump, their new debt will be far more expensive. High interest rates can make some corporate debt essentially unpayable, leading to bankruptcy.

COST PUSH: This is a theory that helps explain why inflation happens. It focuses on forces that push up the cost of things, thereby making prices rise. For example, back in the early 1970s, OPEC imposed an oil embargo that pushed up the price of oil at the same time that labor unions were pushing up the price of labor by negotiating for higher pay levels. A different theory of inflation is called demand pull, which puts more emphasis on central bank actions.

DEMAND PULL: This is a theory that helps explain why inflation happens. It posits that central banks pull up demand for things when the banks print more money and make it easier to get in the form of low-interest-rate loans. The phrase that best captures this is that it creates too many dollars chasing too few goods, hence driving up the price of those goods. An alternate theory of inflation is described as cost push.

DERIVATIVE: At its core, a derivative is any financial product that is based on the value of something else. A futures contract, for example, is a contract whose price is based on the future value of commodities like oil. In this case, oil is the asset, and the futures contract is the derivative. Over the years, the word *derivative* has become a catch-all term to describe an endless supply of exotic financial instruments, including CDOs and hedging contracts on interest rates.

DISCOUNT WINDOW: A term used to describe the Federal Reserve's emergency lending program to banks. This is one of the Fed's core jobs and is a central reason for its existence. During times of financial panic, even healthy banks can go bust because people take their money out of the bank in a senseless stampede. The discount window is designed to stop such panics. In times of panic, otherwise healthy banks can get emergency loans from the Fed's discount window at an interest rate below the market rate. This low rate is the "discount" rate, meaning it is cheaper than the panic-induced high rates in the marketplace. And no, there is no actual window.

ECB: European Central Bank. The bank was founded in 1998 to be the central bank for European Union members. Like the Federal Reserve, the ECB manages monetary policy for its member states along with some bank supervision.

FDIC: The Federal Deposit Insurance Corporation is a regulatory agency that was created in the immediate wake of the Great Depression. It is best known for offering insurance on the retail bank deposits of normal people, up to a value of $250,000. The FDIC is also a key regulator of the entire banking system. It oversees the financial health of the system by examining how much money banks have on hand compared to how much they have lent. Famously, the FDIC can dissolve failed banks.

FED FUNDS RATE: In essence, this is the short-term interest rate controlled by the Fed's FOMC. When the FOMC "sets" interest rates, what the committee is really doing is setting a target rate for the Fed Funds rate. This is the interest rate that banks charge one another for an overnight loan, so it is a core interest rate that ripples out into all other interest rates. When you raise the Fed Funds rate, you are basically raising the cost of money. When you lower it, you are lowering the cost of money.

FED PUT: Wall Street slang for the widely held belief that the Federal Reserve will always intervene to maintain asset prices above a certain unspecified level. The terminology refers to a "put" contract, through which someone agrees to buy an asset at a certain price, even if the market price is lower. A put contract effectively puts a floor beneath that asset price for the contract holder. Investors believe there is a Fed Put based on their observation that the Fed steps in when markets crash and creates more money to allay the volatility. Also known as the Greenspan Put, the Bernanke Put, the Yellen Put, and the Powell Put.

FISCAL POLICY: This is government policy that has anything to do with collecting taxes and spending state money (including borrowed state money). For the purposes of this book, fiscal policy refers to almost all economic policies passed by democratically controlled government bodies, such as state or federal legislatures, as opposed to monetary policy, which is controlled by the Federal Reserve.

FOMC: The Federal Open Market Committee is the policy committee at the Fed that sets a target for short-term interest rates. The FOMC meets every six weeks to debate where short-term interest rates ought to be set, along with other policies the Fed can impose such as quantitative easing. The FOMC has twelve members, which always includes all seven members of the Fed's board of governors. This includes a permanent seat for the most important governor: the chairman of the Fed. Another seat is permanently reserved for the president of the New York Federal Reserve. (The New York Fed president gets special treatment because that bank is the most important of the Fed's twelve regional banks. The New York Fed conducts the open market operations that control interest rates, and it is close to the most important Wall Street banks.) The other four seats on the committee are filled on a rotating basis by the Fed's regional bank presidents. These executives rotate on and off the FOMC as voting members for one year at a time. The regional presidents are the least powerful members of the FOMC. Even if they vote as a block, they can always be outvoted by the seven governors.

FUTURES MARKET: The market where futures contracts are bought and sold. Futures contracts are derivatives that carry a price to be paid at a given future date for a wide variety of products, like corn, oil, or even shares of stock.

HAWKS AND DOVES: These terms are used to define the basic political orientation of any voting member on the Fed's FOMC. Hawks try to restrain the Fed's intervention and limit its easy-money policies. Doves are more comfortable with bigger interventions and keeping interest rates lower for longer. Hawks are associated with America's conservative political movements, while doves have become associated with liberal political movements.

INTEREST RATES: An interest rate is basically the cost of a loan. It is the periodic payment attached to the loan, always measured as a percentage of the loan amount. It is a crucial way to measure the underlying risk of a loan. If a loan is safe, the interest rate is lower. If the loan is risky, the interest rate is higher. You can think of this as the fee that someone has to pay for the privilege of borrowing money. If I am a super-sketchy borrower, then I might need to offer someone a 19 percent rate to convince them to lend me money. If I am the U.S. government, I might only have to offer someone 1.1 percent to persuade them to lend me money.

INVERTED YIELD CURVE: A condition in which debt markets enter the rare state when interest rates (or yields, as they call them) paid for long-term debt become lower than interest rates paid for short-term debt. Most people interpret an inverted yield curve as a signal that a recession is about to happen.

JUNK BOND DEBT: A form of corporate bond that is so risky it is considered "junk." Junk debt carries high interest rates to compensate for the high risk of making the loan. Ratings agencies like Moody's essentially deem what is junk debt by giving the debt a low rating.

KEYNESIAN: The school of economic policy thinking named after the famous economist John Maynard Keynes. For the purposes of this book, "Keynesian" is a shorthand term for a very simplified description of Keynes's view. It holds that the government should step in and spend money during times of economic distress in order to replace the lost demand in the private sector. The goal is to cushion the blow of inevitable downturns and ensure they don't become needlessly protracted or deep. In terms of the Fed, the central bank becomes a Keynesian tool to stimulate the banking system during a downturn, supplying cheap credit or extra cash to spur lending or investment.

LEVERAGED LOAN: A form of corporate debt that is very similar to a corporate bond. The key difference is that leveraged loans are not standardized and traded on open exchanges in the same way a corporate bond is traded. Leverages loans are more "bespoke" in the sense that each one is effectively a single contract, or loan agreement, between a lender and a borrower. But leveraged loans are still bought and sold by traders on Wall Street, even though they aren't as standardized as bonds.

MONETARY POLICY: This refers to policies implemented by the Federal Reserve Bank that affect the supply of money. They are different than fiscal policies, which are controlled by democratically elected politicians and involve taxing and spending. Monetary policy includes the control of interest rates, which is basically controlling the cost and supply of money.

NEGATIVE-INTEREST-RATE DEBT: This should be an oxymoron. With negative-interest-rate debt, a lender is actually *paying* somebody to borrow money from them. It is hard to imagine a world where someone will pay you to borrow their money, but we have lived in such a world since about 2012. That's when European central banks started experimenting with negative-rate debt. The idea was to implement a radical policy that would punish people for saving their money. Shockingly, a lot of lenders didn't care they were being punished and they rushed at the opportunity to pay governments or other entities to borrow their money, kind of like paying someone to hide money under their mattress. By 2019, about 29 percent of all global debt had a negative rate.

NEW DEAL: This term refers to a sweeping collection of interlocking laws and regulatory agencies that were passed right after the Great Depression and which defined American economic life between the 1930s and roughly the late 1970s, when the U.S. government began to repeal key parts of the New Deal. The New Deal did three important things: It put Wall Street on a tight leash, it empowered workers and labor unions, and it reduced the power of monopolistic corporations. Huge parts of the New Deal, then, were aimed squarely at Wall Street and big banks. The new deal created the FDIC and the Securities and Exchange Commission (which regulates stock trading) and it included the all-important Glass-Steagall Act, which divided American banking into commercial banks that held deposits and investment banks that made risky bets.

OPEN MARKET OPERATIONS: The trading operations through which the Fed actually controls interest rates or achieves other policy goals like quantitative easing. The operations are conducted by a trading group based at the New York Federal Reserve Bank who buy and sell assets like U.S. Treasury bills on the open market. The key thing here is that the Fed traders can buy things by creating money out of thin air, thereby increasing the supply of money. When the Fed wants to make money cheaper, it buys things using newly created dollars and floods the system with cash. When the Fed wants to make money more expensive (which is just another way of saying that it wants to raise interest rates), it can sell assets and then take that cash onto its balance sheet, keeping it out of circulation.

OPERATION TWIST: A Fed program that is basically a "lite" version of quantitative easing. Operation Twist aims to lower long-term rates for reasons that are laid out in the definition of "compress the yield curve," but it does so without injecting billions of new dollars into the financial system. The Fed does this by purchasing long-term debt, which compresses the yield on that debt. But, crucially, the Fed simultaneously sells an equal amount of short-term debt. This means that the Fed is injecting cash into the market when it buys the long-term debt, but then it is sucking cash out of the market by selling the short-term debt. The goal is to lower yields without increasing the total amount of new cash in the system.

PRIMARY DEALER: This refers to a group of twenty-four specially designated financial institutions that can do business directly with the Fed. When the Fed does open market operations, it does it with one or more of the primary dealers. The primary dealers include well-known banks like J. P. Morgan Securities, and more obscure companies like Mizuho Securities. The Fed decides which companies are eligible to be on the list, and it periodically removes or adds dealers.

QE: Slang term for quantitative easing.

QUANTITATIVE EASING: An experimental program the Fed first implemented during the crash of 2008. The goal of quantitative easing is to flood Wall Street with new cash at a time when interest rates are low in order to spur new lending and boost asset prices in hopes it will stimulate economic growth. To do this, traders at the New York Fed purchase assets like Treasury bonds or mortgage bonds from primary dealers. The Fed buys the assets with newly created dollars, then holds the assets on its balance sheet. As a result, new dollars are deposited in the primary dealers' reserve accounts at the Fed. There were four major rounds of QE. The first round was an emergency measure during the Global Financial Crisis of 2008. Then, in late 2010, the Fed initiated another round of QE, known as QE2, that pumped $600 billion into Wall Street with the goal of spurring economic growth during the anemic recovery. In 2012, the Fed initiated a third round, known as QE3, which was the largest to date, at $1.6 trillion. Starting in late 2019, the Fed did about $400 billion in QE after the repo market froze up. In March of 2020, the Fed initiated a near-permanent QE program that pumped roughly $2 trillion into Wall Street at first, and then settled on a monthly flow of about $120 billion a month during 2021. All told, the QE programs started with QE2 in 2010 expanded the size of the Fed's balance sheet from $2.3 trillion to $8.2 trillion and rising in mid-2021.

QUANTITATIVE TIGHTENING: This is the only way to unwind the impact of quantitative easing. Under this program, the Fed sells assets and sucks dollars onto its balance sheet, thereby taking them out of circulation. Quantitative tightening has only been tried once, and it was a failure. The Fed began to slowly sell off assets in late 2017 and accelerated the sell-off in 2018. The Fed was able to draw down the value of assets on its balance sheet (which it had purchased through QE) from almost $4.5 trillion to a little less than $3.8

trillion. Then the financial system short-circuited. The Fed halted tightening and eventually resumed quantitative easing, boosting its balance sheet above $8 trillion.

RESERVE ACCOUNT: The account that banks hold inside the Federal Reserve. The reserve accounts discussed in this book tend to be those of the primary dealers, who can sell assets to the Fed and collect new dollars in their reserve accounts.

RESERVE CURRENCY: The U.S. dollar has been the global reserve currency since the end of World War II, meaning that it is the currency that nations and national banks use to conduct international transactions with one another. This is what gives the dollar its supreme place in the global economic system. In times of stress, everyone needs dollars because so much debt and trade is denominated in dollars. Being a reserve currency helps shield the dollar from market pressures faced by other national currencies, which can see their value plummet if other nations or banks decide they don't want to own that currency any longer.

SEARCH FOR YIELD: The economy-wide phenomenon caused by the Federal Reserve when it pinned interest rates at zero for almost a decade while flooding Wall Street with trillions of new dollars from QE. The net result of these policies was to reduce the yield of things like 10-year Treasury bonds, which banks or other firms had once used to safely store their money. As a result, big institutional investors went out into the marketplace searching for anything that might yield them money. In other words, it was a way to push investors to make more risky loans and purchase more risky assets.

SHADOW BANK: This is a broad term that refers to financial institutions that do "bank-like" functions such as providing credit to large institutions. A shadow bank, for example, can be a hedge fund that provides a big cash loan based on the collateral of opaque financial instruments. Shadow banking became really big business after Congress passed the Dodd-Frank Act, which regulated banks more tightly. Shadow banks can engage in the same business lines with fewer regulatory headaches.

SPV: A special-purpose vehicle refers to a set of emergency programs launched by the Fed in order to inject money into different parts of the economy. These carry a wide variety of complicated names, but they are basically the same type of structure. They create a corporate entity that allows the Fed to buy or sell securities like municipal debt or corporate bonds.

SWAP LINE: A Federal Reserve program under which the central banks agree to trade dollars at a fixed exchange rate with a foreign central bank for that bank's currency. This program is basically a way to flood foreign nations with dollars at times of economic panic. It's important because so much global debt is denominated in dollars, so dollars are needed in times of crisis. The swap lines ensure that foreign central banks have access to dollars at a much cheaper exchange rate than the market would offer.

T-BILL: Slang term for Treasury bill.

TREASURY BILL OR BOND: Debt issued by the U.S. government. The Treasury bill is the foundation of the global financial system, largely seen as the safest investment that exists. There are several varieties of Treasury bills, depending on how long the debt will take to pay off. There are really short-term bills, which get paid off in a month. Then there are two-month, three-month, one-year, five-year, and ten-year bonds and on down the line, including a thirty-year Treasury. The longer-term debt typically pays higher interest rates to compensate for the hassle of having your money tied up for so long. Treasury bonds work a lot like corporate bonds. The U.S. government issues the bond and gets all the cash up front. Then the government pays periodic interest payments on the bond until the final date the bond is due, at which point the government either pays the full amount or "rolls" the bond by taking on new debt and paying off the existing debt with the cash from that sale. This is why the U.S. government's debt burden can rise if interest rates rise—the Treasury will need to roll its existing debt into higher-interest debt.

YIELD: For the purposes of this book, the term *yield* refers to interest payments that are made on any kind of debt or investment. If a Treasury bill pays 1 percent, for example, it is said to have a 1 percent yield. Yield is a term that traders use all the time to talk about how much money they can earn from buying certain kinds of debt or assets.

YIELD CURVE: This is a representation comparing the yield on different kinds of debt. In terms of corporate bonds, for example, the yield curve rises from left to right as it goes from very low yields on safe corporate debt to very high yields on risky junk debt.

ZERO BOUND: This term once signified the theoretical limit of the Fed's power. The Zero Bound referred to an interest rate of zero, which was thought to be the lowest level the Fed could achieve. Quantitative easing was seen as a way to push monetary policy past the zero bound by pumping new dollars into the financial system after the zero bound had been reached. Another way to break past the zero bound is to issue negative-interest-rate debt, which the Fed has refrained from doing.

ZIRP: This refers specifically to the Federal Reserve's zero-interest-rate policy.

More broadly, financiers use this term to describe the Fed's policy between 2008 and roughly 2017, when the Fed kept interest rates pinned at zero, or very near zero, while pumping more cash into the financial system through quantitative easing. These were the most extreme easy-money policies in the history of the central bank.

ACKNOWLEDGMENTS

I am indebted to one person in particular for spurring me to write this book. I met him in 2016. He was a source for an earlier reporting project, and he talked with me on condition of anonymity, so I can't name him here. This source was brilliant and fascinating. Everyone who worked with him confirmed that he was probably a genius. Our first interview lasted eleven hours. During the first four or five hours, we talked about the subject of my earlier project. But as the day wore on, this source wanted to talk about other things, which he considered to be far more important. He wanted to talk about asset prices. This gentleman, who sometimes goes by the initials Z. C., was extremely generous with his time and his insights over the ensuing years. I am grateful, sir, for your help.

Thomas Hoenig was remarkably generous with his time over several years as I pursued his story. Hoenig deals with reporters in a way that I believe is rare these days. He doesn't seek attention, but he answered all the questions I put to him, even when they were adversarial and argumentative. My sense is that Hoenig felt an obligation to answer questions from a reporter because that is part of being a public servant. I am grateful for his candor.

I am also profoundly grateful to each and every current and former official and employee of the Federal Reserve who agreed to speak to me for this book, both on and off the record. It is simply impossible for a reporter to learn anything without such sources, and my sincere hope is that I was able to synthesize all these interviews into the best available version of the truth.

This book would not have been possible without my agent, Lauren Sharp, who has the very difficult job of trying to sell book ideas. Lauren couldn't have been thrilled when I said I was becoming obsessed with quantitative easing and wanted to write a book about it. But she heard me out, and from the earliest days she encouraged me to keep digging. When it came time to put the idea into concrete form, Lauren worked overtime to help me shape and edit the book proposal. She has been a steadfast supporter every step of the way, and I am so grateful for it.

As always, I am deeply indebted to my editor at Simon & Schuster, Priscilla Painton, who has shaped and guided every book I've written. Priscilla is a steady leader with absolutely impeccable ethics and judgment. She represents the best school of American journalism, and I am grateful every day to learn from her. I am also deeply indebted to Jonathan Karp, president and CEO of Simon & Schuster.

Lucas Wittmann, a senior editor at *Time* magazine, edited my first and only magazine story about the Federal Reserve. Lucas was exceptionally supportive, thoughtful, and smart as he guided the story through a tumultuous evolution. It began as a profile of the 2019 repo market intervention, back in the halcyon days of January 2020. When I went to New York to visit the Fed bank there, people were just starting to wear face masks, and the stock market was beginning to crash. Lucas hung with the story and helped expand it into a profile of Jay Powell and the Fed's unprecedented interventions during the COVID-19 crisis. I am so grateful to have had the opportunity to work with a real pro like Lucas, and the entire team at *Time*. Thank you for the chance to do it.

While I wrote and reported this book, my institutional home was the Watchdog Writers Group, a nonprofit journalism institute based at the University of Missouri School of Journalism. I am thankful, every day, for the generous support the WWG receives from 11th Hour Project of the Schmidt Family Foundation. I am particularly grateful to Wendy Schmidt, Sarah Bell, Joe Sciortino, Amy Rao, and Ellyn Peabody and the entire team at 11th Hour for their tireless work and support. I am also grateful for the support provided to the WWG by the William T. Kemper Foundation in Kansas City, and the help from Jonathan Kemper, Charlotte Kemper, and Sarah Fox. The WWG operates with complete editorial independence and the group's funders were not involved in any way in shaping, guiding, or providing any kind of input for this book or any of my journalism. I am so thankful that the WWG is operating under the guidance of Randy Picht at the Reynolds Journalism Institute, who has been a wonderful mentor and leader for the program. Dean David Kurpius, Mark Horvit, Randall Smith, Katie Swon, Alison Young, Ron Stodghill, and so many others at the School of Journalism have been invaluable in making the program work.

Kelly Dereuck joined the WWG during the summer of 2020 to help me research Tom Hoenig's tenure at the FDIC for chapter 11 of this book. Kelly's weekly memos and reports were simply indispensable to understanding the FDIC itself, along with Hoenig's efforts at the institution. Kelly also helped illuminate the banking crisis of the 1980s, and I couldn't have kept up without her.

Earlier in 2020, Alexander Holt did me the favor of lending his remarkable mind to this effort. Alex helped me in the very earliest stages of my reporting on the Fed, as I began to dig into the repo market bailout of 2019. Alex nimbly surveyed the entire landscape of information about the repo market and the Fed, from scholarly articles to financial analyst reports and news articles. I never would have understood the terrain without him. He spent many an hour at the Panera in Silver Spring helping me understand the mechanics of repos, reverse repos, and, maybe most important, the dreaded kink in the demand curve for bank reserves. It would be impossible to fully tally all the hours we talked about this, and all I can say is that I am so grateful to have had the chance to work with him.

I am also so grateful to work with researcher Susan Bencuya, who fact-checked this book. Sue can find mistakes and inaccuracies with laser-guided accuracy, and she improved the book throughout. Needless to say, any remaining mistakes are mine and mine alone.

This book would not have been possible without access to the outstanding coverage of the Federal Reserve in our nation's leading newspapers: *The Wall Street Journal*, *The New York Times*, and *The Washington Post*. Among the reporters whose work I am most indebted to are John Hilsenrath, Nick Timiraos, and Greg Ip at the *Journal*; Heather Long at the *Post*; and Matt Phillips, Neil Irwin, Jeanna Smialek, and Peter S. Goodman at the *Times*. These reporters are all doing a hero's job, every day, to document what is happening in our nation's financial institutions and markets, and I was so grateful to have been able to rely on their work as I tried to understand what the Fed has done over the last decade. Any office where I work slowly becomes buried in piles of newspapers with notes scribbled all over them, and I am deeply thankful for the luxury of having these papers delivered to my doorstep.

As always, I am profoundly grateful for the entire team at Simon & Schuster. Hana Park was an absolute maestro from beginning to end, helping the entire project proceed under adverse conditions. Samantha Hoback and her team did an exceptional job of editing and improving the manuscript. Robert

Messenger was extraordinarily generous with his time, insight, and editing ability, and his attention made the book much better. Larry Hughes, as always, was simply indispensable in helping get the word out about the book—a very hard job in a media environment that grows more cacophonous by the day.

Muriel Hesler and Michael Whitney literally gave me shelter from the storm by providing me a place to work as I finished this book in the throes of a pandemic. Thank you so much for your generosity, and thank you to Kimberly and Eric Springer for making it happen. Jane and Paul Molloy were so kind to give my family a chance to get away during the heat of it all, and we are grateful for the memories.

My only bridge to sanity during lockdown was the bus stop crew, who evolved into the firebowl crew when everything came to a sudden stop. Thank you so much to Kevin and Kate Gunthert, Damian and Rachel Rintelmann, Andy and Emily Prugar, and Andy Sousa and Caroline Broder for keeping the neighborhood together. Jerry Hovis, Kristy Walmo, Rob and Deb Levy, Lars and Lucy Volz, and Dave and Carly Flanigan made Silver Spring home: Thank you for all the support over the years. Jerry and Kristy—we will all remember to Walk Like Will!

David Givens and Stacey Ricci were fantastic friends and also fantastic sounding boards for my political ideas during my years in Silver Spring. David was kind enough to review my work on the Fed and give me very thoughtful feedback, which helped me see things more clearly. Thank you so much for your time and your very sharp insights.

Steve LeVine and Nuri Nurlybayeva have been great friends and great supporters all along the way. Thank you. As always, I am permanently indebted to Andrés Martinez and Steve Coll for giving me the chance of a lifetime back in 2012, which paved the way for every book I've written.

I hope this book reflects some of the values that were imparted to me by my elders while growing up in Kansas City. We lost too many of them during 2020. My beloved uncle David Launder was a great role model to me, and I thank him for it. I also thank John and Linda Robertson for the example they provided the rest of us about how to live a full and good life. Thank you. As always, Mom, David, and Blythe were the ones I turned to when I really needed guidance. Thank you for always being there.

The first person who reads my books is the most important person in my life, my wife, Josie Leonard. This time around, she was joined by a new editor, my daughter Sophia Leonard. Both of them made this book much better, much sharper, and much cleaner. It was delightful to hear my daughter walk around the house exclaiming things about Paul Volcker. George and Margot were extraordinarily tolerant of my long absences, and my absentmindedness, during the intense period of writing this book. Most important, all of you remind me why I write books in the first place, and you help keep me on the right path. Thank you.

INDEX

ABOUT THE AUTHOR

CHRISTOPHER LEONARD is a reporter whose work has appeared in the *New York Times*, *Bloomberg Businessweek*, *Time*, and elsewhere. He is the author of *The Meat Racket* and the *New York Times* bestseller *Kochland*, which won the J. Anthony Lukas Work-in-Progress Award. He is director of the Watchdog Writers Group, an investigative reporting program at the University of Missouri School of Journalism.